W9-CIF-864

RICKWOOD FIELD

ALSO BY ALLEN BARRA

Yogi Berra: Eternal Yankee

The Last Coach: A Life of Paul "Bear" Bryant

Big Play: Barra on Football

That's Not the Way It Was

Clearing the Bases: The Greatest Baseball Debates

of the Last Century (with Bob Costas)

RICKWOOD FIELD

A CENTURY IN AMERICA'S
OLDEST BALLPARK

ALLEN BARRA

W. W. NORTON & COMPANY · NEW YORK LONDON

Selections from "Rickwood Field" by Debra S. Robertson reprinted
by permission of the author.

For information about permission to reproduce selections from
this book, write to Permissions, W. W. Norton & Company, Inc.,
500 Fifth Avenue, New York, NY 10110

For information about special discounts for bulk purchases, please
contact W. W. Norton Special Sales at
specialsales@wwnorton.com or 800-233-4830

Manufacturing by RR Donnelley, Harrisonburg, VA
Book design by Judith Stagnitto Abbate / Abbate Design
Production manager: Anna Oler

Library of Congress Cataloging-in-Publication Data

Barra, Allen.
    Rickwood Field : a century in America's oldest ballpark / Allen
Barra.
        p. cm.
    Includes bibliographical references and index.
    ISBN 978-0-393-06933-4 (hardcover)
    1. Rickwood Field (Birmingham, Ala.)—History. 2. Birmingham
Barons (Baseball team)—History. 3. Birmingham Black Barons
(Baseball team)—History. 4. Minor league baseball—Alabama—
Birmingham—History. 5. Historic buildings—Alabama—
Birmingham. I. Title.
    GV416.B57B37 2010
    796.35706809761'781—dc22

                                                                2010010896

W. W. Norton & Company, Inc.,
500 Fifth Avenue, New York, NY 10110
www.wwnorton.com

W. W. Norton & Company, Ltd., Castle House, 75/76 Wells
Street, London W1T 3QT

1 2 3 4 5 6 7 8 9 0

THIS BOOK IS DEDICATED
TO THE MEMORIES OF PIPER DAVIS,
PAUL HEMPHILL, AND
CHRIS FULLERTON.

The one constant through all the years has been baseball. America has been erased like a blackboard, only to be rebuilt and then erased again. But baseball has marked time while America has rolled by like a procession of steamrollers. It is the same game that Moonlight Graham played in 1905. It is a living part of history. . . . It continually reminds us of what once was, like an Indian-head penny in a handful of new coins.

– W. P. KINSELLA,
Shoeless Joe

I don't know what it is, but when I was playing at Rickwood Field, I was always itching to get to the ballpark. We played all over the United States, and when we got here, you just loved coming here to play in this park. There was just something about the baseball in that park.

– BILL POWELL,
Black Barons pitcher

CONTENTS

Preface · 1

CHAPTER ONE

Up from the Slag Pile (1815–1909) · 7

CHAPTER TWO

Birmingham Men Do It Right (1910–1917) · 27

CHAPTER THREE

A Team of Their Own (1918–1925) · 47

CHAPTER FOUR

The Golden Age (1926–1929) · 73

CHAPTER FIVE

The Greatest Game Ever Played (1931) · 93

CHAPTER SIX

*"There Was Just Something about
the Baseball in That Park"* (1932–1947) · 113

CHAPTER SEVEN

"Well, I'm Going to the Ballgame" (1948–1949) · 137

CHAPTER EIGHT

"The Barons Were a Memory" (1950–1960) · 163

CHAPTER NINE

Everything Dies But . . . (1961–2009) · 185

EXTRA INNINGS

Appendix 1 · There Used to Be a Ballpark · 207

Appendix 2 · The Baron of Rickwood · 221

Appendix 3 · Voices of Rickwood · 239

Appendix 4 · This Is a Ballpark · 317

Acknowledgments · 335

Notes · 341

Bibliography · 347

Illustration Credits · 351

Index · 355

RICKWOOD FIELD

PREFACE

·ON APRIL 12, 1909, the atmosphere at Shibe Park was that of
a world's fair. The seating capacity for Philadelphia's brand spanking
new baseball stadium, named for majority team owner Benjamin
F. Shibe, was around 20,000, but in the great tradition of Philadelphia sporting events, thousands—one paper suggested as many as
10,000 more—lined up at the entrance on the corner of Lehigh
and Twenty-first Street to pay for standing room only. According
to baseball historian Lawrence S. Ritter, "Additional fans crowded
onto rooftops on the other side of 20th Street, beyond the right-
field fence, because there wasn't room to shoehorn a single additional customer within the confines of the ballpark."[1]

There were so many celebrities at Shibe Park—Diamond Jim
Brady, western silent film star William S. Hart, and frontier law-
man turned sportswriter Bat Masterson were said to be in attendance—that the Philadelphia Athletics' already legendary manager
and owner,[*] Cornelius Alexander McGillicuddy Sr., known to the

---

[*] That is, in 1909 part owner. Mack owned 24 percent of the Athletics, though he was
allowed total autonomy in running the team. In 1913, he would acquire an additional 25
percent and become equal partner with Shibe.

baseball world as Connie Mack,* hardly noticed the slender, soft-spoken southerner in his early thirties who was wearing a straw hat identical to his own.

Ring Lardner, not yet a nationally known sportswriter and writer of short fiction but a reporter for the *Chicago Inter-Ocean*—and also wearing a straw boater—chatted with the young man and took it upon himself to introduce him to the second most famous manager in baseball (behind the New York Giants' John McGraw, of course). They shook hands.

Allen Harvey Woodward, known to his friends for reasons no one could remember as "Rick," had taken the train all the way from Birmingham, Alabama, to witness the christening of Philadelphia's new marvel, the first concrete-and-steel sports structure in America. Might Mr. Mack, the younger man wanted to know, have a while to talk with him about his amazing new ballpark? He was, Woodward told Mack, planning to build a similar structure back in Alabama. Mack liked Woodward immediately; he suggested they have dinner the following night at Philadelphia's most famous restaurant, Bookbinder's.

The next day, following the Athletics' 8–1 victory over the Boston Red Sox, the two men sat down to dinner. Woodward quickly expressed his admiration for his host. Connie Mack was what Rick Woodward wanted to be: a real baseball man. Mack had actually been a ballplayer, though not much of a hitter; he had a batting average of .245 in 723 big-league games, most of them as a catcher. He was,

---

* There was a widespread belief among Philadelphia sportswriters—and who would know better?—that Mack encouraged the short use of his name in order to see it in print more often. He once told the *Philadelphia Inquirer*'s Fred Lieb, "Except when we voted, our people always called themselves 'Mack.'"

however, a smart and good defensive catcher and eventually worked his way up to managing and the nickname of the Tall Tactician.

Most baseball fans, even those who had never seen him, knew that he was one of the few managers to wear street clothes in the dugout and that he often positioned his players by waving a scorecard. They also knew that his Athletics had won American League pennants in 1902 and 1905, where in just the second World Series in baseball history they lost to McGraw's Giants when Christy Mathewson beat them three times by shutout.*

Rick's father, Joseph Hersey Woodward, was one of Birmingham's iron barons; the team would actually derive its name from the "coal barons" of the 1880s, but by the time of Rick Woodward many felt the term "iron barons" was more appropriate. He regarded baseball as a symptom of moral degeneracy. There was some basis for old Joe's fears. Young Rick had caught baseball fever as a boy when his uncle, less concerned about elements of moral degeneracy, had taken his nephew to exhibitions of barnstorming major league players. At the University of the South, Suwanee, he had, like Mack, become a catcher and grown so absorbed in the game that his grades suffered. Joe Woodward yanked his son out of Suwanee, brought him home, then sent him off to MIT for a B.S. in mining engineering—which would help him prepare for his destiny as future owner of the Woodward Iron Company. Had he known what Rick would be remembered for a hundred years later, he would still be spinning in his grave.

---

* Matty's feat had caused Mack to mutter something he perhaps heard somewhere else but just may have coined himself: "Pitching is 75 percent of the game." Several decades later a black lefthander from Alabama who began his career pitching in Woodward's ballpark, Bob Veale, uttered a classic rejoinder: "Good pitching stops good hitting every time. And vice versa."

Mack was supportive but expressed his skepticism. Were there really enough baseball enthusiasts in the South, in Birmingham, Alabama, he wondered, to support a team with such a park? Woodward assured him that there were, that the citizens of Birmingham, white and black alike, were as baseball mad as the good people of Philadelphia or any other city in the sixteen major leagues, which, placed on a map, all fit into the northeastern quarter of the country.

Though Woodward's proposed ballpark would be smaller than the awe-inspiring Shibe—it would be home to Woodward's team, the Barons, a minor league affiliate of the Southern League—it still promised to be an enormous undertaking. But Woodward's mind was set. Mack promised to visit Birmingham and lend his expertise, and, within a couple of months, he would be as good as his word.

Woodward was delighted and now more determined than ever to build the first steel-and-concrete ballpark in the South—in fact, in all of minor league baseball.

There was no way either man could have known that Rickwood Field, its name appropriated from syllables in the owner's first and last name, would outlast not only Shibe Park but every other major and minor league ballpark standing in 1910. Nor could they possibly have envisioned that its grass would be touched by the cleats of more great players, both dead-ball era and modern, American and National League, white, black, and Hispanic, than any other park the game has ever seen: Babe Ruth, Ty Cobb, Rogers Hornsby, Dizzy Dean, Josh Gibson, Satchel Paige, "Cool Papa" Bell, Willie Mays, Hank Aaron, Reggie Jackson, and Frank Thomas to name just a few.

Little more could they have known or even understood that the little ballpark would survive the Great Depression, segregation, and the decline of the industrial age.

Old Birmingham

UP FROM
THE SLAG PILE

BASEBALL AND BIRMINGHAM arrived in Alabama at the same time, both early products of what would come to be called the New South. The term was coined by the managing editor of the *Atlanta Constitution*, Henry Grady, baseball's biggest booster in the Southeast. Grady passionately believed baseball would be a positive influence in pulling the states of the Old Confederacy into the mainstream of the modern United States and was determined that the South would not take a backseat to the North in the appreciation of what was already being called America's national game.

Grady had his own city in mind as the social and commercial leader of this New South. Atlanta had been incorporated in 1847, but after the Civil War was starting all over again, courtesy of General Sherman. In 1871, six years into Reconstruction, Birmingham was born. The two cities were rivals almost from the beginning.

Birmingham, though, was even newer than Atlanta. When the first white settlers came to Jones Valley in north central Alabama in 1815, they didn't even find Indians there. Cherokee were to the east, Chickasaw to the west, and Creek to the south, and all manner of wild game, but there were no people in Jones Valley. Later, after the settlers solved the basic problems of existence enough to care about such things, mounds were discovered in the northern part of the valley, but the small world the Mound Builders created had ended several hundred years before Europeans first came to American shores. Birmingham, with no Indians to take the land from, was born in peace.

The valley was named for John Jones, who, in addition to being recognized by many as the first homesteader, saved Davy Crockett's life when he treated him for a fever after an Indian companion brought him to Jones's dwelling.* Jones had led the way through the surrounding mountains into the valley, and many, having made the passage, chose to live on the western side of what would become known as Red Mountain, named for the color of the dust from which Indians made ceremonial paint; neither red nor white man yet had the slightest intimation that this was iron ore. Around 1818 Crockett became the closest thing to a celebrity to visit the area. He liked it and went back home to Tennessee and advised his friends to move there. Since football had not yet been invented, there was nothing to keep the Alabamians and Tennesseans from getting along.

By 1819 the great immigration had deposited enough people in the territory for Alabama to apply for statehood; the most heavily

---

* Thus Alabama would make two major contributions to the legend of the Alamo. William Barret Travis, commander of the fort's garrison, lived in what is now Monroeville when he left to fight for independence in Texas.

populated area, Jefferson County, named for the third president, was consolidated, and as far as history goes, it was pretty much a straight shot from there to Rickwood Field.

Jefferson County grew slowly during the antebellum period. This was true of much of northern Alabama; in Jefferson County, for instance, only 20 percent of the black population were slaves at the time of the Civil War. In some of the Black Belt counties to the south, the population was up to 80 percent black.

The late Paul Hemphill, one of the greatest journalists to come out of Birmingham, would always tell me, "Birmingham is *not* a southern city. Don't call it a *southern city*." When I graduated from high school in the wealthy and isolated suburb of Mountain Brook and got out to see more of the South, I understood what he meant: Birmingham wasn't a *typical* southern city. In his 1993 autobiographical book, *Leaving Birmingham: Notes of a Native Son*, Hemphill explained it this way:

> Never for a moment in its brief and tortured life has Birmingham been a genuinely "southern" city. True, it lies in the north-central part of Alabama, "the Heart of Dixie," only a hundred miles up the road from Montgomery, "the Cradle of the Confederacy." True, people there say "y'all" and on the surface would seem to share many traits with the rest of the Old Confederacy: they are churchgoing, flag-waving, slow-moving, and conservative to the point of being paranoid about people and ideas that deviate from the status quo. True, Birmingham has been associated with many icons that are considered, for better or for worse, southern: Bear Bryant, the Ku Klux Klan, the "Dixiecrats," George Wallace, the Confederate flag. But even southerners know that on the one hand

there are Memphis and Charleston and Mobile and Natchez, old cities truly tied to the agrarian South, that gossamer myth of *Gone With the Wind*, and then there is Birmingham. No, Birmingham isn't southern except by geography.[1]

Its geography, though, would have made Birmingham a natural base for much needed industry for the Confederacy, but because of transportation limitations nearly all of the antebellum ironworks were developed in counties on the southern rim of the mineral belt, most notably Shelby and Bibb counties.

Daniel Pratt, an inventor and manufacturer from New Hampshire, moved to Alabama in the 1830s and founded the Pratt Gin Company as well as a town, Prattville, in south Alabama. Before Fort Sumter was fired upon, Pratt's factory was turning out more than fifteen hundred cotton gins a year, making it the largest manufacturer of the machine in the world. He also owned an iron factory, a flour mill, and a tin smithy.* Had Pratt been able to establish a railroad tie through Jefferson County, Birmingham might have rivaled Atlanta as the commercial center of the New South, or even a southern rival of such northern industrial cities as Pittsburgh.

In 1870, by which time the Civil War had been over for five years and Reconstruction was winding down, Mobile had over 49,000 people and Montgomery nearly 43,000, but there were only about 12,000 in all of Jefferson County. A visitor in the 1870s would have had a hard time distinguishing Birmingham from a Wild West min-

---

* The tin shop manufactured cans, and Prattville became the major fruit canning center in the United States. In Gabriel García Marquéz's great novel *One Hundred Years of Solitude*, the fruit picked in the fictitious town of Macambo was shipped to "the United Fruit Company" in Prattville, Alabama.

ing town of about the same period, such as Tombstone, Arizona, or Deadwood in the Dakota Territory. Local lawmen, occasionally assisted by Pinkerton detectives, hunted notorious outlaws,* and most of the buildings were ramshackle storefronts with wooden plank sidewalks. The unpaved streets, like those in any cattle or mining town, were an ungodly mess after rain or snow. Stagecoaches identical to the ones that carried passengers to western cities were common in Birmingham streets. (Early entrepreneurs such as Robert Jemison made fortunes manufacturing the same model stagecoaches ridden by passengers in the western territories.)

· HISTORIANS MAY ARGUE about the true origin of baseball, but there isn't much doubt about the genesis of baseball in the South: it started with the Civil War.† Baseball in a crude form was played by Union soldiers from the Northeast and in turn passed on to Union soldiers from other parts of the country, who then taught it to Confederate soldiers. Many of these were prisoners in camps, but occasionally soldiers from both sides got together during lulls in the fighting and played baseball to combat boredom. Before the war was out, southerners were playing the game in their own camps.

---

* Rube Burrow and his brother Jim were the most famous local train and bank robbers of this period, the Frank and Jesse James of Alabama. Rube and Jim were pursued by Pinkertons though Texas, Arkansas, and Mississippi and even through Birmingham up to Blount County, just to the north. Rube was finally killed in a shootout in Linden, Alabama, in 1890. On the way to burial, his body was shipped through Birmingham, where it was photographed in a coffin Old West style with his Winchester and Colt revolvers.

† There were baseball clubs in New Orleans as early as the 1850s, but like so many things that happened in the South's wickedest city, what happened in New Orleans stayed in New Orleans.

For decades historians argued for three different versions of how blacks came to learn the game, all of them plausible. The first is that slaves and, later, free blacks learned it from former Confederates; the second is that many black soldiers in the Union army picked it up from their white comrades. A third possibility is that blacks simply saw white men play the game as spectators and then went home and played it themselves. Chris Fullerton, in his groundbreaking *Every Other Sunday*, wrote, "During the war thousands of runaway slaves sought refuge in federal camps throughout the South, and many learned baseball from the frequent games played in those military posts. In 1862, 40,000 people at a Union encampment at Hilton Head, South Carolina, watched the championship game for the camp's baseball league. Among the crowd of soldiers and camp followers were hundreds of freed slaves, many of whom made baseball just as much a part of their post-bellum world as their former owners."[2]

Perhaps the biggest boost for baseball in the South came in an interview in the *Lynchburg Daily Virginian* shortly after the war: Robert E. Lee told the paper's editor, Charles Button, that he enjoyed watching "base ball." By the following year teams from Charleston and Savannah were playing each other for a title called the Baseball Championship of the South. The South started late, but by the 1880s leagues and associations of "baseballists" were playing the game from the Mason-Dixon Line in the Northeast all the way over to Texas.

• DESPITE BIRMINGHAM'S lack of refinement, the city had, in the autumn of 1872, an illustrious visitor, Charles Stewart Parnell, the future Irish Nationalist hero and leader of the Home Rule Party in Ireland. His brother John was already living in Jefferson County, making a fairly good living out of peach farming. The brothers were considering investments in the nascent Birmingham steel industry, and, according to University of Alabama at Birmingham professor Kieran Quinlan, Parnell "changed his plans when his train was derailed outside Birmingham, an ill omen for the superstitious future leader of the Irish Home Rule party, a man destined to be celebrated as the 'uncrowned king' of his country. According to one account, it was even his brother's discontent with the indignities of Reconstruction that sharpened Parnell's own perception of English-Irish injustices."[*3]

Though the Parnells were charmed with Alabama and thought Jones Valley rich in natural beauty, they were not impressed by the city that was growing up there. Many years later, in a biography of his brother, John Parnell wrote that Birmingham "had one small, dirty wooden hotel, full of adventurers who had come there in the hope of getting work on the railroad and mines. The hotel was a miserable place and very crowded, and we were constantly in dread of having five or six not too cleanly strangers sleeping in the same room."[4]

Jones Valley's role in the Civil War had been inconsequential; its heart was simply not with the Confederate cause. As Paul Hemphill put it,

> There was no middle class to serve as a buffer between them [the upper class, mostly coal barons and a handful of plantation owners] and the slaves, who earned not a penny

---

[*] Apparently Parnell was even thinking of settling permanently in Alabama. Had he done so, he would have averted the famous scandal over his affair with a married woman, Katharine O'Shea, as well as a forgettable 1937 film with Clark Gable. After O'Shea was granted a divorce, Parnell married her, was condemned by the Catholic Church, and died in 1890 of a heart attack, at age forty-five.

for themselves, and the great sprawling mass of poor whites, whose average income was less than one hundred dollars a year. Little wonder, then, that when the call to arms was sounded, when time came for Alabama to secede from the Union, the slaves and the dirt farmers were much more interested in killing planters than in killing Yankees. Thus was born the Free State of Winston (near Walker County, whose seat is Jasper, an old lumbering and mining town on the railroad lines some fifty miles northwest of Birmingham), on the grounds that, as they say in those parts, "we ain't got no dog in that fight."[5]

Late in 1869 a group of capitalists who had taken note of the rich mineral deposits in Jones Valley—the most prominent were Colonel James R. Powell, John T. Milner, Dr. Henry Caldwell, and William S. Mudd—met with a Montgomery banker to organize the Elyton Land Company "for the purpose of buying land and selling lots to build a city in Jefferson County." They purchased over 4,100 acres of land at the crossing of the Alabama & Chattanooga and South & North Alabama railroads, which they controlled, for the staggering sum of $100,000. The first business in Birmingham, a country store and trading post called Yielding's, went up at the crossroads.

The birthday, the day of incorporation, was June 1, 1871. So, in Alabama it came to be said that "Birmingham was born in Montgomery." There's a brass tablet in Montgomery on the site where the big four had their meeting.

Colonel Powell was the wealthiest of the group and the most influential. Just before the meeting, he had been visiting England

and spent considerable time gathering information in the country's iron center. On his return he began telling people that the new city should be named after England's industrial giant, Birmingham. "The Duke of Birmingham," as he came to be known, gave the city a nickname it cherishes to this day, "the Magic City." Powell, more than any other man, made Birmingham, even though he did not live to see it flourish. In 1875, frustrated in some of his efforts to bring new business to Birmingham, he moved to a plantation in Yazoo, Mississippi. His friends and former business partners persuaded him to come back and run for mayor in 1878. He did, but was defeated by a man named Thomas Jeffers, a foreman on the railroad of which Powell was part owner. Embittered, Powell returned to Mississippi and five years later, in a Yazoo tavern, was shot and killed by a young man who claimed to have been insulted by him.

The colonel failed in many of his personal ambitions, but he definitely succeeded in one: birthing a major city. Within two years of its inception, the population of Birmingham rose to 4,000, but dropped temporarily during a cholera epidemic that alerted city officials to the importance of clean water and sewage facilities. There were numerous freshwater springs in the valley, but a layer of limestone under the topsoil tended to run the water off into springs, creeks, and wells instead of allowing it be absorbed into the ground. The springs and wells soon became contaminated, and thousands fled the city until a proper sewer system could be built. Doctors worked tirelessly to treat the sick; the entire town area resembled the scene in *Gone with the Wind* where Confederate wounded are laid out in the streets of downtown Atlanta.

At least 128 died and were buried in Birmingham's first cemetery, Oak Hill; barrels of burning tar were placed on the street corners at night as a disinfectant, and the dead were buried during torch-lit night processions to the cemetery.*

The cholera passed, and Colonel Powell renewed his efforts to boost Birmingham. In 1874, a year after the epidemic, Powell invited the New York Press Association to meet in what he touted as the Magic City. The meeting place was a huge saloon called the Crystal Palace, named for the glass-walled structure from the exposition of 1851 in London. Birmingham's version had no side walls and a wooden shingle roof; it was built on the Southside, rapidly becoming the fashionable end of town.

The gathering took place in 1875, and the New York press was duly impressed by the city's bustle and mineral wealth. With the approval of the New York papers, investors took notice and capital began to flow into Birmingham. By the end of the decade, Birmingham was on its way to being the only major industrial city in the South, a status that went unchallenged even during the 1884–85 financial panic in New York.

In 1880 the city's first blast furnace—Alice No. 1—was fired up, and the industrial revolution was on. Paving of the streets finally began in 1887, and by the end of the year Southern Bell reported that Birmingham had more than three hundred subscribers for telephones. By 1891 the city had electric streetcars.

Six years before the streetcars, however, professional baseball

---

* The legend of Lou Wooster, Birmingham's most famous madam of the 1870s, grew at this time. Miss Wooster tirelessly treated the sick, paying little heed to her own personal safety. Many years later, in her *Autobiography of a Magdalen*, the Belle Watley of Birmingham, a onetime social outcast, wrote of "being kindly received by rich and poor alike in this dark hour of Birmingham's great need" (p. 117). She would later be buried in Oak Hill Cemetery, near F. B. Yielding, proprietor of the first trading post, which was located about three blocks from her establishment.

had already begun thriving in Birmingham. Blacks and whites had been playing the game all over Jones Valley, but in 1885 Birmingham baseball became organized. The Southern League of Professional Baseball Clubs, the child of Henry Grady, was formed, connecting Birmingham with several cities in Georgia—Atlanta, Macon, Columbus, and Augusta—along with Chattanooga, Nashville, and Memphis. Grady, of course, was the league's first president and ran the league from his office at the *Atlanta Constitution*. All league members were cities with a population of 25,000 or more. Not surprisingly, the Atlanta franchise, with the most money to spend, won the league's first title. Birmingham established a long and frustrating tradition of finishing behind its eastern rival. In time, New Orleans, Mobile, and Little Rock would join the Southern League.

It was the first professional baseball league in the South. In a makeshift ballpark in Smithfield, about two miles west of downtown Birmingham—you could ride to the game on the Pratt City "dummy" streetcar line, drawn by horses or mules—a twenty-two-year-old pitcher from Cherry Flats, Pennsylvania, named Charlie Parsons gave the Birmingham Barons their first piece of history by throwing the first no-hitter in the Southern League, on May 29, 1885. Two years later Parsons pitched for the New York Metropolitans of the American Association. He had been a steelworker in Pennsylvania and picked up the trade in Birmingham, getting off from work early every few days to pitch. He was perhaps the city's first local baseball hero. In other parts of the country, much of the baseball talent would be produced by colleges and social clubs whose members were from the leisure class. In Birmingham, from the very beginning, players, both black and white, were nearly all from the working class.

Two years later the Barons moved their games to a Southside

location, Lakeside Park. Starting in 1893, to the irritation of the
Barons loyal, they occasionally had to share the field with devotees
of the football teams of the University of Alabama and the Agricul-
tural and Mechanical College of Alabama (later Auburn University).
Fortunately for the baseball fans, college football attracted relatively
few spectators, mostly noisy college students. Not that baseball fans
of that period were out for just a day at the park. When protesting
calls against their team, minor league fans everywhere were not merely
vociferous but quick to resort to sticks, rocks, empty bottles, and even,
at times, handguns. More than one minor league game in the South
ended with the players rushing from the field in fear of their lives.

No small part of the animosity between fans and visiting players derived from the fact that many of the players were yankees, veterans hoping to make a few bucks before catching on with a bigger
team in the Northeast. They did not take kindly to insults from
southerners, whose resentment toward the North hadn't softened in
the decades since the end of the Civil War. Southern League fans,
though, had no trouble with northerners' playing on their teams—
they were *their* yankees—at least if they won.

For all the enthusiasm displayed by Southern League fans,
though, Grady's league was poorly organized and faded the year he
died, 1889. Three years later, however, the Southern League was
revived to fanatical fan support, and the Barons won their first pennant. But progress came in fits and starts; transportation between
cities was unreliable at best, and little if any thought was given to
makeup games in case of inclement weather. To the enormous dis-
appointment of baseball-crazy fans, there were no organized games
at all in 1897–98.

Baseballists began to think seriously about how a league should
be managed, and the Southern Association, which would last for six

decades, was organized. Since the baseball fans in Birmingham were so numerous and enthusiastic, the league held its first meeting there in the fall of 1900. Traveling secretaries were hired by the teams to manage schedules and assist the players with personal problems—for instance, with money to be sent home to their families. Plans were made in advance regarding the best dates to reschedule rainouts. In the spring of 1901 the Barons began fierce and bitter rivalries with the Atlanta Crackers, Memphis Chicks—the Chickasaws, though after a couple of decades most fans forgot the team's original name—Nashville Volunteers, Mobile Bears, New Orleans Pelicans, Little Rock Travelers, and other league rivals whose nicknames would survive everything except the invasion of major league baseball.

There was, however, one major problem: the Birmingham Coal Barons (as many still called them) had no real ballpark to play in. Most Southern Association teams were in the same situation, frequently with a couple of rented fields owned by local colleges or rickety wooden stands that often collapsed and sometimes burned down. Birminghamians felt that something was needed to show off the city's increasing wealth and prestige to visitors and prospective investors. Officially they played their home games at West End Park; unofficially, the field was known as the Slag Pile, named for fans who watched the games for free while sitting atop piles of slag outside the fence.

The Slag Pile wasn't even owned by Birmingham. It was the property of the TCI (the Tennessee Coal and Iron Company), which leased it to the Barons' owners, who added a few rows of wooden seats. For some reason—a good guess is that the Slag Pile lacked that indefinable element of glamour that first-class cities look for in their sports teams—Birmingham baseball enthusiasts were itching for something better.

They were also ready for better teams. For nine seasons Birmingham's professional baseball clubs were second-rate, with the exception of the 1906 pennant-winning team, nicknamed the Vulcanites after the huge cast-iron statue of the blacksmith of the Roman gods that had been Birmingham's entry in the 1904 World's Fair in St. Louis.

The local papers railed against a tight-fisted apathetic leadership. Someone energetic, they said, would be needed to forge the Barons into a team worthy of representing the Magic City—a city of more than 130,000 people, nearly 70 percent of whom had arrived since the turn of the century. The success of the Barons was critical for the citizens of

THE STATUE OF VULCAN, *the Roman god of fire and metalworking, was cast to represent Birmingham in the 1904 World's Fair in St. Louis. Like much of Birmingham, its restoration was owed to the Roosevelt administration. In 1936, after years of standing in disrepair at the Birmingham Fairgrounds, Vulcan was refurbished and installed in its present home on top of Red Mountain, overlooking Jones Valley. In 1999 a second major restoration was initiated.*

Birmingham, whose very esteem depended on their fledgling baseball club. And so in 1910 Rick Woodward went to Philadelphia.

• FEW OF THE NEW STEEL BARONS—the men whose sons and grandsons would become the Big Mules of Birmingham industry and politics—were born in Alabama. Most, like Stimson Harvey Woodward, had made their fortunes in the great industrial cities of the Ohio Valley. (Woodward's was estimated at a breathtaking $400,000.) In 1869 he visited Jefferson County and was quick to spot the opportunity, purchasing several iron ore–filled acres in Jones Valley. In 1881 Stimson's sons, Joseph Hersey and William, founded the Woodward Iron Company.

It soon became clear that Joseph was the sharper and more aggressive of the two, and he quickly assumed leadership of the company. He was a conservative man who, unlike some of his newly rich counterparts, chose to downplay his wealth and influence. Rather than build an imposing antebellum-style mansion on the fashionable Southside, he purchased the large but relatively modest brick home of Jacob Sloss, a German immigrant who had made a fortune in early iron production in his Sloss Furnaces.[*]

By pushing Rick into the family business, Joseph Woodward

---

[*] The Sloss Furnaces still stand near downtown Birmingham after years of work by historic conservationists to prevent the structure from being torn down. Today a National Historic Landmark, Sloss Furnaces is a popular tourist site that hosts concerts, cookouts, and an annual Halloween Haunted event. In 1983 I interviewed Mel Gibson at Sloss Furnaces between shooting scenes for the movie *The River*. And Sloss Furnaces is not just a location for Hollywood feature films. In November 2009 the popular show *The Ghost Hunters* aired a segment shot there; the show identified it as "the scariest place on earth."

had hoped to steer him away from the frivolous game of baseball. As it turned out, he had pushed him in entirely the wrong direction. This was an age when company teams were becoming the breeding ground for professional baseball talent. Rick regarded the team of the Woodward Iron Company as an important part of his workers' morale; he played with them, managed them, and took great pride in their success. However, when his team narrowly lost the 1908 championship, some of the players complained openly that management had been too stingy in providing bonuses, benefits, and better work clothing, particularly during the winter months. The most vocal of the men in the ranks were Woodward's own players. Rick Woodward was smart and progressive; he understood, as his father did not, that baseball was not a distraction from work but a unifying influence. He listened to his workers and gave them much of what they wanted—better workers made better ballplayers, and a better baseball team was good public relations for Woodward Iron.

He also understood—again, as his father did not—that baseball was not just a game but a business. In the fall of 1909 he offered Jay William McQueen, the majority owner of the Barons, $20,000 for ownership of two-thirds of the team. The deal was finalized on January 24 of the following year. Rick Woodward, thirty-three years old, was not merely an iron baron but the owner of a professional baseball team in the largest—and, really, the only—major industrial city in the South.

Woodward's thinking was in line with that of other professional baseball team owners around the country at the time. The country was booming, and baseball reflected that prosperity and power. Now the national game required showcases worthy of the game's popularity.

From 1909 through 1915 a dozen new steel-and-concrete ballparks—some owners dared to call them stadiums—were erected. Shibe was the first; then ground was broken for Forbes Field in Pittsburgh, which, according to many, bore a strong resemblance to Connie Mack's palace. In quick succession, Fenway Park in Boston, Tiger Stadium in Detroit (called Navin Field for the first few years), Ebbets Field in Brooklyn, Comiskey Park in Chicago, League Park in Cleveland, and Wrigley Field (actually christened Weegham Field) in Chicago were completed. Birmingham wasn't

A. H. "Rick" Woodward *(right) and friend and golfing partner R. H. Baugh. Son of one of Birmingham's "Big Mules," Rick loved baseball and journeyed to Philadelphia in 1909 to meet A's owner and manager Connie Mack. Mack came to Birmingham the following year and advised Woodward in the construction of his baseball park, Rickwood Field (the name chosen by fans in a contest by combining Rick and the "Wood" in Woodward). Woodward loved the sportsman's image, often playing golf and hunting with visiting managers and players, including Ty Cobb.*

as big as those northern cities, but it was no less proud and their fans no less devoted. In 1910 the term "minor league" carried no pejorative connotation: "major league" did not mean richer or more prestigious; it meant that the league simply had more teams. Woodward was determined to see that his minor league team had a major league home.

Immediately after acquiring the controlling interest in the Barons, Woodward told reporters of his plans for a modern ballpark; a newspaper contest was conducted to let local fans name the new park, and one entrant suggested a combination of the owner's first and last names, Rick and Wood. Everyone liked Rickwood, and the name stuck. In March, just before the beginning of the new season, Connie Mack kept his promise to visit Birmingham and, to the frenzied delight of local fans,* brought the Philadelphia A's with him.

Nothing like it had ever happened in the Magic City. The old slag heap was trod by such future Hall of Famers as second baseman Eddie Collins, a .347 hitter in 1909, third baseman Frank "Home Run" Baker, and pitchers Chief Bender and Eddie Plank. In fact, all four members of what would soon be called the $100,000 Infield (which besides Collins and Baker included Stuffy McInnis and Jack Barry) were on the roster. The A's had finished second in the American League in 1909, and there was a growing consensus that they were the best team in baseball and the favorites to win the World Series in 1910. That feeling proved more than correct. (They would win the World Series three of the next four seasons—1910, 1911,

---

* Judging from the newspaper coverage in most southern cities, fans in minor league towns spent as much time keeping up with American and National League teams as with their own Southern Association teams. Almost every fan in the South knew the names of the top hitters and pitchers of nearly every big-league team.

and 1913.) The exhibition game dominated newspaper headlines for days before and after it was played, selling out well before the Athletics' train arrived. The Barons' unofficial bleachers, the slag piles, were so packed that fans were slipping off and tumbling to the ground.

The reception that the city gave the soon to be world champion Philadelphia A's put out the word to major league teams—Birmingham was a first-class baseball town and would soon have a ballpark the equal or, in most cases, the superior of any in the American or the National League. The visit from Eddie Collins, Eddie Plank, and the rest of the A's set a precedent: for the next half century big-league teams heading north from spring training would stop off in Birmingham for a game and southern cuisine such as fried chicken, okra, fried green tomatoes, homemade biscuits, and blackberry cobbler before boarding a northbound train. And so fans who had only read of the exploits of Ty Cobb, Tris Speaker, Shoeless Joe Jackson (who had just missed seeing Birmingham in 1910 when Mack traded him to Cleveland right before the season began),* Babe Ruth, Rogers Hornsby, and many others would now see them play in the flesh.

The day before the game, Woodward and Mack rode out to the site of the new ballpark, a few miles west of downtown Birmingham. Mack, according to legend, walked off the infield area, suggesting that the first base line run south, parallel to Twelfth Street West. And that line would remain long after Mack's own stadium, Shibe Park, and every other ballpark built during that storied time had fallen victim to the wrecking ball.

---

* Cleveland immediately sent Jackson to New Orleans, where he helped lead the Pelicans to the Southern Association pennant. Thus Shoeless Joe played in Rickwood Field before Cobb, Speaker, or Hornsby did.

THE MACK: Cornelius Alexander McGillicuddy, "Connie" Mack, owner and manager of the Philadelphia A's for half a century. His teams won nine pennants and four World Series. Rick Woodward sought him out when Mack oversaw the building of Shibe Park, the nation's first steel-and-concrete ballpark in 1909. Mack came to Birmingham the next year to help supervise the building of Rickwood, and over the next four decades brought his A's teams, including Frank "Home Run" Baker, Jimmy Foxx, and Mickey Cochrane, to Rickwood many times for exhibition games.

BIRMINGHAM MEN
DO IT RIGHT

O VER THE DECADES Birmingham fans would argue about which major league park Rickwood most resembled. There were no aerial shots of the early major league ballparks and, oddly, few good interior shots from their early years. For the most part, we know the grand old parks that were compared to Rickwood from firsthand accounts of old-time players and managers: Philadelphia's Shibe Park (opened in 1909 and demolished in 1976, though a 1971 fire pretty much razed it), Pittsburgh's Forbes Field (also born in 1909, torn down in 1970), or Cincinnati's Crosley Field (1912–72). All four parks were very much alike, and only later renovations (such as the famed high left field wall in Forbes Field, over which Bill Mazeroski hit his dramatic home run in the 1960 World Series) distinguished them from each other.

Gone were the flimsily constructed grandstands that stood

RICKWOOD FIELD, *aerial view, 1958, clearly shows the covered grandstands and open bleachers in the outfields. You can also see the original fences that so intimidated sluggers before General Manager Eddie Glennon installed shorter fences to encourage batters to swing for home runs.*

like enormous fire hazards in the centers of major cities; the new ballparks, erected just before and after World War I, were built to last. Rickwood Field would be, too. Connie Mack suggested many of the same features for Rickwood that had gone into the building of Shibe Park, including wooden louvers between the top row of the grandstand and the ballpark roof; like the ones in Philadelphia, these louvers were angled to diffuse the setting western sun in the late afternoon—though some joked that Rickwood didn't need them because the clouds of sulfur-filled smoke from the nearby mills accomplished that.

AERIAL VIEW *of Rickwood's big brother, Shibe Park in Philadelphia. This picture was taken in 1965, by which time it had been renamed Connie Mack Stadium in honor of the A's longtime owner and manager.*

Mack also recommended that the distance between home plate to the backstop be the same as in his own park, 90 feet. (The rules specified only the distance from the mound to home plate and around the bases; there were no rules regarding the distance from home plate back to the grandstand or from the infield to the outfield fences.) This disturbed a couple of Woodward's associates; what, they asked, might happen with a runner on third base if the ball got past the catcher? The runner would score, Mack replied. Runners from *second* base might also score. But it would keep your catchers smart and your pitchers alert when it came to covering home. Besides, Mack reminded them, drawing on nearly three decades of baseball experience, your pitchers would soon appreciate all that extra space when they saw how many foul pops their catchers could haul in, balls that would have sailed foul into the stands in most ballparks. You see the occasional run allowed by a passed ball, he told them, but you don't always see the extra runs prevented by catchers grabbing all those foul pops. Mack had spent his entire playing career in organized ball as a catcher, and he thought like a catcher. And like all good catchers, he thought that whatever was good for the catcher was also good for the pitcher.*

Like Shibe Park's, Rickwood's field dimensions were enormous by modern standards. Shibe's center field wall was 515 feet from home plate—with no record of a hitter's putting a ball over that wall until many years later when the fences were brought in—and around 400 feet down the left field line. (The center field wall at Forbes Field was 462 feet from home.) As in many urban ballparks in those years, the length of the outfield fences was shaped by the city block the park was built on. Most of the original northeastern city ballparks were built on rectangular lots with more space out toward left field—hence the expression "out of left field." Shibe, like many of the new stadiums, had a much more limited amount of

---

* "For most of its life," wrote Lawrence S. Ritter in *Lost Ballparks*, "Shibe Park retained an abnormally long distance from home plate to the backstop, putting it in the same league with Comiskey Park [in Chicago] and Forbes Field, both of which had the reputation of favoring pitchers over hitters" (p. 179).

In Pittsburgh's Forbes Field, the distance was actually 110 feet, almost twice as long as in some ballparks. Sportscaster and historian Art Rust Jr. once claimed with some legitimacy that at Forbes Field the catcher was actually a fourth outfielder. Some old-timers indeed maintained that the Forbes Field distance was too much territory for the average big-league catcher to cover and that the expanse really worked to the hitters' advantage.

space facing right, toward Twentieth Street, so the right field fence was just 340 feet from home plate.

Rickwood was constructed along similar lines. The center field wall was over 500 feet to straightaway center, virtually the same distance as at Shibe. The left field fence was even farther than in the Philadelphia park, 470 feet down the line, and right field almost exactly the same, 335 feet.

The dimensions of both parks raise two questions. First, why were center and left fields so far out, particularly when compared with those of modern parks? The answer is simple: because it was the dead-ball era. This was a time when the home run was disdained, particularly by managers who didn't consider it proper baseball strategy. Managers, players, and fans thought it far more exciting to keep the ball in play and to see outfielders running down enormous fly balls in cavernous left and center fields. That would change in the mid-1920s and 1930s when fans discovered that the game transformed by Babe Ruth was even more exciting.[*]

The second question is why Rickwood, which was not located in a downtown area and had more surrounding space than Shibe, had a relatively short right field porch. The simplest answer is probably the correct one: it was short because the one in Shibe Park was short.

Mack also advised that the diamond be angled to minimize the sun's effect on fielders. And so it was, as were the diamonds in Shibe Park and as would be those in the ballparks of Pittsburgh and Cincinnati.

---

[*] In 1945, for instance, both center and left fields were brought in nearly 50 feet, and right field about 10.

Less than a week after Connie Mack trod the turf of the ballpark in progress, the blueprints were completed. The Connie Mack–
Shibe Park influence could not have been more obvious from the
plans, but the *Birmingham Age-Herald* began a rumor that persists to
this day, that Forbes Field was the primary influence for Rickwood.
Woodward was friendly with Pirates owner Barney Dreyfuss, but
the only known connection between Rickwood and Forbes was that,
according to historian Timothy Whitt, Forbes architect Charles W.
Leavitt later designed the estate grounds for Woodward's colossal
mansion on Red Mountain.

Unlike most team owners then and today, Woodward had a
good deal of engineering experience, holding a degree from MIT
and several patents for industrial machinery. He saw the sound-
ness in Mack's thinking—the same basic principles that were going
into several other new ballparks—and took control of the design of
Rickwood Field himself. The steel columns of the grandstand were
forged from the same Red Mountain iron ore whose distinctive hue
had made an impression on the first settlers of Jones Valley. The
grandstand covered more than 3,000 seats from first to third base;
there was just one deck, but the columns were built in a curve, like
those of Shibe Park. For who knew that Birmingham wouldn't continue to grow into a big-league city?

The slag piles of the old West End Park were now just a memory. In addition to the grandstand, Rickwood's gleaming new bleachers could seat over 1,000 fans on each side of the field, and there
was enough standing room to take in nearly 2,000 more; in fact, on
opening day an estimated 10,000 fans packed the park. There was
just one problem associated with Rick Woodward's new jewel, and
it was proving to be an enormous one. The original cost of the ball-

park, funded by bond sales, was estimated at $25,000, but midway through construction, as Woodward made improvements to the original design, it became obvious that the cost would be closer to an unheard-of $75,000. Additional bond sales were initiated to cover the cost overrun, putting a severe strain on Woodward's finances.

But the cost to field the Barons involved more than the new ballpark. The $75,000 budget didn't include the cost of the blue-chip ballplayers Woodward wanted for his team. The Barons would soon have one of the most beautiful ballparks in the country, and Rick Woodward would not be satisfied until it showcased a winning baseball team.

• "THERE IS NO DOUBT but that Birmingham is 'baseball-wild,'" wrote the *Birmingham Age-Herald* on August 17, the day before the first game was played at Rickwood Field. Many thought the atmosphere was similar to that of November 2 of the preceding year, the biggest day in the city's thirty-nine-year history, when President William Howard Taft had paid a visit.

On August 18, opening day, downtown businesses closed at three o'clock so that fans would have time to reach their streetcar stops for the trip out to West End; the *Birmingham News* reported that fifty-seven extra cars had been put into service to meet the demand. Blach's department store, in an ad in the *Age-Herald*, advised, "Everybody should attend the opening ball game at Rickwood Field," and predicted that "all patriotic citizens" would be there. Blach's did its share for patriotism by distributing a block of tickets to its employees. (Blach's, like several other local businesses, was a sponsor of the

Dedication of Rickwood Field

Thursday, August 18, 1910

The Scoreboard Indicates by Number the Player at Bat

No.	MONTGOMERY.	1	2	3	4	5	6	7	8	9	10	11	12	R	H	E
7	Daly, lf. - - - - -															
8	Whiteman, cf. - - -															
5	McKay, ss. - - -															
6	Yohe, 3b. - - - -															
4	Pratt, 2b. - - - -															
9	Burnett, rf. - - -															
3	Greminger, 1b. - -															
1	Miller, c. - - - -															
2	Hickman, p. - - -															
10	Thomas, p. - - -															
11	Duggleby, p. - - -															
12	Juul, p. - - - -															

2 bh._____3 bh._____base on balls_____struck out_____hit by pitched ball
_____double plays_____stolen bases_____

No.	BIRMINGHAM.	1	2	3	4	5	6	7	8	9	10	11	12	R	H	E
4	Marcan, 2b. - -															
9	Messenger, rf. - -															
8	Molesworth, cf. - .															
7	McBride, lf. - - -															
3	McGilvray, - - -															
1	Elliott, c. - - - -															
10	Ryan, c. - - - -															
5	Ellam, ss. - - - -															
6	Emery, 3b. - - -															
2	Coveleski, p . -															
11	Fleharty, p. - - -															
12	Wagner, p. - - -															
13	Stockdale p, - -															
14	Bauer, p. - - - -															

2 bh._____3 bh._____base on balls_____struck out_____hit by pitched ball
_____double plays_____stolen bases._____

Scorecard *from the first game at Rickwood Field, August 18, 1910. Owner Rick Woodward, dressed in a Barons uniform, threw the first pitch—not a ceremonial pitch but one that counted in the game. It was a ball. Despite this, the Barons beat the Montgomery Climbers 3–2.*

team and reserved a section in the bleachers for "Blach's Boosters.")
An advertisement placed in the papers by the Cox Shoe Company
urged fans, "Go to Rickwood Park today in a pair of Nettleton's."
(Sportswriters at the time alternated between the use of the terms
"field" and "park"; by the 1920s Rickwood Field had won out.)

A story in the opening-day edition of the *Age-Herald* boasted of
the new ballpark, "In every detail, it is modern and as near-perfect
as skill and money could make it." The *Birmingham News* summed it
up this way: "When Birmingham men do a thing, they do it right."

As Timothy Whitt described it, shortly after lunchtime "the
fans arrived in force. They overflowed the grandstand and the
bleachers, and the standing room as well. Part of the playing field
was roped off for spectators. The throng, conservatively estimated
at 10,000, approached the all-time Southern Association record"—
and the Association included several cities such as Atlanta with
larger populations than Birmingham.[1]

The crowds at Rickwood could be distinguished from those of
the industrial cities of the Northeast in at least one significant way:
many in attendance were female. Big-league baseball was considered
too vulgar an experience for genteel white women in pre–World
War I America. But in the South, except for the baiting of players of
opposing teams and the harassing of umpires who made calls unfa-
vorable to the home team, professional baseball was more refined.*

---

* Ben Cook, in *Good Wood: A Fan's History of Rickwood*, unearthed a fascinating nugget of
Rickwood's history. On August 19, 1915, the park hosted "Suffrage Day." Female employees of Southern Bell, the telephone company, played a one-inning exhibition game
against a female team from Bessemer, a small town a few miles from Birmingham. "The
Bessemer girls, so we were informed, won," according to the *Birmingham Age-Herald*, "but
as the press box does not boast of an adding machine, no score was kept. Still it was very
amusing" (p. 17).

Before the first pitch, Whitt noted, "the crowd began to get its money's worth ... as the Barons starters Harry Coveleski and Bob Messsenger"—Woodward's other big acquisition, having been purchased from the Chicago White Sox, like Coveleski, for $1,000—"briefly engaged in fisticuffs in front of the home team dugout, buoyed by the raucous cheers of the overflow crowd."[2] By the time the game was over, the altercation had been forgotten, written off to an excess of high spirits.

Workmen under the stands continued to hammer and saw as the fans poured in and Rick Woodward stood on the mound of his dream ballpark to throw the first pitch in Rickwood Park.* The umpire called it a ball. Woodward, having fulfilled the fantasy of a lifetime, stepped off the mound, handed the ball to his newly acquired ace pitcher, Harry Coveleski, and went to his seat in the owner's box.

It would have been hard for any game to live up to the hype that preceded Rickwood's inaugural home game. Carlton Molesworth, a Maryland man whom Woodward had hired to be the Barons manager, was also in the lineup. Molesworth had been Woodward's second choice for manager; the first was Miller Huggins, often called "diminutive" by baseball writers, since he stood just 5' 6½"—though Molesworth was just 5' 4" himself.[†] Huggins came to Birmingham and liked the city, the ballpark, and the owner but finally decided against leaving the big leagues. His decision would pay off several

---

* In the first decade of twentieth-century America, in order to evoke the pastoral mood of the 1890s, every new athletic facility was called a "park."
† A second baseman with the Cincinnati Reds who had batted just .214 in 57 games, Huggins didn't develop a reputation as a good hitter, but did develop one as a smart baseball man, going on to a seventeen-year managing career, five with the Cardinals and twelve with the Yankees. He would also live on in baseball legend as the man Babe Ruth held over the back of a moving train by his ankles.

years down the road when he became the manager of the New York Yankees and won six pennants (including three World Series wins) en route to a plaque in the Hall of Fame.

And so Molesworth was given the job, which he would hold through the 1922 season, managing the Barons to their first two pennants. He scored the first run ever in the new ballpark, but Derrill Pratt, a household name to much of the crowd, having been a former star football player at the University of Alabama, got two hits for the Montgomery Climbers, who led 2–1 going into the bottom of the ninth. Bill Duggleby, a former Philadelphia Phillies pitcher on the mound for the Climbers, hit the leadoff Baron with a pitch. Molesworth then called for a classic exhibition of pre-Ruthian baseball, signaling for four consecutive bunts. Roy Ella tied the game for Birmingham with a tap that dribbled down the third base line.

Then, to the thunderous approval of the crowd, Lou Emory slapped a ball past the slow-moving Duggleby, and the Barons had won the first game played at Rickwood Field. The standing-room-only crowd, far from disapproving of such old-fashioned offensive techniques, was thrilled; this was baseball as they were taught to appreciate it—a tight, well-pitched defensive struggle in which bat control, base stealing, and moving runners were cardinal virtues.

The victory was satisfying in no small part because it came at the expense of the team from Montgomery. The snooty old-moneyed city to the south might have had bigger mansions and fancier carriages, and its citizens' manners might have been a shade more genteel, but they didn't have a brand-new steel-and-concrete ballpark that was the envy of the Southern Association.

An elderly gentleman seated in the owner's box couldn't hear the cheering fans—he was deaf—but he could see his fellow Birminghamians on their feet gesticulating wildly. For the first time, the old man understood baseball's power to bring people together. He clapped heartily, approving the Barons' thrilling victory. Joseph Hersey Woodward had become a baseball fan and made the decision to purchase Rickwood Field's bonds, eliminating his son's debt.

• HARRY COVELESKI, the Barons starter that day and the team's great star, was one of Woodward's big player signings for the 1910 season; purchasing his contract cost Woodward an eye-opening $1,000, paid to the Cincinnati Reds. Coveleski, from the coal-mining town of Shamokin, Pennsylvania, was from a great baseball family; his younger brother Stan, who outlasted him in the big leagues fourteen seasons to nine, was a pitcher of near–Hall of Fame caliber. Stan Coveleski won 20 or more games in five different seasons, led the American League twice in shutouts and earned run average, and won 215 games with a career won-lost percentage of over .600.

Harry didn't put up career numbers like that, but at his best he was better than his little brother. Though he spent parts of four seasons trying to find himself, he had flashes of brilliance before coming to Birmingham. In 1908 the twenty-two-year-old lefthander deprived John McGraw's powerful New York Giants of the National League pennant, defeating them three times in five fateful days, with the third coming against the great Christy Mathewson. The next season Coveleski developed arm trouble (as well as, said the rumors, a drinking problem). He was not pleased about going to the minor leagues, and he wasn't shy about telling the local press that he regarded pitching for the Barons as a demotion.

But by July 17 Harry had adjusted to the climate, the food, and Alabama girls enough to wow the state with a no-hitter, at least for nine innings, though he ended up losing in extra innings. That won him the hearts of Barons fans, and he justified it just two weeks later when, on July 31, he pitched another no-hitter, this time getting the victory. From late summer through the end of the season, he was virtually unhittable, winning eleven straight decisions with a microscopic 1.55 ERA. It wasn't his fault that the Barons couldn't catch the New Orleans Pelicans, who were buoyed by the fabulous young Joe Jackson, who led the Southern Association in runs, hits, and batting with a .354 average,[*] but by the next season he had left the Barons.[†]

The year 1910 would not be one of those pennant-winning seasons, but the euphoria from the opening of the new ballpark almost made the pennant seem like an afterthought.

· **FOR ALMOST** three glorious weeks in the early spring of the next season, Birmingham baseball fans thought they were in heaven. In early 1911 the New York Giants, New York Highlanders, Philadel-

---

[*] Coveleski did, however, get a measure of revenge, gaining his 21st win by shutting out the Pelicans 1–0 on the final day of the season, holding Joe Jackson hitless in four trips to the plate.

[†] The strange career of Harry Coveleski continued in Chattanooga, where the Barons had dealt him in 1911 following an arm injury. After two undistinguished seasons in which he won 25 and lost 37 for the Lookouts, he apparently developed some kind of new pitch and rebounded in spectacular fashion in 1913, leading the Southern Association with 28 victories. Detroit purchased his contract, and Coveleski had three sensational years with the Tigers, winning over 20 games each season and 65 overall. Then he hurt his arm again and by the end of 1918 was out of big-league ball. Harry was one of those blazing stars who is just a footnote to modern fans but who might have been a Hall of Famer in an era of pitching coaches and team physicians.

phia Phillies, and Detroit Tigers—four teams that had finished over
.500 the preceding year—stopped off in the Magic City on their
way home from spring training to play the Barons. Lucky fans got to
see such distinguished players as "Wahoo" Sam Crawford, Ty Cobb,
Christy Mathewson, Rube Marquard, Grover Cleveland Alexander,
and "Prince" Hal Chase, widely regarded by Walter Johnson and
other great stars as not only the best-fielding first baseman of his
time but also the most corrupt. Perhaps the most dishonest player
of his time, the "Prince" was widely known to be a gambler who fixed
big-league contests.

In 1916 the Barons actually won two of their games against the
big leaguers, including a stunning victory over the great Mathewson,
at the time the leading baseball hero in the country, Honus Wagner
and Cobb not excepted. Matty had led the National League with 27
victories in 1910, the fourth time in six years he had led the league
in wins, and would win 26 more in the 1911 season. But the Barons pounded him for eight hits in five innings; the *Birmingham Age-
Herald* noted that, of the two New York pitchers the Barons saw,
Mathewson was the less impressive.*

Birmingham sportswriters had a way of playing down the greatness of visiting big leaguers. Ty Cobb, not merely the American
League's batting king in 1910 but the batting crown winner for twelve
of thirteen seasons from 1907 to 1919, was described by a Birmingham reporter as an "ordinary mortal" after a game in which he had two
hits, one of them a triple into Rickwood's spacious left center field, but
made an error. Cobb had other problems while playing in Birming-

---

* Perhaps the writer was angered at Mathewson's criticism of the easy availability of pros-
titutes in the streets of Birmingham. A devout Christian, Mathewson earned a stained-
glass window at St. Patrick's Cathedral in New York.

ham. As the biggest sporting celebrity in the South (and second in the country only to Christy Mathewson), Cobb was invited to play golf with Rick Woodward and his business partner, R. H. Baugh, who served as the Barons' secretary and hacked Birmingham's first golf course out of the rocky soil of North Birmingham. Cobb and Woodward got along well until, on a hunting trip in the fall, Cobb shot one more pheasant than was allowed under state gaming laws; since the site they were hunting on was owned by Woodward, Cobb thought his host should have looked the other way. But Alabamians being more law-abiding than Georgians, Woodward said no, and an angry Cobb stomped off and refused to speak to Woodward for years.

During the regular season the baseball was uninspired. A first baseman, William McGilvray, was the team's only .300 hitter, and the Barons fell to third place behind New Orleans and Montgomery. Rick Woodward, it turned out, wasn't too fond of his manager, particularly after a newspaper poll in which the majority of Barons fans indicated that they wanted Molesworth out. If New York Yankees fans in the 1970s and 1980s thought George Steinbrenner was intrusive in on-the-field affairs, they would have been interested to know that Woodward, in the fashion of many team owners of the period, sat in the dugout doling out advice while wearing a Barons uniform.*

Whether Woodward's presence spurred Molesworth to greater efforts the following year is dubious, but it certainly helped him to have a speedy young center fielder named Jimmy Johnston, a second-year man who hit .296 and set a Southern Association record of 81 stolen

---

* Connie Mack might be included in that number because he managed the Philadelphia A's while owning half the team's stock.

bases, which lasted to the end of the league.* A right-hander named Raymond Boyd also helped take the heat off Molesworth by winning 23 games and pitching in all four crucial games against the Mobile Sea Gulls in a series the Barons swept, ensuring the 1912 pennant.

Rick Woodward was a fortunate man indeed; he had now achieved virtually everything he had set out to do: building a first-class stadium, winning a pennant, and even throwing a pitch in a professional game.[†]

· IN LATER YEARS it would be commonplace to hear knowledgeable fans say that Satchel Paige was the greatest pitcher ever to play in a Birmingham uniform. Indeed he was, but Burleigh Grimes, the Barons' first Hall of Famer, was, at least for a few seasons, a close second.

Burleigh Arland Grimes is remembered today as the answer to a trivia question: "Who was the last legal spitball pitcher?" What is often forgotten is how well he threw it along with a mean fastball and curve, neither of which he had any qualms about whizzing below a batter's chin.[‡] In truth, Grimes threw the spitter no more

---

* Johnston lives in the collective memory of Brooklyn Dodgers fans. He spent ten of his thirteen major league seasons with the Bums, 1916–25, and retired with a career batting average of .294, almost exactly what he hit with the Barons. Dodgers fans loved him for his ability to play every outfield and infield position.

† He also did some things he probably hadn't planned to do. After a game in 1912 in which Woodward vociferously disagreed with umpire "Bulldog" Williams, Woodward pursued him to the first base tunnel underneath the stands and picked a fight. Apparently the altercation took place between innings of a game, because the *Birmingham Age-Herald* reported that Woodward was merely "ejected" from the ballgame.

‡ The spitball, whether treated with spit, tobacco juice, petroleum jelly, or tree sap, wasn't invented by any one man, but was just something that evolved. A spitter from Carl Mays

"TAKE ME OUT TO THE BALLGAME" *was the caption for this 1915 photograph taken by the Chamber of Commerce to promote the Barons. Birmingham trolley cars averaged 135,000 passengers per day; these numbers would soon be reduced by "jitney" buses and private cars. This trolley stop, headed for Rickwood Field, was on the corner of Twentieth Street in front of Loveman's Department Store.*

in 1920 is still largely believed responsible for killing Cleveland's Ray Chapman when the pitch struck the popular Indians player in the left temple. More likely is that what killed Chapman was a combination of Mays's deceptive "submarine" delivery and the late afternoon shadows of the Polo Grounds.

Because so many pitchers were throwing some form of spitter and because so many defensive-minded managers defended the pitch—indeed, taught some of their pitchers to throw it—it wasn't banned all at once. Actually, the movement to ban the spitball preceded the death of Chapman; before the 1920 season, managers had already voted to partially ban spitballs, allowing each club to designate no more than two pitchers who would be allowed to throw it. After Chapman's death, it was banned outright except for pitchers who were already throwing it; they were permitted to use it until they retired. Sixteen other pitchers besides Grimes were okayed to throw doctored balls, but Grimes outlasted them all, throwing his last pitch for the Yankees near the end of the 1934 season, fourteen years after Chapman was killed.

than many other pitchers of his time; he was simply more discrimi-
nating about the way in which he lubricated it, not with saliva at all
but with the sap from slippery elms.

The Barons' pitching had been so good in 1914—Charles
"Curly" Brown, Omar Hardgrove, Dick Robertson, and Artie Johnson won a combined 79 of the Barons' 88 victories (in a season of
151 games)—that they scarcely needed Grimes, a brash twenty-
year-old from Emerald, Wisconsin. But Molesworth had heard
reports about how good Grimes was pitching up in Richmond in
the Virginia League and got Woodward to engineer a trade.

For the next two seasons Burleigh flourished. He won 17 games
in 1915, keeping the Barons in contention for much of the season.
He was so hot, Barons fans joked, that Woodward had installed the
ceiling fans to relieve the heat coming off the mound (actually, the
fans were installed before the season began). The next year he won
20; the Barons slipped to third and were a sub .500 team on days
when he didn't start.

Burleigh, who had a reputation as erratic and hot-tempered,
went on to great success in the big leagues. Before the season was out
in 1916, Woodward, drawing on his friendship with the Pittsburgh
owners, sold Grimes's contract to the Pirates for a substantial sum.
He went on to win 270 games in nineteen seasons with several major
league teams; in nine seasons with the Brooklyn Robins (so named
for their manager, "Uncle" Wilbert Robinson), he won over 20 games
five times. He led the National League in wins in 1921 and 1928, and
everywhere he pitched the smell of slippery elm was in the air.*

---

* Burleigh later replaced Casey Stengel as Brooklyn's manager and finally became a scout
for the Yankees. In 1964 he was elected to the Hall of Fame. In his *Historical Baseball
Abstract*, Bill James ranked him 62nd among baseball's all-time starting pitchers in the

• • •

· TEN DAYS BEFORE CHRISTMAS of 1917, Joseph Hersey Woodward, the silent hero of Birmingham baseball, died at his home on Highland Avenue. Though he never entirely understood the appeal of baseball, he at least managed to derive some pleasure from both the game and the prestige that owning the Barons conferred on his family. In terms of baseball, he missed little over the next four seasons; the Barons would finish just third, fourth, seventh, and fourth in the league during the rest of the decade. There is no telling how he would have reacted had he known that his son, beginning in 1920, would be taking on some tenants of a different color at Rickwood Field.*

---

nineteenth and twentieth centuries. Alabama baseball historian Tim Whitt concluded "that his record as a Birmingham Baron strongly suggests that he was the finest pitcher ever to wear a Barons uniform."

* Fifty-seven years after the old man's death, in 1974, I was a student at the University of Alabama at Birmingham, living in an apartment off Highland Avenue, perhaps one Willie Mays–length baseball throw from the Woodward house. On the night of April 8, I opened my door to the sound of tumultuous cheering from students and locals when Hank Aaron, who had played some of his most memorable ball at Rickwood Field, hit his 715th home run to pass Babe Ruth's record.

"BLACK BARONS TODAY": *Front gate at the corner of Twelfth Street West and Second Avenue West. Patrons line up to buy tickets. The sign was displayed to be sure everyone knew which of Birmingham's teams were playing that day.*

A TEAM
OF THEIR OWN

U NLIKE OTHER major southern cities, Birmingham did
not start the twentieth century with a large population of
former slaves. In fact, Birmingham itself didn't have a large black
population. Most blacks lived in industrial communities at the edge
of the city, many of them to the west. If life in these communities
was somewhat less dehumanizing than in much of Georgia, Louisiana, Mississippi, and even south Alabama, it was because most of
the men had jobs in the mills and foundries; the towns were more
or less self-sufficient and in most ways independent of Birmingham.
In the black neighborhoods there were schools, churches, restaurants, and even movie theaters that were black owned and operated
(though the movie houses got the films only after they had run in
the downtown white theaters).

Children who grew up in these industrial communities—such

as Piper Davis and Willie Mays—later noted a relative lack of racial tension compared with other parts of Jefferson County. Davis pointed out another factor that made relations between the races a little easier:

Baseball. After the companies got government contracts, there was integration more or less. I don't meant that there was any kind of regular fraternizing, but there was contact between black and white men on an everyday basis, and if you were on break and drinking some coffee or eating an apple, sometimes, say, two black guys would be talking about a ball game they had seen and a couple of white guys would come over and start talking about the game, asking some questions about players they had heard of. Sometimes you talked to white guys who played ball for the company teams. They knew the game and had been to Rickwood to see the Black Barons—sitting behind the chicken wire, of course.

The right field bleachers, commonly called the "Negro bleachers" but also used to seat white fans during Black Barons games, were separated from the rest of the park by chicken wire.

I ain't sayin' that we were friends, not really, cause after work we went back to our own neighborhoods. But there were a lot of black and white men in those factories who were friendly, and that was something.

Though nearly every black person could trace his or her ancestry to slaves, much of the black population had come to the Magic

City from somewhere else, and usually for economic reasons. In *The Other Side: The Story of Birmingham's Black Community*, a booklet published by a cultural project called Birmingfind,* a researcher wrote,

> Most slaves in Jefferson County belonged to farmers who owned only a few Negroes and usually worked alongside them. The relatively poor soil discouraged large plantations like the ones in the Alabama Black Belt which were cultivated by large numbers of slaves. Eight planters, however, owned more than forty slaves in 1860 and one, Williamson Hawkins of Thomas, had 107.

But by the standards of the rest of the South, Birmingham planters weren't, either figuratively or literally, walking in tall cotton.

At the end of the Civil War, Birmingham's population already included free blacks, such as those who belonged to Obadiah Washington Wood, who first settled the community of Woodlawn, a few miles east of downtown Birmingham. Wood gave all his former slaves small parcels of land, for which they agreed to be faithful members of the Baptist Church—and the Masonic order. The area where the free blacks lived became known as Zion City; the community was still on the map until the late 1960s, when most of the homes were bought and then demolished to make room for expansion of the Birmingham airport.

---

* Birmingfind proved an invaluable and still largely untapped treasure trove for research not only on Birmingham's black and Anglo-Saxon citizens but also on its Italian, Lebanese, and Jewish communities. A history and culture project sponsored by the Birmingham Alliance for the Humanities and funded by the National Endowment for the Humanities, Birmingfind published thirteen studies on Birmingham culture in 1980–81.

Most of the Anglo-Saxon and Celtic population of Jefferson County had come from the east, their ancestors starting in Virginia, going south through the Carolinas and Georgia and then westward into Jones Valley. The great black migration following the Civil War headed north to Birmingham from the large plantations of the Black Belt, named not for the men and women who toiled there but for the color of the rich loam itself. In the years right after the war, thousands of blacks poured into Jefferson County to mine coal and work in iron smelters and steel mills. These were the livelihoods of the men, while their wives and daughters often found work as domestic servants in white homes. Women who needed to stay home to tend their children took laundry in to earn money; during the summer they canned fruits and vegetables from their own gardens for the winter months. There were jobs in white homes, too, for men as gardeners and carriage and wagon drivers. But these jobs paid little compared with those in the mines and mills. The drawback of the industrial jobs was that they were subject to economic disruptions: recessions, strikes, and lockouts.

Nonetheless, the black population continued to grow, from an estimated 2,500 five years after the end of the Civil War to twice that by 1880. By 1890 it was around 30,000 and by 1920 more than 130,000.

Clarence Dean, who arrived in Birmingham in the early 1920s, recalled that his father came to Birmingham and found work in the mines, and then sent for his family down in Hopeville, Alabama:

My mother told me that we're going to Birmingham, where all them bright lights is.

The Terminal Station was lit up like a big mansion or

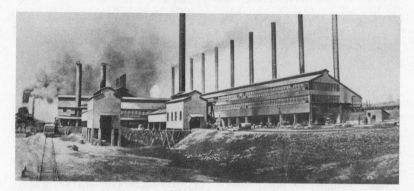

STEEL MILL IN ENSLEY, *outside Birmingham, circa 1900. In Birmingham, steel was king, and the men who owned the mills were "Barons." At the beginning of the twentieth century, Birmingham's potential seemed unlimited, but in 1907, Teddy Roosevelt inexplicably allowed U.S. Steel to buy the Tennessee Coal and Iron Company (TCI), a merger that put Birmingham's key industry under the control of an absentee landlord. This monopoly crushed the local economy during the Great Depression.*

something. It was a sight to see. When I stepped off the train, they had to catch me because I'd never seen nothing like that before. I pointed and told them, "Pretty lights. Pretty lights." They were beautiful. Being a little fellow, it looked like heaven to me.[*][1]

Clarence would quickly find out that while life in Birmingham marked an improvement over life in Hopeville—you got paid cash and had something to spend it on—it was far from heaven. In 1933,

---

* Birmingham's Terminal Station, opened in 1909, was a magnificent Byzantine-inspired Beaux Arts structure that was demolished in 1969 with the approval of a city government looking to attract new businesses. The site is today a freeway right-of-way, and the loss of this landmark continues to sadden local preservationists. The needless destruction of the terminal may be one reason why people in Birmingham have worked so tirelessly to preserve Rickwood.

when he was eighteen, he got a job at Sloss Furnaces; considering
that the Great Depression was in full swing, he was lucky to get it.
"When I was there," he told historians forty-seven years later, "it was
a man-killer. When you go in and hit the clock in the summertime,
you'd be wet . . . till you go back out."

Another black laborer, Will Battle, found employment at one
of the Ensley steelwork plants in 1906. "When I first started," he
recalled nearly three-quarters of a century later, "you didn't have no
day off. If you could make 365 days a year, you'd make 365 days. . . .
1911 was when we went to the off days. Work six days and rest
and another crew came on. One shift at night, one shift at day. It
revolved, twelve hours a day."[2]

The day off was Sunday, and that day meant baseball.

• FROM THE END OF WORLD WAR I through about 1950, if
you wanted to find the great heroes of Birmingham black ball on a
Friday or Saturday night, you'd look around Fourth Avenue from
Fifteenth to Eighteenth Street, the social hub of the city's black
community. The area was Birmingham's Harlem, with black-owned
banks, butcher shops, mortuaries, pool halls, clothing stores, barber
and beauty shops, and restaurants (specializing in barbecue and
what would later become known as soul food). There were four
banks, including the Penny Savings Bank, which was instrumental
in making loans for businesses and homes. At Tom's Real Shine
people waited in line to get "the best shine in town." And from 1908
to 1941 you could go out in style at Elsie Bradford's Funeral Home,
where the Cadillac hearse was accompanied by a full-length flower

car. There were movie theaters, such as the Carver* and the Lyric, and nightclubs that showcased some of the greatest black talent of the era.

Social life among the men centered on organized clubs like the Knights of Pythias, whose headquarters were across the street from the Lyric Theater. The Masonic Temple was not only the home of the black Masons but also housed offices for many black firms and professionals and even a branch of the library—for blacks only, of course. The Masonic Temple Ballroom featured social and athletic events in addition to weekly dances. Count Basie often played there, and Duke Ellington was featured once a year.[3] After a visit in 1926 Ellington went back to New York and wrote "Birmingham Breakdown."

Black Birmingham didn't just inspire but also made great music, most notably native musician Erskine Hawkins's hugely popular "Tuxedo Junction," named for the streetcar crossing at Tuxedo Park in Ensley, west of Birmingham.† In almost every material way, black Birmingham, which comprised about 40 percent of the population, lagged behind white Birmingham, but it can be said with certainty that musically it was light-years ahead.

For better or worse—most historians today would argue the latter—much of the popular image of Birmingham's black culture between the two world wars is due to a writer named Octavus Roy

---

* Today the Carver Theatre for the Performing Arts is the home of the Alabama Jazz Hall of Fame.

† Trumpeter, bandleader, and composer Erskine Ramsay Hawkins was born in Birmingham in 1914 and died in 1993, at the age of seventy-nine. Revered by Duke Ellington, Count Basie, and other period greats who often played with him, Hawkins lived long enough to hear his own music celebrated before integrated audiences.

Cohen. Scarcely anyone remembers his name today, but from 1919 through the early 1930s he was one of the country's most popular novelists, screenwriters, and short story writers. One of his favorite subjects was the culture black people had created for themselves on their side of Birmingham.

Born in 1891 in South Carolina, Cohen went to Porter Military Academy and then Clemson University. Like so many popular magazine writers of the period, he worked through a dizzying series of newspaper jobs, mostly in New Jersey but for a while at one of the smaller papers in Birmingham, the *Ledger*. He seems to have possessed one undeniable literary quality: curiosity. Most white journalists would have avoided Birmingham's black sections, even if they hadn't been wary about going there, but Cohen, a Jew and an outsider who had spent considerable time as a reporter in the North, found grist for his mill in life around Fourth Avenue.*

His "Darktown Birmingham" column for the *Saturday Evening Post* featured a character—caricature would be more accurate—named Florian Slappey, a wheeler-dealer of the type Cohen met and probably shared beer and barbecue with on Fourth Avenue. Slappey, a bumbling comic private eye, was roughly the black equivalent of a Damon Runyon character and very nearly as popular as some of Runyon's creations, appearing regularly not only in the *Saturday Evening Post* but in several short films, for which Cohen is believed to have written the scripts under the pen name Alfred A. Cohen.

Cohen's 1925 novel, *Bigger and Blacker*, involved the misadventures of the Midnight Pictures Corporation, a company of comical

---

* The bulk of Jefferson County's Jewish population lived in the prosperous suburb of Mountain Brook, not in the city proper. Most of Birmingham's major department stores, particularly Blach's, whose owners did much to support the Barons, were owned by Jews.

semiprofessional filmmakers specializing in two-reel comedies. For years after the book's publication, white newspapermen visiting Birmingham asked for the address of Midnight Pictures.

Cohen, who later achieved more commercial success as a writer of detective stories and screenplays for Hollywood B films, was no Damon Runyon and apparently never met a black man in Birmingham who could say "that" instead of "dat" or "Yes, sir" instead of "Yas suh." He also never seemed to find a black person who had a care in the world aside from where he was going to scrape together enough loose change to go to a dance hall or bet on the Black Barons at Rickwood Field. Cohen barely scratched the surface of the richness and complexity of black life in Birmingham in the 1920s and 1930s, and he never really understood the role baseball played in it.

The reality, the way blacks saw themselves in the period, was very different.

· BASEBALL WAS AN INTEGRAL PART of Birmingham's black community before Rickwood Field was built, in fact, even before the Negro Leagues were organized. In 1904 a dynamic and enterprising black man named Charles Isham Taylor arrived in Birmingham from South Carolina. Born in 1872, Taylor had worked his way from a dirt-poor background to an education at Clark College in Atlanta and had served in the U.S. Army during the Spanish-American War.

Taylor was a baseballist, and he came to Birmingham to put together a black baseball team from the talent being groomed by the town's industrial leagues. As far back as the turn of the century, Birmingham industrialists realized the importance of baseball for both their black and their white employees: it provided great exercise and improved morale enormously, and shirts with company names and logos were effective advertising. In 1908, after four years of staging and promoting baseball games in and around Birmingham, Taylor and his three brothers formed the Birmingham Giants.

Lorenzo "Piper" Davis, whose name is now virtually synonymous with the history of the Black Barons, told me in a 1987 interview,

> There is a lot to be said about the way the companies treated us. It was the closest thing that a black man could get to a square deal. They paid for bats and gloves and uniforms, and they even paid for our travel expenses to go play other company teams, and that's more than the Negro traveling teams did. We were pretty conscious of what the white guys got that we didn't get, but I'd have to say that on the whole the companies gave us pretty much what they gave them. Everything but a chance to play white teams.

He was speaking of a time, of course, more than three decades after Taylor came to Birmingham to put together a team. But even then, in the early 1900s, one could see the genesis of a mighty movement. "See," Davis told researcher Theodore Rosengarten in 1977, "your better ballplayers were right here working, they had experienced life on the road a little bit. I played at ACIPCO [the American Cast Iron and Pipe Company, one of the area's largest foundries] with Artie Wilson [later a star in the Pacific Coast League who made it to the big leagues with the New York Giants in 1951 long enough to have a cup of coffee]. Ed Steele, guys that played later in the Negro Leagues. [Bill] Powell, too, and Herman Bell, the catcher. We were on the ACIPCO ball club. That's five Black Barons on the same company team."[4]

Simply put, the heart of the black baseball world was Birmingham, and it was forged in its mines and mills. In time it would produce perhaps the greatest all-around player in baseball history.

Building on company team talent—he had no other resources to work with—Taylor fielded the Birmingham Giants, who barnstormed through the Midwest, beating teams as far north as Chicago. The Giants were hugely popular with the black community in Birmingham, but Taylor quickly realized that although his talent might be Alabama grown there was far more money to be made north of the Mason-Dixon Line. In 1910, the year Rickwood opened, Taylor decided to move the Giants to a town in Indiana called West Baden. Many black fans in Birmingham were heartbroken; a black paper, the *Birmingham Reporter*, continued to follow the Giants, now renamed the West Baden Sprudels.* For one brief shining moment, the Sprudels won immortality: on September 11, 1911, in an exhibition, they defeated the National League's Pittsburgh Pirates 2–1. The Pirates had the greatest all-around player the game had seen up to that point: Honus Wagner had led the National League that year in batting with a .334 average. Wagner was gracious in defeat and praised the Sprudels, earning him a reputation in black ball as a decent fellow. But the game received little publicity outside of black newspapers, as though "white folks' ball," as Piper Davis would later call it, didn't want to acknowledge that a black team could beat a white major league ball club.

In time, Taylor would find even West Baden too small for his operation and moved his club to Indianapolis, where, sponsored by

---

* The origin of the name has never been clearly established, though a "sprudel" was a fizzy soft drink of the period made with mineral water, and apparently in some midwestern states a popular soft drink, possibly an early competitor of Coca-Cola.

the American Brewing Company, it was renamed the ABC's.* The
ABC's would become one of the first teams in the Negro National
League, and Taylor would be almost as influential a figure in the
nascent Negro Leagues as the great Rube Foster.

Back in Birmingham, professional black baseball, still fed by
industrial-league talent, began to reform. Teams of Birmingham
All-Stars found ready opponents in black teams from other Alabama cities. Rick Woodward immediately recognized the economic
value and rented out his ballpark to black teams for a percentage of
the gross ticket sales—when, of course, the white Barons were on
the road. And so, black ball, especially every other Sunday, became a
Birmingham tradition. In 1919 a Labor Day doubleheader at Rickwood between black teams from Birmingham and Montgomery
drew an eye-opening gate of 15,000—and not all of them black, as
the right field bleachers (the "Negro bleachers" during white Barons
games) were filled with white fans.

Fans were happy to sit or stand in roped-off areas in the outfield. For once, the white world took notice of black ball: the *Birmingham Age-Herald* reported that the doubleheader saw "the largest
crowd of Negroes that ever attended a ball game in the United
States and next to the largest, irrespective of color, that ever jammed
into Rickwood."[5]

Woodward also rented Rickwood Field to the Ku Klux Klan
for its rallies.† The arrangement may seem cynical, but if Wood-

---

* West Baden, though, continued to be a popular spot for black sports, and in the 1930s
Joe Louis, the first black heavyweight champion since Jack Johnson before World War I,
trained there.

† The Klan wasn't as visible in Birmingham as in many other southern cities, possibly
because most integration in Jefferson County was in factories with government contracts,
and there was nothing the Klan could do about it. The KKK's headquarters, though, was

ward had not accommodated the Klan while also dealing with black teams, Rickwood Field might not be standing today.

• BY 1920 BIRMINGHAM counted 178,806 residents and had more than doubled its coal and pig iron production from the turn of the century. It also boasted a baseball park that was the envy of much of the baseball world and two professional baseball teams, even if the fans of one didn't know much about the other.*

The post–World War I era saw major changes come to baseball in Birmingham. The fans were ready to shake off the doldrums of the war years, which saw the Barons, like every other professional team in the country, cut back the number of games. The year 1920 saw a curve-balling pitcher named "Jughandle Johnny" Morrison† win 26 games, tying a Barons record, and though the team finished no better than fourth in the Southern Association, attendance was over 177,000. In comparison 1921 began in a whirlwind—two whirlwinds, actually. On April 16 a tornado ripped through Birmingham's West End—the second time a tornado hit the park—

---

just down the road in Tuscaloosa, and every so often they would put on a public spectacle in Birmingham just to make its presence known.

* This was the logical result of the 1910 Greater Birmingham Act, which allowed the city to annex many of the growing suburbs, including Avondale, Woodlawn, East Lake, and West End, where Rickwood was located. It also had the unintended effect of making the new ballpark officially part of the city of Birmingham.

† Morrison's nickname reflected his favorite postgame activity, frequenting one of Birmingham's numerous speakeasies, most of them located in the annexed neighborhoods. Great things were predicted for John, but alcohol got the best of him, as it did of so many promising ballplayers of the era. A teammate, on hearing a couple of years later that Morrison had strained his arm, wryly commented, "It was probably strained from lifting that jug so often."

"Diamond Kings Meet in Birmingham" *read the headline in the Bir-mingham* News *on March 18, 1922, when Ty Cobb (with the highest recorded career batting average in major league history, .367) faced off against Rogers Hornsby (with the highest career batting average in National League history, .358). Cobb had three hits in the game, but Hornsby had four.*

and slammed into the wooden outfield fence and bleachers. Repairs on the estimated $30,000 damage started the same day, and two days later Rickwood had a temporary fence in place for a series with Little Rock.

A tornado, however, didn't stir up Birmingham the way the

New York Yankees and Brooklyn Dodgers did. Twelve days earlier, on April 4, the Magic City was electrified by an exhibition game between the two New York teams. The Dodgers, with their popular manager Wilbert "Uncle Robbie" Robinson and their great left fielder Zack "Buck" Wheat, a future Hall of Famer, would have been enough to sell out Rickwood. But there was also the triumphant return (though he did not pitch that day) of Burleigh Grimes, who had won 23 games for the Dodgers in 1920. Grimes brought the crowd to its feet simply by grinning and waving his cap from the dugout. But all this was peanuts compared with the main attraction.

By 1920 Babe Ruth had changed America's game forever, obliterating all previous home run records when he hit 54 home runs that season, nearly three times as many as the entire Barons team. While Barons fans couldn't wait to see him in person, many were rooting for Rickwood Field and its immense center field to contain the Babe—if, that is, they could keep him from pulling the ball to right field. Ruth put on a spectacular show in batting practice, hitting balls over both the right and left field fences and very nearly reaching the top of the center field wall. In the game, though, he was held in check, going hitless in four at-bats, including a called strike three in his final time at the plate. Babe, assuming that final pitch was ball four, tossed his bat aside and started to stride to first base before home plate umpire George Moriarty barked out his call a second time to Ruth's obvious anger. The capacity-plus crowd didn't feel cheated, though, as both the Yankees' Bob Meusel[*] and the Dodgers' Zack Wheat hit homers.

---

[*] Meusel's brother Emil "Irish" Meusel had played for the Barons in 1916 and batted .312 that year. For his career Irish batted .310 and his brother Bob .309.

It was Wheat's home run that is still talked about—or rather, the home run he didn't hit. With the Yankees leading 7–5 in the top of the ninth, Wheat slammed a pitch into the crowd in the overflow seating in left. He gleefully circled the bases, thinking he had hit his second home run of the game. That's what the crowd thought, too. Moriarty, however, making his second controversial call of the game, waved the Dodgers' star back to second base. It had been agreed before the contest that a ball hit into the left field crowd would be a ground rule double. Fans along the third base line were outraged and started throwing their seat cushions onto the field. Some flipped them backhand, surely the first instance of Frisbee tossing ever seen at Rickwood. One hit Moriarty in the face. Incensed, he suspended the game before the Dodgers had their final outs and quickly fled into the tunnel.

• HAROLD JOSEPH "PIE" TRAYNOR—the nickname came from the way he fielded ground balls, as easy as pie—is regarded as the greatest third baseman in major league baseball in the first half of the twentieth century, but on the Barons he played short-stop. Signed by Pittsburgh Pirates owner Barney Dreyfuss and sent to Birmingham in 1920 for seasoning, he hit .336 with 13 triples and 47 stolen bases. His only apparent flaw was that his arm was too strong for a shortstop, and his throws often sent the ball into the right field stands. The Barons had a good season in 1921, winning 90 games, but they were never really in the pennant race as the Memphis Chicks rolled to 104 victories. Traynor's major league image would be that of a consummate gentleman, but on the Barons

PIE TRAYNOR (LEFT) AND TEAMMATE JOHN GOOCH. *Harold Traynor was nicknamed for his ability for making tough plays look "easy as pie." A shortstop with the Barons, he went on to become perhaps the outstanding major league third baseman in the first half of the twentieth century.*

he was such a talker that, according to a visiting Pittsburgh journalist, "he led the Southern Association in heckling."*[6]

---

* Why Traynor went from a loud-mouthed bench jockey in the minors to "the nicest man in baseball," as he was often called, in the majors has never been explained, but it probably had something to do with the influence of his manager on the Pirates, Bill McKechnie, a devout Methodist-Episcopalian nicknamed the Deacon by the Pittsburgh press. McKechnie was one of the few managers in baseball who thought that harassing the other

Twenty-seven years later, after compiling a .320 batting average over seventeen seasons with the Pirates and a reputation as the best-fielding third baseman up to that time, Traynor became the first former Baron to be elected to the Hall of Fame.

· THE TERM "NEGRO LEAGUE" was born in February of 1920 when Rube Foster, together with C. I. Taylor and several other black team owners, founded the Negro National League.[*] (John Leslie Wilkinson, generally known in print and to his friends as J.L., owned the Kansas City Monarchs even though he was white; he was allowed into the league because he had earned the trust and respect of his black colleagues.) Within a short time the Negro National League was rolling; by 1923 just under 410,000 tickets had been sold—the overwhelming majority to black fans, but nearly every ballpark where black teams played had sections for white fans, too.

At Sunday baseball, in the words of Negro League historian Mark Ribowsky,

---

team with verbal abuse was not only unsportsmanlike but often riled the other team into playing even harder.

[*] In his chapter on the Negro Leagues in *The New Bill James Historical Baseball Abstract*, Bill James sums up the complex history of black ball: "When we speak of the Negro Leagues, we often mean something more than the leagues themselves. Segregation in baseball dates back at least to 1867; Cap Anson's famous refusal to play against black players, which came twenty years later, is more properly described as a time when efforts to break the color line were turned back, rather than a time when the color line was established. From 1867 forward, when African Americans wanted to play baseball, they had to play it, in the main, within the walls of segregation" (p. 167).

BIRMINGHAM BLACK BARONS, 1927: *At the top left is Satchel Paige in his first known photograph.*

the black *glitterati* intermingled. A Sunday ball game was a place where the black brought out the cream of high-toned ebony society. The big leagues had Ladies Day, but the Negro Leagues had Easter every Sunday, a saints day that might feature Bojangles Robinson hoofing before the game and Lena Horne throwing out the first ball. By owning a black ball team, as Bojangles Robinson and Louis Armstrong both did, esteem in the black community could be had at a very small price.[7]

About two months after Foster and the owners met to establish the NNL, the Indianapolis ABC's, who had begun their existence as the Birmingham Giants, traveled to Birmingham for their spring training. For the first time Birmingham fans got to see the legendary Oscar Charleston, the man regarded by many as the greatest all-around player in black ball or perhaps anywhere else. According to *Baseball: The Biographical Encyclopedia*, "Many players have been compared to a great one—to Babe Ruth, Tris Speaker, Willie Mays, or Ty Cobb. But only one player was compared to all four. He was Oscar Charleston." Bingo DeMoss, a great second baseman in his own right, said, "Oscar was the only player I've ever seen who could turn twice while chasing a fly and then take it over his shoulder." Another outstanding center fielder, Hall of Famer James "Cool Papa" Bell, thought that Charleston had greater range than Willie Mays in center field.

Birmingham's black community was as enthralled by the presence of Charleston as white fans would be the following spring when Babe Ruth came to town. Not only did the game with the ABC's sell all available seats, but ropes were stretched across the outfield to accommodate more fans.

There may have been doubters in other cities, but among Birmingham black ball fans there was no doubt: they had to have a team of their own. Birmingham, though, had no wealthy black celebrities, and there was some doubt among Negro National League owners in the North whether Birmingham could support a team. For that matter, there were not that many black businessmen around with the capital to support a team. Frank M. Perdue, a white businessman, became the first owner of the Black Barons in the new Negro Southern League. It was a convenient arrangement for all, since Perdue had money and as part owner of the Barons had easy access, through Woodward, to Rickwood Field; the Black Barons' other owner was Oscar W. Adams, a black businessman.*

And so the Black Barons were born. Officially they were called

---

* Adams's son, Oscar W. Adams Jr., would become the first black supreme court justice in the state of Alabama. I had the honor of sitting next to him at one of the Barons' last games at Rickwood Field, in 1987.

the All-Stars, but no one called them that. Black company teams had
been called the Black Barons for years. It was common throughout
the South to simply affix "black" to the name of the local white team.
Thus in Atlanta the Negro team was the Black Crackers, a name that
seemed a contradiction in terms. The All-Stars were the Black Barons to their fans, and within a couple of years they were called nothing else.

Black Barons fans quickly latched on to the team's first two genuine stars. George "Mule" Suttles and Norman "Turkey" Stearnes,
both terrific hitters and fine fielders. Suttles, who was 6' 6" and
weighed 230 pounds in his prime, had developed a tremendous
upper body from digging coal as a youth in north Alabama. At age
eighteen he had begun working for ACIPCO and playing ball for
its team. Black sportswriters were pretty much in accord that he was
black ball's leading long-blaster. Suttles was said to have hit a ball
nearly 600 feet while playing in Havana's Tropical Park.*

---

* Suttles's most famous home run was hit at the East–West All-Star game at Comiskey
Park on August 11, 1935. *Pittsburgh Courier* sports editor William G. Nunn wrote about
the game; here, in his best Grantland Rice mode, is his description:

> For the West, Mule Suttles at bat!
> That's the resonant voice of the announcer, through the new public address
> system of the park.
> The M-U-L-E!
> Reverberating through the reaches of this historic ballpark and bounding and
> rebounding through the packed stands comes the chant of some 25,000 frenzied
> spectators.
> They're yelling for blood! They're yelling for their idol, the bronzed Babe Ruth
> of colored baseball to come through.
> It's more than a call! It's a chant! It's a prayer!

Suttles's home run, hit off the New York Cubans Martin Dihigo, was said to have landed
475 feet from home plate. "It was a Herculean feat," wrote Nunn. "One of the greatest in
baseball" (*Pittsburgh Courier*, August 12, 1935).

Norman Stearnes, at about 170 pounds, didn't hit home runs as far as Suttles did, but he hit more of them. Black ball historians credit him with more recorded home runs than even the great Josh Gibson, generally considered the greatest hitter of all the Negro Leaguers. A star in Montgomery before coming to Birmingham, Stearnes was described by Mark Ribowsky as "a cobralike outfielder ... All arms and legs ... a pastiche of oddities; in his batting stance he leaned way forward and his back foot pointed straight up. When he ran, his elbows flapped in and out—thus his nickname. He choked up on a light, thin bat, yet he hit moon-shot home runs."[8] He would have a twenty-year career in black baseball.

Buoyed by two of black ball's best sluggers and the best home ballpark of any Negro League team, the Black Barons were ready for the big time: at the end of the 1923 season, they applied for and were granted a berth in the Negro National League. The move seemed like a natural, but problems soon revealed themselves. The Barons did well enough at home, but transportation was expensive and time-consuming, and once they were on the road in the North they were forced to spend weeks without playing a home game. Other teams had to travel, too, but few teams in the Negro Leagues had as much ground to cover as the Black Barons. Their road trips, especially for young black men starting out in the game, could be exhausting and draining.

· BABE RUTH CARRIED a portable holiday with him. At the end of March in 1925, both white and black Birmingham were once again electrified as Babe and the Yankees passed through town on

THE BABE AND YOUNG FANS: *1933 photo of the Babe with young fans Sam Burr, Jack Cuniff, Bob Leland, and Tom Brown (identity of fifth boy is unknown). The Babe was a huge favorite at Rickwood. According to legend—dubious legend—he hit the longest home run in history over Rickwood's right field stands.*

the way to New York from spring training. In 1924 the Yankees had finished second in the American League, two games behind the Washington Senators, but to many fans they were the only team in the league: they had Babe Ruth, and in 1924 Babe had led the league in batting (.378) and home runs (46). In 1921 Ruth hadn't given the crowd what they wanted, but this time he was determined not to disappoint. According to the *Birmingham Age-Herald*, "It was a dramatic moment when the mighty slugger stepped to the plate with the sacks fully populated and his own team two runs in the rear. And then the Babe delivered in true Ruthian style, the drive going in a line over the right field wall—and four pairs of hoofs dented the plate."[9]

Birmingham's black fans got a bonus that day. During batting practice Ruth slammed several balls into the Negro bleachers in right. On this day, at least, there was an advantage to being segregated.

In one of Ruth's appearances at Rickwood—or so the story goes—he hit what was reputed to be the longest home run in baseball history. The ball cleared the right field roof—again, so the story goes—and landed in either an open boxcar or coal tender, depending on which version of the story you hear. It did not reach the ground again until the train stopped in Atlanta a couple of hours later. No one knows what year or off which pitcher Ruth hit this mighty shot, because the story is, of course, apocryphal. For one thing, Ruth would have had to hit the longest home run in baseball history just for the ball to reach the train tracks, which, by one estimate, were at least 700 feet from Rickwood's home plate.

Where, then, did the story originate? There's no record of such a home run ever having been hit, at least not in any Birmingham paper, and no known player or manager or sportswriter ever said he was there. Perhaps more to the point, no one has ever surfaced who claimed to have retrieved the ball from the train after it arrived in Atlanta.

Ruth inspired so many whoppers that it's hard to tell, but this one can probably be laid at the feet of popular sportswriter, radio personality, and myth-monger Bill Stern, who loved telling the story even though he never saw any game at Rickwood Field, let alone one with Babe Ruth on the field. Why would he have set this fabled home run in Rickwood? Probably because when he told the tale in New York in the mid-1930s, he wanted to be sure he placed it far enough away that there could be no credible witnesses to deny it.

Babe Ruth hit several titanic shots at Rickwood Field, but the one he didn't hit became the subject of a folktale that helped make Rickwood Field famous all over the baseball world.

VIEW FROM THE FRONT: *The Spanish mission–style entrance was added in 1928. When former Los Angeles Dodgers manager Tommy Lasorda came to Birmingham in 2006, he proclaimed, "I feel like I'm back home!"*

THE GOLDEN AGE

T HE GOLDEN AGE of Birmingham baseball was the second half of the 1920s. Steel was king, industry boomed, and unemployment was rare. These were the most prosperous years in Birmingham's history. No one could have anticipated that in a few short years the very economic factors that had caused Birmingham to flourish in such a short time would, in an even shorter period, lead to near-devastation. On the surface, life was placid and the future bright with promise. Black and white were separate though not equal, but for tens of thousands of blacks who had come to Jones Valley from the Cotton Belt equality was not yet the overwhelming issue it would become in the next two decades.

In 1926 whites and blacks were living better on the whole than their parents, the majority of whom had been farmers and even sharecroppers, could have ever imagined. Baseball had no rival. On

January 1, 1926, the University of Alabama football team, led by their sensational halfback (and future western film star) Johnny Mack Brown, thrilled the entire state by defeating the heavily favored University of Washington Huskies in the Rose Bowl, capturing college football's mythical national championship. It was far and away the most colossal sporting event for Alabama up to that time. But football was a sometime thing that occurred a few weekends in the fall. White workingmen could not afford tickets to football games in Tuscaloosa—and black workingmen were not allowed, even if they had the money for tickets. Baseball, though, was for every man for most of the year. In early spring fans in Mobile, Montgomery, and Birmingham began anticipating the arrival of the major league teams as they headed north to begin the season, wondering which major league immortals would be playing at Rickwood Field.

The sports pages of both white and black newspapers devoted nearly all their space to profiles not only of new players on the local teams but of those who would be visiting Birmingham through the Southern Association and Negro National League circuits. It was affordable entertainment for the workingman, for entire families. The games were like mini-holidays, and the radio broadcasts, at least for the games of the white Barons, were a unifying theme for Birminghamians of both races. Piper Davis, who, like many black kids, listened to the Barons' radio broadcasts by Eugene "Bull" Connor, recalled Rickwood Field as one of the few places where blacks and whites, at least a few of them, relaxed and enjoyed something together. "My dad and I would go to games and, while standing in line for tickets, actually talk to white men about baseball—pennant races, famous players. I don't just mean Black Barons games, but the white Barons, too. Until I was grown and in college, I don't remem-

THE VIEW FROM CENTER FIELD: *The "Crow's Nest" on the grandstand roof, flanked by the unusual cantilevered lights, which ESPN.com's Jim Caple described as looking "as if they were peering over the roof for a better look."*

ber talking to a white man, really having a conversation with him, about anything except baseball."

Rick Woodward was determined to polish his ballpark into a jewel befitting the times. Fans continued to flock to Rickwood Field in the early 1920s, and the main attraction certainly wasn't the Barons, who finished third, fifth, and fifth in the first three years of the decade. It dawned on Rick Woodward that whether or not he produced a winning team, he had a winning ballpark. He had built it, and the fans were coming whether the Barons won or not. He was determined to accommodate even more of them and make the fans—the white fans, at least, as the Negro bleachers were left uncovered—as comfortable as possible in the brutal Alabama summer heat. In 1924 he contracted with the Paul Wright Company to cover the right field bleachers by extending the grandstand roof and also to design new steel bleachers beyond the concrete bleachers in left field. New box seats were added along the first base side. In 1927 Woodward brought in the architects Denham, VanKeuren, and Denham* to extend the grandstand roof down the third base line, bringing shade to the concrete bleachers, as well as adding box seats along the third base line.

The next year Woodward again chose the Paul Wright Company for another round of renovations. The covered grandstand that extends all the way down to the right field foul pole, curving around the pole, was constructed, leaving only the black patrons sitting unprotected from the blazing sun. A more distinctive addition, one that has been identified strongly with Rickwood over the last eight decades, was the 40-foot-high scoreboard installed in left center (it would be moved closer to center about twenty years later by the team's new general manager, Eddie Glennon). To modern fans, the manually operated scoreboard, with drop-in slots for hand-painted numbers, is old-fashioned, but in 1928 it was a radical idea: there were spaces for scores from big-league games around the country, so when updates came in over the wire Rickwood fans could follow the fortunes of the New York Yankees, Brooklyn Dodgers, and Connie Mack's Philadelphia A's.

The year 1928 also brought the change to Rickwood that has become its signature. In architecture Spanish colonial revival style or Spanish mission style, as it became popularly known, began in Florida and evolved into a national craze following the release of the

---

* Within forty years the firm would evolve into Davis Architects, who has continued to work on Rickwood Field renovations into the twenty-first century.

No ELECTRICITY REQUIRED: *The manual drop-in scoreboard may be Rick-wood's most enduring symbol. Five of the big-league franchises on the scoreboard are no longer in their original cities. The scoreboard fell into disrepair and was eventually replaced with an electronic version, but one of the first projects of the Friends of Rick-wood was to re-create the original in the early 1990s.*

hugely popular 1910 film *Ramona*, directed by D. W. Griffith and starring Mary Pickford. The story was set in old Spanish Califor-nia, and several of the buildings used in Griffith's production weren't movie sets but surviving examples of period architecture. The trend swept across the country, with many notable examples in the Los Angeles/Beverly Hills area, especially the El Capitan Theater, built directly across the street from Grauman's Chinese Theatre in 1926. Huge mission-style homes were built for such celebrities as west-ern film star William S. Hart and Buster Keaton, Joan Bennett, Carole Lombard, and Loretta Young. After the Depression, the houses became the favorites of budget-minded stars who wanted to live comfortably and fashionably but sensibly, such as Loretta Young (who starred in the 1936 film version of *Ramona*). They are almost identical in style to the houses still standing throughout the country.

A handful of cities, including Birmingham, had entire Spanish-mission-style neighborhoods. A section of Homewood, a Birmingham suburb on the south side of Red Mountain, was originally the town of—fittingly enough—Hollywood, a 1926 residential development featuring mission-style houses. Most of Hollywood, Alabama, remains intact today and is one of the area's most popular tourist attractions. Many of the houses are indistinguishable from those in and around Hollywood, California. In the 1920s Rick Woodward built his own mission-style mansion on Red Mountain, copying a famous home in Pasadena, California. (The Woodward

"No Betting in This Park": *Warning along the leftfield line, which was seldom obeyed.*

home was for decades said to be the most expensive private home in Alabama.)

So it was in keeping with the trend that Rickwood's front gate was transformed into a Spanish-mission-style façade facing Twelfth Street West and Second Avenue West, which had just been paved. The new one-story entranceway, replete with arched openings and plaster ornaments, was set off with stucco walls and a red clay tile roof. The "arcade," as it is still called, connected to a two-story building that housed the Barons offices. Between the entrance and the grandstand was an open breezeway called a "privileged man" where gentlemen smoked and talked.

Eighty years later Rickwood's Spanish flavor continues to open the eyes of first-time visitors. When former Los Angeles Dodgers manager Tommy Lasorda visited Rickwood Field in 2006, he exclaimed, "I feel like I'm back home!"

• RICKWOOD FIELD got dressed up just in time to welcome the greatest pitcher in Black Barons history. In the spring of 1926, while playing the Black Lookouts in Chattanooga (the Chattanooga Giants, actually, but even the press called them the Black Lookouts), the Black Barons got their first look at a gangly 6' 3½" right-handed pitcher by the name of LeRoy Paige, who just happened to be pitching in his first professional baseball game. No one called him LeRoy; he called himself Satch, short for Satchel, which he said he got from stealing purses and briefcases back in his native Mobile. So that's what everyone else called him, too, and the way his name appeared in the box scores of Chattanooga's black paper. Later, Paige would claim that he had shut down the Black Barons that day, although the record shows they hit him well enough to lose by only one run, 5–4. But the Black Barons' brass was convinced they had seen something—a potentially great pitcher as well as a great drawing card. They offered Paige a hefty $275 a month to pitch for the Black Barons in 1927, a whopping $225 more than he was making with the Black Lookouts. "Birmingham," Satch noted in his autobiography, *Maybe I'll Pitch Forever*, "looked mighty good."[1]

Satchel Paige was the Black Barons' ticket back to the black major leagues. In *Bases Loaded with History*, Timothy Whitt described in captivating detail Paige's debut with the Black Barons. Tied 1–1 with the Stars in St. Louis, Paige clunked the batter, the Stars' catcher, in the head with a fastball. The St. Louis player exploded in anger, picked up his bat and charged the mound: "Paige took off for the safety of the Birmingham dugout, but did not make it. Murray [the St. Louis catcher] heaved his bat at Paige, striking the pitcher in the back just above the hip. A near riot ensued, with fans taking the field, some carrying knives and blackjacks. Police officers had to restore order, and the game was called, bringing to a close Satchel Paige's first NNL start."[2]

Incomplete records show that Paige won at least 8 and lost at least 3 in 1927, with 3 recorded shutouts. It was enough to give the Black Barons the second-half championship of the NNL. They then played the winners of the first half, the Chicago American Giants, for the NNL championship. They lost, but it had been a fabulous season, which proved that the Barons belonged with the best teams in black ball.

"Birmingham," Paige told writer David Lipman in his autobiography, "showed me a new world of baseball." Part of that world was the side money a talented kid could make when not pitching in league games: "When I wasn't throwing for Birmingham, [Black Barons manager] Bill Gatewood would rent me to another club so I could pick up a piece of change and get him some."[*3] Paige was in such demand elsewhere because the Birmingham black press doted on him and followed his every move. He made sure that Black Barons fans knew who he was from his opening start. He wanted to re-create his old barnstorming stunt of bringing his outfielders to the infield and seating them on the ground while he disposed of the opposing batters, a bona fide crowd-pleasing stunt. Paige knew, however, that Gatewood would have none of it—these weren't exhibitions; it was real professional baseball, and Gatewood wanted his players to understand that. No barnstorming stunts would be allowed by anyone wearing a Black Barons uniform, so Satch thought of another way to make himself the center of attention.

In his first game at Rickwood, he would later recall, he bragged to the other team that he was going to strike out the first six batters. The patrons in the box seats along the first and third base lines howled and cheered in appreciation and passed the news back until all of Rickwood Field knew of Paige's boast, exactly as if it had been announced on a PA system. A hush followed as Satch prepared to make good on his promise; he then yelled it out a second time; the crowd roared.

"The whole place was jumping," he said, "when the first guy

---

* Paige said many times that he pitched for other teams under aliases—which brings up the intriguing question of how he could have done this while being perhaps the best-known player in southern black baseball. Barons star of the 1940s Willie Lee, who grew up on Satchel Paige lore, suggests that many, if not all, of the teams Satchel pitched against knew very well who he was and were quite willing to look the other way because Paige was such good box office that everybody made money on the deal.

came up against me." He started the first batter with a curveball that broke on the inside corner for a strike. "I fired in close to him and he couldn't untangle himself. He struck out quick. The next two batters also struck out." He didn't throw a single ball in the inning. He struck out all three batters on ten pitches, allowing just one foul ball. After the third whiff, the crowd gave him a standing ovation.

When going out for the second inning, Paige recalled, "I pulled off my hat and waved to them. They liked that." The ladies pulled off their hats and returned the compliment. After a foul on the first pitch, Satch effortlessly fanned the next batter on two "jump balls." The next hitter went down on a fastball. Then, from the opponents' dugout, came a white towel tied to the handle of a bat waved back and forth so everyone in the ballpark could see. Paige looked over at the enemy and grinned: "They'd surrendered."

The Black Barons went wild, and Satch knew, "I was in around Birmingham."

The next batter popped up. As they ran off the field, a team-mate kidded Satch, reminding him that he hadn't struck out the sixth batter as promised. "They'd already surrendered," Paige told him. "When ol' Satch needs a strikeout, he gets it."[4]

Paige, though, wasn't the best pitcher on the Black Barons in 1927. By consensus, the best was a fastballing sidearmer named Harry Salmon, who, in his day, was as much of an Alabama hero as Satchel Paige. Salmon was a *recorded* 14–6—he might have won more games that year, but Negro League teams couldn't afford their own scorekeepers, and baseball historians have been forced to dig box scores and accounts from the often incomplete archives of black newspapers. Paige was at least 8–3 for the season. Salmon reminded Paige, who had seen them both, of Ewell Blackwell, the 6' 6" Cincinnati Reds whip-like sidearmer who, for at least one season before he hurt his arm (1947, when he led the National League with 22 wins), was regarded as close to unhittable, at least by right-handed batters. "Harry Salmon pitched from the side like Ewell Blackwell," Paige once told an interviewer. "He was hard to hit. He tickled me. All the batters would jump out of the way when he went into his act."[5]

Sometime in the early 1970s Salmon was discovered by Negro League researcher John Holway to be living in Pittsburgh, and Holway recorded the only known extensive interview with him. Salmon, who was born in Warrior, Alabama, about eighteen miles outside Birmingham, in 1895, drifted from mine to mine around the Birmingham area playing for company teams. He became a Black Baron in 1920, the team's first year.

Like many of the black players, Salmon spent a considerable amount of time observing his white counterparts and comparing them with the men in his own league. "Pie Traynor," he later recalled, "played for the Pirates, came up the same year I did, '20. He was playing short for the Birmingham Barons, the white team. I saw him play a lot of times. No, I never played against him. They wouldn't allow that. Sam West was playing outfield for the Barons, too. Went up to the Washington Senators."*

Best of all, Salmon remembered Satchel, whom he had met in 1926 when Paige was pitching for Chattanooga and Salmon for the

---

* West just missed hitting .300 by a point over sixteen major league seasons, most of them with the Senators. He was a five-time All-Star who twice led the American League in fielding average.

Black Barons. He beat Paige twice that year, both complete-game 2–1 victories. He recalled beating him again in 1932 while he was pitching for the Homestead Grays against Paige's Pittsburgh Craw-fords. "I can't remember a game that he ever beat me," said Salmon.

They were teammates when Satchel came to the Black Barons in 1927, and Salmon claimed to have taught the younger man a few things. In the beginning, Paige "wasn't much of a curve ball man," mostly sending hitters down with a fastball. The two of them would "practice, practice" together. "We used to get out and throw and see how many strikes we could throw . . . when the years go by, you learn how to pitch more with your head than with your arm. That's what he became—a good-headed pitcher."

The Satchel Paige with whom Salmon played and roomed with on the road "was full of fun—you know how youngsters are. He was our showman. He even played a jew's harp at times. He'd entertain us back in the hotel."[6]

The crowds loved Satch's style—the slow long-legged stride off the mound, the whip-like release of his amazing right arm, his quips to the fans and to the opposition, and the colorful stories—some of them actually true, or at least partly true, that they had read in their local papers. Paige quickly established himself as the biggest box office draw in southern black ball. In 1928 he won at least 12 games for the Barons; no one knows how many games he may have won for other teams under various aliases. He pitched at least three shut-outs and is known to have walked only 19 batters in 120 innings. (An impressive figure no matter how you look at it, though, as Piper Davis pointed out to me in an interview, in black ball fans wanted to see the ball in play, so batters did not go to the plate expecting to work the count for a walk.)

He may have been even better in 1929. On April 29, at the Black

Barons home opener, he struck out 17 batters, and later in the season duplicated that feat in Detroit. He went on to set a record for confirmed strikeouts by a Negro League pitcher with 184, though his known record slipped to 12–11, possibly because at this point the Barons couldn't field an effective team to back him up. He started and won the Black Barons' final two games of the season, a doubleheader against the Memphis Red Sox. When asked by novelist William Price Fox why he had allowed himself to be worked that hard, he said, "They knew I'd keep the fans in the park for that second game, so they slipped me a little extra."[7] The next year he did what Turkey Stearnes and Mule Suttles did when they found out you could make more money playing for northern teams (and pitching in integrated barnstorming exhibitions): he went north to pitch for the Baltimore Black Sox. When the money proved disappointing, he came back to Birmingham, posting at least 12 wins for the 1930 season.*

In 1931 Satchel Paige went north again, and the Negro National League collapsed. Rube Foster, the most important man in the history of black ball, died of a heart attack at age forty-nine on December 9, 1930, after being confined in a mental asylum in Kankakee, Illinois, for four years. In 1925 Foster had been nearly asphyxiated by a gas leak, and although he recovered and returned to baseball, dementia marked by erratic behavior plagued him for years before he was committed. His wife told of how he would suddenly jump out of bed, yelling that he was ready to pitch in the World Series. Many believed that had Foster lived and not suffered mental ill-

* Timothy Whitt's research credits Paige with at least 15 wins for 1930, 3 with Baltimore and 12 with Birmingham. Whitt estimates Paige's four-year winning percentage from 1927 to 1930 at .667.

ness, the man who organized the Negro Leagues could have held it together through hard times, but according to Mark Ribowsky this view "overlooked the league's failing condition when Foster left, and the alienation he left behind."

Probably nothing, not even a healthy Rube Foster, could have helped black ball survive the first wave of the Great Depression without damage. By 1931 Satch was gone, and so was the Negro National League. The Black Barons survived as a name and as an entry in the Negro Southern League, a minor league. It would take both the Barons and the league six years to recover. Satchel continued on his convoluted road to the major leagues, to the Hall of Fame, and, finally, to his place as an American folk hero. So far he remains the only professional baseball player after whom Woody Allen has named a son.

In future years ballplayers would measure their own greatness by how they performed against Satchel Paige, and those who missed the opportunity regretted it. Mickey Mantle was always proud of the fact that he had faced Paige twice and was able to hit a home run off him. In his 1988 autobiography, Willie Mays recalled his first meeting with Paige:

Now, you've got to remember that this was the late 1940's—and he already had been famous *since the 1920's*. The man was the most interesting player I had ever come up against. He stood six four and weighed about 170 pounds. His rules for staying out of trouble and in shape hadn't become famous yet. The one I like best went: "Don't look back, something might be gaining on you. . . ." He was about forty when the Indians brought him up as a rookie, but he was no rookie to me. He showed me the darnedest stuff I ever saw, along with some of the screwiest motions and combinations of different speeds. Old Satchel could really drive you crazy.

He had a knuckleball, a screwball, an assortment of curves—and his hesitation pitch. He'd pump his arm around like a windmill, and bring it over his head and you expected to see the ball coming down, because that's the point at which a pitcher would throw. But nothing happened. He would be almost in his follow-through when all of a sudden the darn ball would appear and you would be swinging way in front of it.

Yet during this first meeting with the legend, I got a double off Paige my very first time up. I stood on second, dusting myself off, feeling pretty good. Paige walked toward me.

"That's it, kid," he muttered.

I didn't know what he meant—was he angry? Did he mean I had had it for the day?

It didn't take long to find out. My next time up I went *whoosh*, *whoosh*, and *whoosh*. I never saw a fastball from him, only those crazy curves....[8]

William Price Fox noted that Dick "Night Train" Lane, a Pro Football Hall of Fame cornerback for the Detroit Lions,* began his career as a professional athlete playing in the minor leagues. In Council Bluffs, Iowa, his team was scheduled to play against

---

* Also husband of Hall of Fame jazz vocalist Dinah Washington.

Paige, but the game was canceled owing to rain; Lane sat on a curb-stone outside the ballpark, soaked to the skin, crying, because, he explained, "I'd never get another chance to bat against him. I tell you, it almost broke my heart. That's how important he was to me." Bob Feller called the prewar Satchel Paige "the best I ever saw, and I'm judging him on the way he overpowered or outwitted some of the best big players of the day."

William Price Fox, who got to know Satch better than any of his earlier biographers, wrote, "The press who'd made up [Paige's] slogans and 'Rules To Live By' and his not eating fried foods and his Uncle Tom demeanors had trivialized him and made him more comic than heroic. And in doing so they had done Satchel Paige and all baseball, black or white, a grave injustice."[9]

The only ballplayer to surpass Satchel Paige as a folk hero in post–World War II America, Yogi Berra, recalled showering in the clubhouse with Paige after the American League All-Star game in 1949. He noted that Paige didn't use ice after a ballgame, but in the manner of Oriental sports medicine, mostly heat. "I never knew a man who could put water that hot on his arm the way he did. That stuff would be smoking and would have scalded the average man. But Satch loved it." Yogi also said, "I hit him a few times toward the end of his career, and he still had plenty of stuff on the ball. I wish I'd gotten to bat against him earlier."[10]

• EVERY BASEBALL FAN knows the name Satchel Paige, but scarcely anyone recalls the name of the man who was probably the greatest hitter during Rickwood's golden age, Elliot Bigelow.

Rickwood's renovations did something to change conditions

for hitters. No one is quite sure what. Perhaps the roof over the grandstands affected the wind currents, or perhaps the center field wall allowed hitters to see better when the pitcher released the ball. Maybe the mound was lowered a couple of inches. Perhaps it was just another sign of the times. The late 1920s are regarded by many sports historians as the golden age of American sports, the era of the big hitters, and at no time did they hit bigger than the second half of the decade—Babe Ruth and Lou Gehrig in baseball, Red Grange in football, Jack Dempsey in boxing, Bill Tilden in tennis, Bobby Jones in golf—and, in minor league baseball, Elliot Bigelow.

No one is certain, but *something* dramatically changed the balance between batters and pitchers at Rickwood. In 1927 the Barons, after years of frustration, were back in the pennant race and won 91 games, finishing second to the New Orleans Pelicans. They did it with six .300 hitters in the lineup, the best of whom was Bigelow at .361.* "Babe," or "Gilly," or "Sandy"—he was apparently called all three nicknames by friends and teammates—led the Southern Association in runs scored with 137 and runs batted in with 143. He also won the home run title with the amazing total of 19. It would be interesting to know how many of those were hit in Rickwood, which still had dead-ball-length outfield fences.

The next year the Barons, under new manager Johnny Dobbs, won the Southern Association pennant with a superb 99–54 record and an entire lineup of .300 hitters—in fact, five part-time players also hit over .300. Bigelow hit .395 and struck out only 19 times.

---

* I'm using the spelling of Bigelow's first name that is given on www.baseball-reference .com; in *Bases Loaded with History*, Timothy Whitt uses that spelling as well. STAT's *All-time Major League Handbook* gives him two *t*'s, as does *The Southern Association in Baseball, 1885–1961*.

For the first time in the league's history, the split-season format—where the leader of the first half of the season played the leader of the second half—was implemented; the Barons won the first half, the Memphis Chicks won the second, and then the Barons wiped Memphis out in four straight games to take the flag. The topic of conversation around the South and even up North was Birmingham's bombers: what exactly were the Barons eating for breakfast to produce such astonishing numbers? The reason for the hitting explosion has never been determined; perhaps it was nothing more than more talented players imitating the aggressive big-league-style hitting of Babe Ruth, Lou Gehrig, and Rogers Hornsby.

Whatever spurred the Barons' hitting that season, they made minor league history. Southern Association historian Marshall D. Wright concluded that, in retrospect, "Birmingham's stratospheric 1928 team batting average stacks up well against other top level league record holders." The 1928 Barons, Wright added, were "the best hitting top level team in minor league history."[11]

The next season Elliot Bigelow's contract was picked up by the Boston Red Sox, for whom he played 100 games in 1929. He never got another chance to play professional ball. He was thirty-one when he finally got his shot, and after the season the Red Sox released him. No explanation was offered at the time; most assumed that Bigelow, who would have been thirty-two the following season, was too old to have a future in the big leagues. From 1925 to 1928 Bigelow had an astonishing four years with Chattanooga and Birmingham in which he never hit less than .349. In 1930 he was back in Chattanooga, where he hit .331 but played in only 57 games. Bigelow's old friends were puzzled at his short season in Chattanooga. Two years later they found out why, when he died of cerebral meningitis. The bacterial infection, exacerbated by drinking, had apparently been contracted in Boston.

Elliot Allardice Bigelow, with a .359 career average, was, according to the Society for American Baseball Research (SABR), the all-time batting king of the Southern Association. His flower was born to blush unseen, except by those who saw him in his prime at Rickwood Field.

DIXIE SERIES GAME, B'HAM, ALA. OCT. 2, 1929.

RICKWOOD IN THE GOLDEN AGE: *The Barons play the 1929 Texas League champions, the Dallas Steers, before a packed house with the legendary manual scoreboard presiding over the proceedings.*

THE GREATEST GAME
EVER PLAYED

WIRE ME 150 WORDS every day on Dizzy Dean," the
sports editor of the *Birmingham News*, Zipp Newman,
wrote to a colleague in Houston. "What does he do to pass time?
What does he eat? Let's have all the dope. He's started a stampede
here for tickets. His name has already become a household word in
Birmingham. From what you hear, you would think he's the whole
Houston ball club. The common impression around town is 'What
do you think Dizzy will do in the series?' And the answer is 'Pack
Rickwood Field.'"

There was nothing like the Dixie Series in all of the South, east
or west, and almost nothing else like it in the entire nation. There
was no pro football, and college football mostly ignited interest only

in those who had been to college.* The World Series, of course, was bigger to the entire country, but it's doubtful that in the states that made up the Southern Association, and in Texas, which had a league all to itself, even the fall classic between the American and National Leagues was of more significance.

The 1929 Dixie Series championship had set the state on fire. The Barons had sold over 200,000 tickets that season, just as they had done every year since 1925. The pitching staff for the 1929 team included a little-used veteran named Ray Caldwell, who had pitched only 65 innings, but most of them brilliant, and compiled a 4–2 record with 1.80 ERA, easily the lowest on the team. Caldwell, born in the nearly abandoned mining town of Corydon, Pennsylvania, was already forty-one years old that season.† His first year in the majors was 1910, the year Rickwood Field and Dizzy Dean (in Lucas, Arkansas) were born. Caldwell pitched for twelve years in the big leagues, all of them in the American League, nine in New York. He had done well, winning 134 games and losing 120 for teams that were far from powerhouses, winning 19 games in 1915 for New York and 20 for Cleveland in 1920. His career highlight was a no-hitter for the Red Sox. (He was also a respectable hitter, with a career batting average of .248, eight

---

* That would begin to change during the 1934 season, when quarterback Dixie Howell, throwing to the great Don Hutson and his other end, Paul "Bear" Bryant, won a stunning 29–23 victory over mighty Stanford in the Rose Bowl, giving the Crimson Tide their first national championship. "The only way to think about the Rose Bowl back then," says sports historian Bert Randolph Sugar, whose book *The SEC* chronicles the history of the conference through 1978, "is to see it as the Super Bowl of the Depression era." It's safe to say, though, that the Dixie World Series of 1931 was the biggest sporting event in Alabama and the entire South before the 1935 Rose Bowl, and probably a bigger event all through the South.

† A Dizzy Dean biographer, Vince Staten, says in his 1992 book, *Ol' Diz: A Biography of Dizzy Dean*, that Caldwell was referred to as "Old Man." I have yet to find corroboration for this.

home runs, and 46 doubles.) By the time he reached Birmingham, he was clearly playing out the string. As with so many grizzled big leaguers of his day, the bottle and late hours had taken their toll. One apocryphal story was that his manager in Cleveland, Tris Speaker, had put a clause in Caldwell's contract requiring him to get drunk the night after his turn in the rotation, the idea being that then he would certainly be ready when his turn came around again. Like many such stories, this one contained a grain of truth: Caldwell tended to rise late in the afternoon after his pitching turn and usually did not come to the ballpark at all the day after a start. By 1929, though, his drinking was more under control, and he had put his life back together, marrying an Alabama girl—his third marriage—and making it known to local fans and press that he was grateful for the opportunity to close out his career on a top-level minor league team.

In 1930 the Barons slipped to third place (attendance dipped as well, to about 183,000), but Caldwell, surviving on a steady diet of slow curves and an occasional knuckleball, was the franchise's most valuable player, winning 20 games. In 1931 he was even better, with a 19–7 record. The Barons dominated the Southern Association, finishing 10½ games in front of the Travelers of Little Rock. But no one, not even Ray himself, compared Caldwell to Dizzy Dean.

Jay Hanna "Dizzy" Dean was the most colorful character to visit Jones Valley since Davy Crockett. In 1931 he was a year or so away from joining the St. Louis Cardinals and beginning his rise as an American folk hero,[*] but he was already the biggest box office draw

---

[*] Actually, Dean *re*-joined the Cardinals in 1932; he had pitched one game for them in 1930, after winning 25 games for two teams, in St. Joseph, Missouri, and Houston. The Cardinals brought him up to pitch the final game of the year. He allowed just three hits in a complete game victory over Pittsburgh.

DIZZY DEAN *and former New York Yankees star Ray Caldwell shake hands before their legendary meeting in the 1931 Dixie World Series. Caldwell was forty-three and began his career in 1910, the year Rickwood was built. Dean was twenty-one and born in 1910.*

in southern baseball. No one else was even close. In 1931 the Buffaloes drew 229,540, the highest attendance in either the Southern Association (Birmingham, Little Rock, Memphis, Chattanooga, New Orleans, Atlanta, Mobile, Knoxville, Nashville) or the Texas League—for that matter, higher than the number of fans who attended St. Louis Cardinals home games, a fact not lost on the Cards' front office. Houston management attributed much of that to Dean, who pitched to standing-room-only crowds in nearly every game, both home and away. His season was amazing: 26 wins (giving him 51 in two minor league seasons) and 303 strikeouts. A few big leaguers actually thought he threw as fast as Walter Johnson, the Big Train. One of those was the Barons' manager Clyde Milan, who had spent sixteen seasons in center field watching Johnson pitch.

Birmingham fans had been inflamed by Dizzy's predictions, which had appeared several days before the start of the series in Birmingham papers. At a Houston civic luncheon in honor of the Buffaloes, Dean swore, "If I don't beat them Barons, I'll join the House of David and grow a beard and never, never shave it off. It would hide my shame."[*][1] The remark drew laughs from Birmingham fans, but the next day Dean ruffled some feathers when he told reporters, "Beating the Barons will be just a breeze, just a breeze. I suppose Birmingham has a pretty fair minor league club, but it must be remembered Houston has a major league club. At least the pitching staff is as good as most major league twirling staffs."[2]

What Diz meant, of course, was that the Buffaloes had Dizzy Dean, and he was headed for the major leagues. So was Houston's best hitter, Joseph Michael "Ducky" Medwick, a stocky slugger from Carteret, New Jersey.[†] The Barons had no one as good as this future Hall of Famer—Medwick would play for seventeen years, most of them with the Cardinals, bat .324, and lead the National League in RBIs three times—but in 1931 they had an outfielder named Art Weis who played in every regular season game and had the year of his life, batting .369 with 102 RBIs and 20 home runs, just 5 of them at Rickwood Field—that's how intimidating the park's left and center field fences could be.

The Barons did have a few other things going for them, includ-

---

* The House of David began early in the twentieth century as a barnstorming baseball team whose mission was to raise money for a Jewish colony in Benton Harbor, Michigan. By 1930 several of the players were non-Jewish free agents who were sometimes required to grow beards to maintain the team's image; one of the ringers who wore a false beard was female pitching sensation Jackie Mitchell, who, in a 1931 exhibition game at Engel Stadium in Chattanooga, struck out Babe Ruth and Lou Gehrig. (See page 323.) Texas sportswriter Mickey Herskowitz relates that Dean's remark drew raucous laughter from Texas Jews. "My dad quipped that Dizzy would have to change his name to 'Izzy.'"

† Recalling the idols of his youth during an event at the Yogi Berra Museum and Learning Center at Montclair State University, in New Jersey, Yogi told how he had sold newspapers to Medwick near the Hill area in St. Louis while Ducky was on his way to Cardinals games. Years later, in 1946, Berra, much to his joy, received outfield instructions from his idol during spring training.

ing three starters—Bob Hasty, Jim Walkup, and Caldwell—who won 60 games, and a double play combination of shortstop Shine Cortazzo and second baseman Billy Bancroft, dubbed by Zipp Newman "the Gold Dust Twins," for their skill in making double plays.

More than 20,000 tickets were sold for the first two games at Rickwood Field, 6,000 more than even the most optimistic sportswriter had predicted. Robert Gregory, Dizzy's best biographer, wrote, "When the standing room was gone, the fans spilled onto the field. First along the foul lines, then in front of the left and right fields."[3] A *Houston Post* writer phrased it this way: "Depression or not, people are scraping up the price of a ticket. They want to see the Great Dean and will go without a meal to do it."[4]

Birmingham was baseball mad in the fall of 1931, but there were dark clouds on the horizon, and they were not just a product of the soot and fumes belching from the smokestacks of the city's steel mills. Within a short time the powers that ruled U.S. Steel in Pittsburgh would shut Birmingham's mills down, and an economic dark age would descend on the Magic City. Already many locals, white and black, were feeling the pinch, a tighter pinch in Birmingham than just about everywhere else in the country. Social tensions were frequently strained to the breaking point. By the end of 1931 there were 148 murders—at least 148 *reported* murders—earning Birmingham the tag of "the Murder Capital of America."

• ON SEPTEMBER 15, the morning before the start of the Dixie Series, Zipp Newman wrote, "People will watch Dizzy Dean today who've never seen a baseball game, and they won't care about the outcome. They'll be here just to see him. If Tex Rickard"—the legendary fight promoter who created "the Million Dollar Gate" for heavyweight champion Jack Dempsey—"had had a boxer like Dean, who could have backed up what he said, he would have three million dollar gates instead of 500,000.* Dean is the greatest showman of his day."[5]

One of those people who had never seen a baseball game—that is, a professional one—was seated in Rickwood for the first time out in right field in what was called the Negro bleachers. Fourteen-year-old Lorenzo "Piper" Davis would become the most important man to wear a baseball uniform in Birmingham.† The game was his introduction to what he would later call "white folks' ball," but, as he told me in a 1988 interview, "I didn't think of it that way at the time. All I knew is I was gettin' to see the great Dizzy Dean, and he *was* great."

Like the man he was destined to be compared to and contrasted with, Satchel Paige—the two had so much in common that they almost seemed like black and white bookends—Dizzy Dean made for great copy. On the train ride from Houston to Birmingham on the Southern Pacific, Dizzy kept reporters and teammates enthralled with a nonstop stream of stories and antics. In the dining car, he pushed the tables over to the side so he could simulate his windup and throw an imaginary ball, then scamper down to the end of the car and pretend to be a hapless Barons batter. After a big swing and a miss, he turned to the invisible umpire in back of

---

* Rickard, friend to such roustabouts as Diamond Jim Brady, Bat Masterson, and Wyatt Earp, had drawn huge crowds promoting fights for Jack Johnson as well as Dempsey, but his magic faded after Dempsey retired and he backed several financial failures—hence the reference to "instead of 500,000."

† Unless one includes Rick Woodward, who donned a Barons uniform for the first pitch in the first game at Rickwood in 1910.

him, shrugged his shoulders, and yelled, "I didn't even see that ball, Mister. Did you?"

The most ballyhooed minor league championship series ever had fans in every Southern Association and Texas League city sitting by their radios waiting for news of the game. Western Union constructed new wire circuits for announcers in other cities for receiving ticker tape accounts and recount each pitch and play.

Dizzy, basking in the glow of all the attention, talked back to hecklers while he warmed up. "It'll be like takin' candy from a baby." When a couple of grinning Barons approached him with a gag gift, a bunch of carrots, "to help improve his eyesight," Diz laughed and said, "Give 'em to Deerfoot, he's the rabbit," referring to the nickname given to Clyde Milan, who had led the league in stolen bases in 1912 and 1913. But though Barons fans hooted, few of them booed; the truth was that having Dizzy Dean in Birmingham was like having a second Fourth of July.

· THE ROAR OF THE CROWD turned to stony silence just three batters into the game when Caldwell gave up two singles before recording an out. The batter was exactly the man whom Caldwell and Barons fans did not want to see up in a situation like this—and Ducky Medwick delivered, slamming a long, high drive deep into left center field. It would have been a home run in most ballparks—indeed, it would have been a home run in Sportman's Park in St. Louis, where Medwick would soon be playing—but this was Rickwood Field, and Barons center fielder Woody Abernathy made a running catch that brought the crowd to its feet. Abernathy stumbled, nearly fell, recovered himself and fired back to his cutoff man in time to keep the runner from advancing to third. Caldwell got the next batter on a pop-up to end the inning.

The experience of working his way out of trouble paid off for Caldwell, who found himself in similar hot water the rest of the game. In every inning the Buffaloes put runners on base, only to find themselves frustrated by Caldwell's elliptical curveballs and occasional spot-on fastballs. Dean, for his part, was having no such problems. For the first six innings he faced only 18 batters, allowing just a bloop single and a walk on a 3–2 pitch (to which he loudly objected, much to the amusement of the crowd). Both runners were taken out on double plays.

It was not until the seventh inning that Caldwell struck out a batter; in the eighth he struck out two more. When the Barons came up in the bottom of the inning, the game was a scoreless tie. Dean, answering taunts of Barons fans by tipping his cap and grinning, got two quick outs and had an 0–2 count on Birmingham catcher Zach Taylor when he committed one of the cardinal sins of pitching: he gave a hitter a good pitch on an 0–2 count. Taylor, protecting the plate, looped a single to right field. There seemed to be no harm in that, since the next batter was Caldwell. Milan, contrary to thousands of managerial advisers in the seats, allowed Caldwell to hit. His reasons were twofold. First, Caldwell had been getting stronger as the game went on, striking out three of the last six hitters he faced. Second, he had been a pretty fair hitting pitcher in his major league career and had nearly as good a chance against Dean as anyone Milan had on the bench.

Caldwell strode to the plate to the chorused cheers of "Hooray!" On Dean's first pitch, he tapped a ground ball that snaked between the second baseman and shortstop. The ball was hit so slowly that Taylor was able to reach third just as the ball was tossed back into the infield.

Next up was Gold Dust Twin second baseman Billy Bancroft, a local fan favorite from his football heroics at Howard College. Dean fired a fastball and Bancroft missed it, strike one. Then, for some reason he never explained, Dizzy chose a curveball. Billy expected the off-speed pitch and hit it hard over third base. The ball skipped into the crowd standing in the roped-off section of the field for a ground rule double. To the delight of the frenzied crowd and thousands following the game on radio—and with Western Union telegraph operators Cowboy Rogers, Halsey Hall, Hy Vance, and Pistol Smith frantically punching out accounts of the action—Taylor scored the game's only run. Dean recorded the third out without more damage, but in the ninth, Caldwell, with a newfound strength, struck out two more Buffaloes to seal the game. Caldwell's wife— they had been married just three weeks before—burst into tears.

Afterward, Milan was gracious in victory: "I thought he'd try to beat us with his speed and be the strikeout artist. But he showed me some brainy pitching out there. He's the best we've ever seen." As Dean climbed into a cab, a Barons fan called out, "Why didn't your boys get you some runs, Dizzy?" Diz replied, "They tried, but ol' Ray was too tough for 'em."[6] He smiled and waved to his admirers and even invited them to show up at the team hotel if they wanted to talk some more.

The next day an editorial in the *Birmingham News* proclaimed the veteran from Pennsylvania "The Proud South's Newest Hero." The editorial also said that the win was all the more satisfying because it had the effect of "humbling Mr. Dizzy Dean."[7] The writer obviously didn't know Dizzy Dean very well.

Perhaps because the Barons won, and because everyone in attendance knew they had witnessed an all-time classic, Birmingham fans
bore Diz no grudge for his outrageous pregame bragging.[*] In fact,
as Zipp Newman wrote the following day, Dean deserved credit
"for 10,000 of that crowd. . . . Everybody swarmed him for his autograph, which he smilingly wrote."[8] It became common in later years
for Birminghamians to claim they were at the game whether they
really were or not. Ticket stubs became collector's items, and autographs from Dizzy Dean and other Buffaloes and Barons became
heirlooms passed on to later generations.

Game Two was somewhat deflating for the Barons and their
fans. Houston pitcher Dick McCabe pitched a four-hit shutout,
and the Buffaloes won 3–0, evening up the series. Barons faithful
grumbled a bit; McCabe had pitched the regular season for the Fort
Worth Cats, but thanks to an obscure rule McCabe was named as
a replacement for Houston's Tex Carleton, who was dropped from
the roster with a blister on his right index finger.[†]

If the loss dampened the Barons' spirits, they were fired up again
the next day when thousands of fans came to the Birmingham train
station to see their boys off on the Louisville & Nashville Mis-

---

[*] And it was bragging, by Dean's own definition. "If you say you're gonna do something,"
he once said during his brief stint broadcasting New York Yankees games, "and you don't
do it, that's braggin'. But if you say you're gonna do something, and you do it, why that's
just plain old predictin'."

[†] Exactly which rule allowed McCabe to pitch for Houston isn't certain. Birmingham
historian Ben Cook says, "It was a common practice for the Dixie Series. Each team
could borrow up to three players from other teams" (*Good Wood*, p. 47). But both Robert
Gregory and Southern Association researcher Art Shaut claim that it was a Texas League
rule that allowed McCabe to pitch for the Buffs. Charles Stewart, an Alabama baseball
researcher, has combed all Birmingham papers that covered the 1931 Dixie Series and
found a mention of McCabe's having been "borrowed" from Ft. Worth but no mention of
any players "borrowed" by the Barons.

souri Pacific Special. Early on the morning of September 18, Rick
Woodward, dressed in a blue gabardine suit, waved his Panama hat
in farewell as the Birmingham police band, the Musical Coppers,
blared "Dixie" and John Philip Sousa marches. (Woodward footed
the expense for the forty-five members of the band to accompany
the team to Texas.)

Much to the irritation of the Barons, the train stopped for
nearly two hours in New Orleans, where Dean made an impromptu
speech and signed autographs. Then, to make up for the time Dean
had cost them, the train streaked the final 270 miles to Houston in
under six hours—at some stretches approaching speeds of 75 miles
per hour—and arrived just before dinnertime. Houston fans who
met the train at the station were impressed by the enthusiasm of the
Barons, the Musical Coppers, and more than fifty Barons followers
who had accompanied their team to Houston despite the $26 round
trip fare. The band formed ranks and accompanied the team to the
luxurious hotel, making everyone in Texas who wasn't deaf aware
that the Birmingham Barons were in town.

But unlike their band, the Barons didn't seem to have arrived.
They were shut out the next day in game three, 1–0, with just one
hit. That made it 18 consecutive innings without a run scored.

Dean would make it 27 consecutive scoreless innings the next
day. This time it was Caldwell's turn to pitch gallantly and lose. He
gave up a single earned run and another on an error. Diz had his
revenge, 2–0, but he didn't treat it that way, walking over to the visitors dugout and slapping Caldwell on the shoulder after recording
the final out. The Barons, who were down three games to one and
had scored just one run in 36 innings, were on the verge of extinc-
tion. Back home, the *Birmingham Herald*'s Fred Smith offered Clyde

Milan a piece of advice: the Barons would score more runs if he replaced his players with the Musical Coppers' tuba players.

The Barons ensured a return to Birmingham by winning game five, 3–1. Then in game six back home at Rickwood, Art Weis, a .369 hitter during the season who had been stifled so far in the series by Buffalo pitching, hit a home run into the "Negro bleachers," two doubles, and two singles in a rousing 14–10 victory. According to legend, after the Barons fell behind early in the game, a note was passed down the dugout from a wealthy fan: if the hometown boys came back to win, it said, he would take Milan and all the players to dinner at Britling's Cafeteria.* Spurred on by this incentive, the Barons roared back to victory.

"What have the stars in store for the Diz?" Zipp Newman asked the following day as the two teams headed back to Houston for the final game, its location determined by the toss of a coin. "If you can read the heavens, then call the turn in the seventh game. What will the great man do? Will he have it? Will the smoke rise? The South waits."[9]

Thousands of Buffalo fans were waiting at the Missouri Pacific Station in downtown Houston, and this time Houston team president Fred Ankeman was prepared with his own band, which rang out with "The Eyes of Texas" to greet the Buffaloes. No president of a major league ball club ever gave his team a more rousing welcome. "Go home and sleep well," Dizzy told them. "Leave it to me. I'm

---

* Britling's was no ordinary cafeteria. It offered its patrons a choice of fresh fried catfish and trout almandine, steak, chicken fried steak, fried chicken, and no fewer than ten different vegetables, including fried okra. There was also homemade cornbread and biscuits—to be used as "push bread" for sopping up gravy—as well as pecan pie and hot peach cobbler à la mode for dessert, all washed down with traditional "southern" sweet iced tea.

gonna win your Buffs some dough for the winter." The Barons, he told the adoring throng, "didn't see me at my best in the daytime, no foolin'. Night time is my best time to shine."* (Actually, Dean's 2–0 shutout against the Barons in game four had been a night game.)

By the seventh game, Ray Caldwell's arm was worn out, and Dean was matched against Bob Hasty, a 21-game winner whose arm trouble put him in the Southern Association after six seasons with Connie Mack's A's. Dean had logged an unusually high number of innings pitched to that point: 304, plus 19 more against the Barons, including a foolish extra inning in the 14–10 slugfest in which he asked to pitch just to stay loose.

For the deciding game, Dean changed his pitching strategy. Amazingly, in the first game at Rickwood, Diz had failed to record a strikeout, the first and only time that happened in his minor league career. His reasoning was that Rickwood's famous left and center fields would swallow any fly balls he served up, and he was right. In the smaller confines of the Buffaloes' park, he went for strikeouts and got all three Barons swinging in the first inning.

Ducky Medwick, who had been held in check except for the game six barn burner, lashed a hard single in the first inning to put Houston on the board to the approval of the frenzied crowd. The hit was regarded by the hometown press box as a good omen since the first team to score had won all previous six games.

But something began to happen in the second inning. Though

---

* Like many of the more successful minor league franchises, the Houston Buffaloes played night games years before the majors did. The first recorded minor league night game was played on May 2, 1930, in a Western League game in Des Moines, Iowa, against Wichita, a full five seasons before the Cincinnati Reds played under permanent lights. Around 12,000 fans attended the game, quite a step up for a team that normally drew 600. Many minor league owners credited night games with helping them survive the Depression.

he collected two more strikeouts, some of Dizzy's pitches were being hit hard by the Barons, particularly Art Weis and Shine Cortazzo, who both doubled to tie the score. Dean reared back and threw harder, stopping the Barons cold while Hasty, like Caldwell in the first game, constantly worked his way out of trouble. Going into the seventh inning, the score was still 1–1.

The Barons took the lead with two shockers—a bloop double right over first base and a weak "seeing eye" single. The Buffs came back on a walk, a sacrifice bunt by Dean, and a single. In the eighth inning Diz got two outs on just four pitches. At this point, he had pitched $26\frac{2}{3}$ innings in the Series and given up only two runs. But his luck was about to turn bad. With two outs Woody Abernathy singled, and Medwick, perhaps already counting the money from his first St. Louis Cardinals paycheck, misplayed the ball, which rolled through his legs all the way to the center field wall. The Barons now led 3–2 and could taste victory.

Trying to redeem himself, Ducky led off the eighth by fouling off pitch after pitch, looking for one he could drive. He found one, sending it to deep left field for an apparent home run, but it landed in some temporary bleachers that were built into the outfield corner to accommodate the overflow Series crowd. Instead of a home run, it was a ground rule double. From the Buffaloes' dugout, Dean encouraged his hitters, telling them that Hasty had nothing left. Two hard-hit grounders, though, failed to produce a run.

In the ninth, Dizzy's roof caved in. Third baseman John Gooch, a .305 hitter during the regular season, laced a hard double to the right field wall. Afterwards, the Buffs' manager, Joe Schultz, admitted that he thought Dean's fast ball had gone and that "the boy's arm was tired."[10] Schultz didn't have the heart to yank Diz after such great pitching, and a single, a walk, and a bad throw on a bunt gave Birmingham four more runs. Houston got a third run in the ninth, and Medwick came to bat as the tying run. As if in a movie, Milan brought in . . . Ray Caldwell. But there was no joy in Houston that night as mighty Ducky struck out. A Buffalo named Homer Peel bounced into a force play to end the game, and the Barons won 6–3.

In the stands Caldwell's wife had broken down yet again as the Barons carried him off the field on their shoulders. The Buffaloes shook their heads and wondered how they had been able to collect thirteen hits but only two with runners on base. The defeat cost them more than just their pride: the winning Barons got a hefty $850 apiece, $300 more than the losing Buffaloes. In defeat Dean was gracious. Cigarette in hand, he told reporters in the clubhouse, "I thought I had too much speed, but they're a good bunch of boys and got to me." Asked whether he regretted his predicting, he forced a smile and said, "Nope." That night the players had a big party, and Dean raised a glass to his veteran opponent in two memorable games, Ray Caldwell. Then, in the morning, they saw their guests to Houston's train station for the ride back to Birmingham.

Caldwell, a grandfather, had pitched his last professional game in a career that had begun a quarter of a century earlier. He retired from baseball and went back to Pennsylvania with the satisfaction of knowing he had pitched the greatest game ever in America's grandest minor league park. Nineteen years later, celebrating the fortieth anniversary of Rickwood Field, the Barons held a pregame ceremony to honor past greats. Ray Caldwell, who had been managing American Legion ball in Hoboken, New Jersey, received the biggest ovation. Dizzy Dean, unable to attend because of his broadcasting duties with the New York Yankees,* sent flowers and a personal telegram to Caldwell, asking for a rematch. Caldwell died in 1967 in Salamanca, in upstate New York, where, into his eighties, he still umpired Little League games. He was always happy to talk about his professional baseball exploits, his favorite story being about the great day in 1931 when, at the little jewel of a ballpark nearly thirteen hundred miles to the south, he beat the great Hall of Famer Dizzy Dean.

"In Houston," wrote Vince Staten more than six decades later, "life had been a big game for Diz. He would have greater seasons"— from 1934 through 1936, he averaged better than 27 wins a year with the Gashouse Gang Cardinals—"and play to greater acclaim, but because he was outside the intense media glare that would later both invigorate him and wear him down, he would never have more fun than he did that second season in Houston."[11]

Except, perhaps, in his barnstorming duels with Satchel Paige. The two men had a respect† for each other that was rare in any age

---

* During Dizzy's three-year stint with the Yankees, 1949–51, he was enormously popular with Yankee fans but unfortunately wasn't the sophisticated sound that Yankees general manager George Weiss wanted. But he caught on with other TV and radio stations; from 1955 to 1965 he worked CBS's *Game of the Week*, often sharing the mike with former Brooklyn Dodger great Harold "Pee Wee" Reese. Reese was from Kentucky, but as sports historian Bert Randolph Sugar put it, "Dean made Pee Wee sound like he was a BBC announcer." Among Dean's most famous on-air statements were "If he'd slud a little harder, he might have had that one" and, worthy of Yogi Berra at his best, "The players will now return to their respectable positions," as well as "Don't fail to miss tomorrow's game." In 1952 he was the subject of a popular film, *The Pride of St. Louis*, with Dan Dailey as Diz and Richard Crenna as his brother, Paul (also known as Daffy).

† Larry Tye, in his definitive biography of Paige, *Satchel: The Life and Times of an American Legend*, relates that Satchel had a special nickname for Dean, Old Homer Bean, though no one ever figured out what it meant (p. 85).

DIZ AND SATCH: *Two American folk heroes and two of the greatest right-handers of all time. Both Dizzy Dean and Satchel Paige had strong ties to Rickwood. Dean pitched one of the most famous games in Southern League history in the 1931 Dixie World Series; Paige pitched many great games there with the Birmingham Black Barons. The white and black southerners got along very well and barnstormed together with their All-Star teams. Dean ranked Paige as one of the greatest of all time, "right behind me and Carl Hubbell." At other times, he called Satch the best he had ever seen.*

and positively amazing for black and white southerners in the 1930s. In later years, reminiscing about his games against Paige, Dean said that it was a shame that Satchel hadn't made it to the major leagues until he was forty-two years old,* because Satch could have been one of the greatest ever: "prob'ly right behind me and Carl Hubbell, because he was just like us with all that stuff a' his and he could

---

* Or forty-one, according to www.baseball-reference.com.

get ever' bit of it over. Not like these fellows today. They're so wild, they couldn't hit my ol' daddy's red barn with three tries. But Satch coulda knocked it down."[12]

Larry Tye, author of *Satchel: The Life and Times of an American Legend*, offered this insight:

> The Dizzy-Satchel contests [stand] as landmarks in American sociology as well as sports. The color-coded pairing of stars gave a human face to the battles between white and black baseball teams that had been playing out in California for twenty-five years. Dizzy was America's darling, hero of the just-completed 1934 World Series and dizziest of the brawling, cursing Gas House Gang. He also was a bigot, or at least that is what a casual observer would have concluded from his roots in segregationist Arkansas and his liberal use of slurs like coon and nigger. It was precisely that redneck image that gave resonance to a racial rivalry with Satchel that was really a rapprochement. On their barnstorming tour, ballparks that normally walled off blacks let them sit where they wanted. It brought in white reporters along with white fans. And when good ol' boy Dizzy Dean praised blackball legend Satchel Paige, followers of all hues pricked up their ears.

In 2006 I sat with Paul Hemphill in seats just over the third base line, watching the Rickwood Classic. "Just think," he told me, "thousands of people all over the country got to see Dizzy Dean and Satchel Paige pitch against each other. What a shame, what a deep, deep shame that no one ever got to see them pitch against each other in this ballpark."

GOOD BOYS *got to see the Barons for free. General Manager Eddie Glennon established a program for honor students to get into the games gratis.*

"THERE WAS JUST SOMETHING ABOUT THE BASEBALL IN THAT PARK"

IN THE WINTER OF 1938, while the rest of the United States was crawling out of the Depression, Birmingham and Rick Woodward were still in the middle of theirs. On February 7 Woodward, age sixty-one, signed the papers that would turn over Rickwood Field and the Birmingham Barons to an undistinguished automobile dealer named Ed Norton. The price was $175,000, perhaps one-third of what Woodward had put into the ballpark over the years in renovations and maintenance. About a third of the money Woodward made on the sale went to the government for back taxes.

In retrospect, the Woodward era was probably doomed as far back as 1930, a year sandwiched between Barons championships. Both Bethlehem Steel and the Republic Steel Corporation offered him $30 million for the Woodward Iron Company. He wanted more;

exactly how much more is not known, and for some reason the deal
was never made. Had Woodward accepted either of the companies'
offers, he would probably have been the richest man in Jefferson
County, if not all of Alabama. Instead, less than eight years later he
was struggling to, in the parlance of the times, hold off the tax man.

· FOR BIRMINGHAM the devil's bargain had been made decades
earlier. In 1907 Theodore Roosevelt, the renowned trustbuster,
made a grievous error of judgment by allowing the Tennessee Coal
and Iron Company (TCI) to be bought by U.S. Steel for a paltry
$35 million. Neither Roosevelt nor the citizens of Birmingham
had any idea of the hardship this merger would someday bring.
What the merger (though it was technically more of a buyout)
achieved was to guarantee that Birmingham would forever—or
as long as steel was king—be subservient to northern steel interests.* The *Birmingham Age-Herald* predicted that U.S. Steel's purchase would "make Birmingham hum as it never hummed before,"[1]
which was true and would be so for at least a couple of decades.
An editorial in the *Birmingham News* proclaimed that the acquisition would "make the Birmingham district the greatest steel manufacturing center in the universe."[2] This view would prove to be
disastrously inaccurate. In later years the truth would slowly reveal
itself: U.S. Steel bought TCI not to expand the economy of Bir-

---

* Eighty-six years after the takeover, Paul Hemphill observed that, as the steel industry in
Birmingham declined, "virtually no new industry, blue-collar or otherwise, had filled in the
gap, mainly because U.S. Steel and the local barons didn't want the competition" (*Leaving
Birmingham,* p. 114).

mingham, or even to increase the worth of their own holdings, but to restrict Birmingham as a competitor to its holdings in Pittsburgh.* Until the Great Depression, no one saw the downside of the takeover, and when U.S. Steel started shutting down the mills to protect its interests in the North, the city, Jefferson County, and virtually all of Alabama were devastated.

For the first couple of years of the Depression, social and economic advances that prosperity had helped make in combating illiteracy and hunger were wiped out almost overnight. Within a year after FDR began his presidency, tens of thousands of Birminghamians were near starvation. The city government was on the verge of shutting down by mid-1933; only a million-dollar loan from the First National Bank engineered by president Oscar Wells kept the city machinery from grinding to a halt. By early 1935 a government study indicated that Birmingham had the highest rate of venereal disease, the highest illiteracy rate, and the lowest per capita income of any city in the United States.

In later decades Birminghamians—or at any rate, most white Birminghamians—would decry the legacy of the New Deal and the increase in government power that came with it. The truth, however, is that Birmingham sprang out of the ashes of the Depression. The city that began to emerge after World War II was the child of the New Deal. The Democratic-controlled Congress gave or lent a staggering $360 million over a four-year period, a colossal stimulus program that included jobs from the Works Progress Administration repairing and improving bridges, buildings, streets, and parks. Birmingham's superb parks and recreation system dates from this

---

* Even railroad rates fixed by the Interstate Commerce Commission were slanted to favor Pittsburgh's iron over Birmingham's.

period. Government money also went to the Red Cross, which set up food pantries and soup kitchens in and around the city.

The most visible lasting proof of the New Deal's gift to Birmingham is its very symbol. The 56-foot-tall statue of Vulcan, the Roman god of fire and metalworking, which had lain in exile at the state fairgrounds after returning from the 1904 St. Louis World's Fair,* had its arm repaired and was placed on a 24-foot pedestal at the top of Red Mountain, from which its rich iron ore had come. It still stands there today. With baseball's inexorable decline, Vulcan was the closest thing the people of Birmingham, white and black, had to an inspiration.

Birmingham's other great symbol, Rickwood Field, suffered through a near-devastating period that brought down many of her sister ballparks. Since the revenue for finding and developing new players was almost wholly dependent on ticket sales, it's not surprising that the Barons' performance often reflected Birmingham's economy. That was particularly true in the ten seasons before the United States entered World War II when the Barons finished as high as third in the Southern Association only once. Once the richest team in the league because of their owner's iron and steel holdings, the Barons now fell behind teams from other southern cities with more balanced economies—the hated Atlanta Crackers, for instance, who won four Southern Association pennants from 1932 to 1941.

The presiding king of southern baseball for more than a quar-

---

* In 1903 the city of Birmingham conducted a big fund-raiser to pay for Vulcan. The man who dropped the first iron ingot into the casting furnace was the New York Giants' great pitcher "Ironman Joe" McGinnity, so-named because he had led the league with 48 starts and 44 complete games in 1903, also leading the National League in victories with 31.

ter of a century, Rick Woodward would go on about the golden age with his sporting pals, but his blue blazers and straw boaters were never again seen at the park he built. From 1919 through the season of the great Dixie Series in 1931, attendance averaged 125,000 per season; over the next ten seasons, it plummeted to around 70,000.

In 1936 Woodward's son-in-law, Jim Burt, tried a daring innovation, or rather followed an innovation of many minor league franchises in the early years of the Depression: lights for night games. In that year attendance shot up to 195,000, the best since the boom year of 1929, spurred by the combination of the cooler night ball and the triumphant return of thirty-eight-year-old Riggs Stephenson, a football star at the University of Alabama who had played fourteen seasons of major league ball with the Cleveland Indians and Chicago Cubs. The Barons' surge was reflected by the city's overall recovery as, for the first time since 1932, demand for steel increased and the fires were stoked in several furnaces.

However, the New Deal faltered in 1937, the nation's economy stalled again, and most of the mills again went dark. The Barons faded to sixth, 21½ games out of first place, and attendance dropped to an all-time low.

Ed Norton lost interest in owning a baseball team and dumped the franchise, selling it to the Cincinnati Reds after just two years— and so the Barons, like Birmingham's steel industry, had an absentee landlord. The Cincinnati Reds' front office did make one important decision regarding the Barons and Rickwood: in time for the 1941 season they put up a wooden fence inside the long left field wall, making a concession to the new lively-ball era, a move that was perhaps ten to twelve years overdue.

• • •

• **THINGS WERE TOUGH** for everyone in Birmingham during the 1930s, but they were even tougher for the 40 percent of the population that was black. Being closer to the poverty line, though, meant blacks had less to lose and could adjust more quickly to changing circumstances. In 1937, while the Barons were treading water, the Black Barons reemerged as a member of the major black circuit under the banner of the Negro American League. It was a struggle—there was no time at which any Negro League franchise didn't have to struggle—but the Black Barons, to paraphrase William Faulkner, not only endured but prevailed.

The Black Barons survived in large part by supplementing their income with barnstorming tours. Even in the South, in defiance of segregation, they sometimes played in front of mixed crowds. Life on the road was grueling. There was little time or opportunity for players to shower after doubleheaders played in brutal summer heat wearing heavy flannel or wool uniforms, and meals were often wolfed down on the run. Air-conditioning, of course, was unheard of on the old buses and in hotel rooms, and long road trips, especially in the dog days of summer, could leave the players enervated.

Segregation left its mark on the players in many ways. "It was kinda funny," recalled Piper Davis, "the way white fans would cheer us on in the ballpark and then ignore us everywhere else. I don't necessarily mean treat us badly, I just mean that on the field we were entertainers, and off the field it was almost like we were invisible."

The Black Barons played local teams (which were often beefed up with players from other professional and industrial teams not using their real names), and they played before crowds that had gathered for medicine shows, music festivals, and carnivals.* As late as the 1940s, Bill Greason remembers, "road games often seemed like holidays. Most of the ballparks were in areas where you could sit in the dugout and smell the cooking—the barbecue and fish frying. Sometimes you could hear music coming from the fairgrounds. The first time I pitched on the road and I heard that carnival music, I thought it was going to be distracting, but it turned out to be lovely and soothing."

Even when the baseball was fun and the players made money, the unrelenting segregation could turn the trips into a grind. Black-owned hotels could be found in larger towns, but, in small ones, players often had to call on friends and acquaintances to find a bed. Piper Davis told Chris Fullerton, "I've stayed in jails twice. No place else to sleep." Always, always, the saving grace was that the players could make a living playing baseball. "We played seven days a week, all summer long," Davis recalled. "See, you had places that didn't have baseball, and they were glad to see you."[3]

Despite the hardships, there was a bond that kept them going. Possibly because of the major league affiliation, the white Barons were constantly being broken up as players were called up to the big leagues. The Black Barons spent more time together and were closer

---

* The story of traveling black teams was told in a pretty good 1976 film, *The Bingo Long Traveling All-Star & Motor Kings*, starring James Earl Jones, Billy Dee Williams, and Richard Pryor. The film was based on a novel by William Brashler, who also wrote the excellent biography *Josh Gibson: A Life in the Negro Leagues*, and was directed by Birmingham's own John Badham, who grew up less than a half-hour drive from Rickwood Field.

as a unit. "We helped each other out," says Bill Greason. "If someone was having family problems, all of us felt it. The veterans helped the younger players learn the game and how to live your life in baseball on and off the field."

When the Black Barons came back to Birmingham, they were treated like kings. Those who weren't from Birmingham usually stayed at the Rush Hotel, owned by Joe Rush, who, not coincidentally, also owned the Black Barons. The Rush Hotel, located on North Eighteenth Street, was about a baseball throw from the heart of the black business district. Though perhaps a 10- to 15-minute walk from city hall, it was an area that few white people knew. The *Birmingham News* wrote in 1936:

> The Frolic Theatre's bright lights twinkle and the Harlem Cafe beckons—where dark-skinned and dapper city boys and lanky cotton hands from the "black belt" gape. . . . A paradise of barbecue stands and pool rooms, of soft drink parlors and barbershops . . . the Mecca for cooks and chauffeurs on Thursday night, a heaven for miners and mill workers on Saturday night.
>
> Many white men have seen Eighteenth Street. Only a few know it. No white man understands it.[4]

During the day the area was a swirl of activity. Black Barons third baseman Willie Patterson recalled, "You had the Carver Theatre and the Frolic, the Famous and the Champion. On that corner they sold records. Anything you want you can get on Fourth Avenue. Watches, anything you want. . . . And Bob's Savoy was open until two o'clock in the morning. Nobody messed with that club; they

LITTLE SAVOY CAFE
The South's Finest; the City's Largest
CHICKEN—STEAKS—DINNERS—SHORT ORDERS—DRINKS—SMOKES
411 N 17th Street, Birmingham, Alabama   BOB WILLIAMS, Proprietor, Phone 7-888?
Phone Us At 7-8883—Booths—Tables—Open All Night

THE LITTLE SAVOY CAFE, *was even popular with white patrons, although they could not mingle with blacks.*

just closed at two."[5] Perhaps Patterson left around two o'clock in the morning, when things got slow, but several other players, including Piper Davis and Artie Wilson, admitted to having sometimes left much later than two.

The Savoy, at 411 North Seventeenth Street, was the undisputed center of black cultural life in Birmingham. Often operating twenty-four hours a day, except on Sundays, when it opened in the early afternoon after church was out, the Little Savoy Cafe, as it sometimes billed itself, was started by Bob Williams, who had moved to Birmingham from New York in 1932. The downstairs was for drinking; the upstairs was for eating: "Chicken—Steaks—Dinners—Short Orders—Drinks—Smokes," boasted the ads. The place was big enough for pool tables and, occasionally, for performances by some of the same great jazz musicians who played at the Harlem namesake. Duke Ellington and Count Basie played piano at the Little Savoy (and played with their big bands at the nearby Masonic Temple Ballroom).* It was also patronized over the years by some of the same black celebrities as the New York club: heavyweight champion Joe Louis, Jackie Robinson, and, when he was old enough, Willie Mays, whose father, "Kitty Cat," was a regular at Williams's club while playing industrial league ball.†

Williams became one of the most influential black men in Birmingham, known by his friends in the Masonic Temple as "the Noble Bob Williams" and an early inspiration for civil rights activists. (In 1949 he helped raise a defense fund to fight race-based zoning laws.) The Little Savoy was such a hot spot for ballplayers that buses on their way out to Rickwood Field made scheduled stops there to pick them up.

As if in defiance of Depression economics, the Black Barons became the focal point of Birmingham's black community. Large church groups scheduled trips to the Sunday games. Long before

---

* Willie Patterson told Chris Fullerton that "Count Basie, Duke Ellington, Cab Calloway, Lionel Hampton" all played at Bob's Savoy, sometimes to white audiences. "See, what they did then, they would play, that evening, they'd play for the whites. At night, the whites that sat there had to go upstairs. The whites had to go upstairs, the Negroes came downstairs."
† Located between 140th and 141st Streets on Lennox Avenue, Harlem's Savoy Ballroom, with its luxurious red carpeted lounges and mirrored wall panels, was nearly a block long and was thought to be one of the first racially integrated clubs in New York. It called itself "the World's Finest Ballroom," and its floor took such a pounding from the hundreds of thousands of dancers who came there every year—"The Home of Happy Feet," it was called—that the club's owner, Mo Gale, who was Jewish, and the manager, Charles Buchanan, who was black, cheerfully told everyone that it had to be replaced at least every three years.

The famous Chick Webb vs. Benny Goodman Battle of the Bands took place at the Savoy Ballroom, and an entire generation of bebop artists such as Dizzy Gillespie, Charlie Parker, and Thelonious Monk regularly played there. The Savoy was a meeting place for black Alabamians when they came to New York; Willie Mays's friends gave a party for him there after his return from the Army in 1954. That same year the Savoy had a visit from a soon-to-be-famous fictitious white man, James Bond, who was taken there by his CIA friend Felix Leiter in Ian Fleming's second 007 novel, Live and Let Die.

white major and minor league teams had special events and activities at their games, such promotions were common in the world of black ball. In 1942, for instance, there was a jitterbug contest during a break between games in a doubleheader between the Barons and the Cincinnati Buckeyes. Beauty contests, particularly Miss Birmingham Black Barons, were big draws. Though baseball was a serious business, the players knew how to have fun. When the Indianapolis Clowns (black baseball's equivalent of the Harlem Globetrotters) visited, Lloyd Bassett would put on an exhibition of catching while swinging back and forth in a rocking chair or somebody would pitch to a batter from second base. Black ballplayers learned how to turn disputes with umpires into shows within a game.* White patrons, who sat in the right field bleachers at Black Barons games, derived much enjoyment from the antics, though, as the Barons' traveling secretary Bob Scranton observed, "they would have been shocked to see things like that going on at white Barons games."

Black Barons didn't receive the same gifts—free shirts or suits—for hitting the ball over the outfield billboards that white players received. But there were rewards. When Ed Steele hit the Black Barons' first home run of the season one year, he received, among other things, two chicken dinners from the Porters Club (being a rail center, Birmingham was a key city for the Porters Union), a diamond-studded watch, and $50 cash (from the Davenport and Handy Funeral Home).

---

* Negro Leagues couldn't afford regular umpires and let home teams supply their own. This led to constant friction with visiting teams on the matter of "hometown calls." In truth, the problem was that most of the black umpires lacked real experience. As Pepper Basset put it, "There was no umpiring, only guesses" (*Every Other Sunday*, p. 74).

• • •

• THERE WAS AT LEAST one compensation for black ballplayers: there was less chance of being drafted. Maintaining black troops
required separate facilities for housing and training, instructors, and
transportation. In some cases black laborers in key industries such
as steel were simply allowed to continue at their jobs. In Birmingham this meant that the quality of baseball didn't suffer as it did
in the white major and minor leagues. So strapped for players were
the Reds during the war years that in 1944 Joe Nuxhall, age fifteen,
became the youngest pitcher to appear so far in major league history,
pitching in one game, allowing one hit and walking five for an ERA
of 62.50. After his one-game tenure in Cincinnati, Nuxhall was sent
to Birmingham, where he pitched in one game for the Barons.*

Help was on the way for the Barons, and just as in 1910, it
came from Philadelphia. In the winter of 1944 the Cincinnati Reds
decided to keep their Birmingham affiliation but to give up ownership of the team. The buyer was Konstantenous John "Gus" Jebeles,
a Birmingham hotel owner. Jebeles was a big baseball fan who had
followed the Barons even before Rickwood Field; as a boy he had
seen them come from behind to beat their archrivals the Atlanta
Crackers at the Slag Pile.† He publicly expressed his desire to restore
the Barons to the glory of the Rick Woodward years and was smart

---

* Longtime *Birmingham News* columnist Bill Lumpkin remembers Nuxhall as "a really
gritty kid, in over his head, but wouldn't admit it." Nuxhall got another shot at the majors
in 1952 and went on to pitch a total of sixteen seasons, winning 135 games, mostly for
the Reds, and making the staff of two All-Star teams. He eventually became a popular
broadcaster for Cincinnati.
† Discouraged Barons fans sometime referred to the Crackers as "the Yankees of the
Southern Association." The Barons and their fans, then, inevitably assumed something of
a Brooklyn Dodgers complex.

enough to realize he couldn't do it on his own: he needed some-one with real baseball savvy. After the 1946 season Jebeles attended the 1946 Minor League Winter Meeting in Los Angeles and asked other team officials for advice about acquiring a general manager.

A man named Frank Longinotti, general manager of the Mem-phis Chicks, told Jebeles he had someone in mind. The man he had in mind had learned from the best: Connie Mack. Eddie Glen-non was his name. Glennon was born on the only Irish block in an otherwise Italian-American enclave in South Philadelphia.[*] When he was fifteen, Glennon's family moved to within a block of Shibe Park, and Eddie became hooked on baseball. In high school he had run track and played baseball and even some football in his junior and senior years. After high school he put in a couple of years of semipro football, then several seasons with the Frankford Yellow Jackets, who paid scarcely better than semipro even though they later evolved into an NFL franchise. But he saw no future in profes-sional football. As a teenager he met Connie Mack, who nicknamed him Shorty, and after a stint selling peanuts worked in Mack's office running out for coffee and cigarettes. After a year he asked Mack for a desk job; Mack was impressed by his confidence but advised him to get some experience, then passed him on to Philadelphia Phillies owner Bob Carpenter, who gave him a job with one of the Phillies minor league teams. Within three years Glennon was back working for Mack as general manager of the Athletics' Wilming-ton, Delaware, team.

---

[*] The area produced at least two other outstanding men, Bernard "Toots" Shor, whose restaurant/saloon became New York's most popular haven for sports stars and celebrities in the 1950s, and my father, Alfred Barra. Shor said his was the only Jewish family in the neighborhood.

Glennon wanted a major league job, but somehow it always eluded him. During the war he had the opportunity to run the New Orleans Pelicans and fell in love with the Deep South. On his first trip to Birmingham, he was delighted to find that Rickwood was modeled on Shibe, the first ballpark he had ever seen. Portly and balding, with big ears and nose, Glennon, with his tailored suits and derbies and ready Irish smile, gave the appearance of a character actor in Hollywood films. He was forty-three when he shook hands with Gus Jebeles, who liked his energy and intelligence. Bob Scranton called him "a ball of energy." Glennon let Jebeles know that he wouldn't come cheap and that if he took the job he wanted the power to make decisions—important ones. Jebeles said yes to everything.

He quickly found that success would not come easily. The Barons were a dismal 68–84 during the 1946 season, good for only sixth place in the Southern Association, so one of Glennon's first moves was to find a new manager. He hired a former major league outfielder named Dick Porter, who had hit .308 in six seasons in the 1930s with the Indians and Red Sox before banging up his knee. But Porter would not press the players the way Glennon wanted, and before the season was over he was replaced by a pitcher who had grown up near Birmingham, Ivy Paul Andrews, who had put in eight seasons with four big-league teams, including the Yankees. Glennon swung some deals for new players with Connie Mack and did everything he could think of to promote the franchise, from reorganizing the concession stand to personally inspecting the restrooms before every game. He brought students to the games with clubs like the Birmingham Bees, which gave honor students free admission to Barons games. He bought beer for sportswriters and shook hands at public functions all over town, taking some locals

aback with his brashness but in the end winning them over with his
Emerald Isle élan.

While he was no civil rights activist, Glennon intuitively
understood that integration was good for baseball. Bob Scranton
was with him in New Orleans when the news came over the radio
that Brooklyn Dodgers owner Walter O'Malley had signed Jackie
Robinson. "He nodded," Scranton recalls, "and said, 'It'll be good for
the game.' That was about the only trouble we had in the South. A
lot of southerners said to us, 'I'll bet you yankees are happy about
this.'" Under Glennon's direction the Black Barons for the first time
had an amicable relationship with the Barons, or at least one that
involved something more than simply renting the ballpark when the
white Barons were on the road. There would be no Ku Klux Klan
rallies at Rickwood Field while Glennon was GM. Black Barons
majority owner Tom Hayes, Scranton says, "was truly a gentleman,
and he and Eddie got along very well. We sold tickets for him and
ran concessions. He didn't gouge black fans by raising prices by so
much as a nickel"—a frequent complaint when the team was under
previous ownership. "We sold hot dogs for just a quarter, and bags
of peanuts and popcorn just ten cents. Cokes were a dime, and not
those chintzy six-ouncers."

Glennon did something else that was relatively unimportant to
most whites connected with the team but made a big impression on
the blacks. For the first time, Black Barons were allowed to use the
same clubhouse as white Barons; the degrading practice of having
them dress in the tunnels or in the bus on the way to the park was
abolished.

But for all Glennon's hard work, the Barons improved by only
five games in 1947. It turned out that most of Connie Mack's prospects weren't that promising after all. A first baseman/outfielder

GENERAL MANAGER EDDIE GLENNON (*left*) *and Traveling Secretary Bob Scranton were both yankees (Glennon from Philadelphia, Scranton from Hartford, Connecticut). Each took to Alabama and baseball at Rickwood Field. Glennon moved in the fences and promoted the team tirelessly, raising attendance to an all-time high. Scranton says Eddie was the first Barons official to establish a good relationship with Rickwood's other tenants, the Black Barons. Here they prepare hot dogs for a visit from the Birmingham Bees, school kids given free tickets as a reward for good grades.*

named Joe Collins was probably his best player; the twenty-four-year-old hit .360 with 6 home runs and 31 RBIs in just 48 games before he was dealt to the Yankees, where he would earn six World Series rings in ten seasons.

One thing Glennon did do was increase attendance: more than 320,000 fans saw Barons games in 1947, an all-time record. (Indeed, postwar attendance was up throughout the Southern Association, but only Atlanta, with its substantially larger population, surpassed Birmingham.) He made Rickwood into a cleaner, pleasanter place to go as well as a more exciting one. He talked Jebeles into changing the outfield dimensions, bringing them once and for all into line with major league standards. "This ain't dead ball," Bob Scranton recalls him saying. "It's time people were hittin' home runs here." The power alleys were still long compared with most big-league parks, but they were 70 feet closer to the batter's box. The new, shorter dimensions made the home run a much more likely occurrence, something a fan could go to the ballpark and actually expect to see.* The scoreboard was moved closer to center field and about 60 feet closer to home plate, so lucky fans could occasionally see the spectacle of a home run ball bouncing off the scoreboard.

Glennon instructed his grounds crew to paint stars on the spots where long home runs had landed. He had his groundskeepers plant thick grass in back of the new left field fence so that fans in the bleachers could see home run balls land—the area was soon dubbed Glennon's Gardens. Best of all, a brand-new scoreboard topped off with a giant clock, forty feet from the ground, became Rickwood's new landmark.

Exercising the authority that Gus Jebeles had given him, Glennon made one more important change. Just in time for the 1948 sea-

---

* Amazingly, many postwar minor league teams still hadn't caught on to the fan appeal of the home run. In Mobile a slight alteration of the fences had allowed George "Shotgun" Shuba, soon to be a Brooklyn Dodger, to hit an eye-opening 21 home runs for the pennant-winning Bears. But in Memphis the dimensions of the Chicks' ballpark were such that Ted Kluszewski hit just 7 home runs in 115 games. Called up by the Reds toward the end of the 1947 season, "Big Klu"—his biceps were so massive he had to cut his sleeves to accommodate them—would go on to hit 257 home runs in thirteen years, including 136 from 1953 to 1955.

son, he dropped the Barons' affiliation with Connie Mack's decaying farm system.* A new connection was established with the Boston Red Sox, whose owner, Tom Yawkey, was willing to spend money developing minor league prospects.

Before the 1948 season the Yankees made their customary spring visit to Rickwood. The occasion was something of a homecoming for Melvin Allen Israel, better known to millions of Yankee fans as Mel Allen. Allen was born in Birmingham and grew up in nearby Sylacauga; he graduated from the University of Alabama, where, among his greatest accomplishments, he helped tutor a young football player named Paul Bryant.

Allen had begun his career broadcasting Crimson Tide football games. Like so many of the most popular major league baseball announcers of the period, such as the Brooklyn Dodgers' Red Barber and the Detroit Tigers' Ernie Harwell, Allen spoke with an unabashed Deep South accent.† He was just coming into his own as a celebrity in 1948; though the Yankees had not yet begun their unprecedented streak of five consecutive World Series titles from 1949 to 1953, his signature phrases—"How about that!" and "Going, going gone!" (for a home run) and "That's a Ballantine blast!" (Ballantine Beer was a longtime Yankee sponsor)—were already well known.

---

* Mack's tight-fisted economic policies had doomed the franchise that had once challenged the Yankees for American League supremacy. By the end of the 1954 season the A's had left Philadelphia for Kansas City—where, many Kansas City fans bitterly complained, they became the Yankees' de facto farm team.

† I was astounded as a boy to find, upon opening my first packages of baseball cards, some of my favorite players' names spelled out: Skowron (Bill), Howard (Elston), and Aaron (Hank). I had assumed from listening to Allen's World Series broadcasts that their last names were Skarn, Haard, and Airn.

Owing to Glennon's influence, the Boston Red Sox also stopped off in Birmingham in 1948, bringing their great star Ted Williams. Williams delighted black fans, as Babe Ruth had done before him, by slamming several dozen balls into their bleachers. At one point during batting practice, a grinning Williams called out to black fans in right field, announcing where he intended to hit the ball. The debate over whether Rickwood was a pitcher's or a hitter's park was never completely resolved, but to Williams there was one undeniable pleasure of batting in Rickwood: "Here you could hear that good sound of the bat against the ball."[6]

Thus in one memorable spring, three of the greatest outfielders in twentieth-century baseball, some would say maybe the three greatest—Ted Williams, Joe DiMaggio, and Willie Mays—all trod the grass of Rickwood. Then the season started, and on May 21 a young giant from Moosup, Connecticut, named Walt Dropo hit a spectacular drive, estimated at 467 feet, over the clock on the scoreboard.* Another estimate put the shot at 479 feet; still another estimate, by the *Birmingham News'* Alf Van Hoose, was 486 feet. As Satchel Paige said, you pays your money and takes your choice. Eddie Glennon had his first and most sensational star painted on the outfield wall.

Glennon did not produce instant winners, but he did stir up new

---

* It's hard to believe, but neither Glennon nor his assistant understood the publicity value of Dropo's home run. According to Bob Scranton, it was *Birmingham News* sports editor Zipp Newman who called and wanted to get a picture of Dropo standing close to where his ball hit the wall. A plaque was placed next to the X that read, "This marks the spot where Walt Dropo's blast hit the concrete wall 467 feet from home plate, 1948." Dropo, who hit .359 for the Barons in 1948, would go on to play thirteen years in the big leagues, winning the Rookie of the Year in 1950 when he hit 34 home runs and had an American League–leading 144 RBIs.

interest among both white and black fans. As the pall cast on the city by the Depression began to lift in the postwar prosperity, Rickwood was once again a jewel, and fans took new pride in it. In an interview preserved in the oral history archives of the Birmingham Public Library, Black Barons pitcher Bill Powell remarked, "I don't know what it is, but when I was playing at Rickwood Field, I was always itching to get to the ballpark. We played all over the United States, and when we got here, you just loved coming here to play in this park. There was just something about the baseball in that park."

· IN THE WORDS of historian Chris Fullerton, "While Eighteenth Street jumped with the sound of big bands, a growing sense of impatience began to swell in the heart of the city's black community."[7] The postwar optimism in Birmingham, with the factories and mills churning and black servicemen anticipating a squarer deal when they got home, did not last long. Paul Hemphill, who grew up in the era, would later write,

> As the black population expanded over the decades, creating competition between the lower-class blacks and whites for jobs and housing and respectability, tensions inevitably worsened. In a sense, the whites got whiter and the blacks got blacker, until Birmingham, by the forties, had become almost as rigidly segregated as South Africa. And the presence of rabble-rousers like Bull Connor and the Klan, doing the dirty work for the Big Mules and U.S. Steel, two groups whose only vested interest in the city was in keeping costs at a minimum, made sure that it stayed that way.[8]

What no one could have anticipated in 1945 was that the great era of the black industrial teams would soon be coming to an end. The New Deal had spent in excess of $2 billion aiding the war effort and reviving industry in Jefferson County. Birmingham's Big Mules wanted the money but not the legislation that went with it. Civil rights advocates had pressured the Roosevelt administration— or more specifically, the Fair Employment Practices Committee (FEPC)—to make integration mandatory for companies receiving government contracts. The mean-spirited response of some company owners was to cut back on programs. They had no choice about integrating their factories, but rather than integrate their baseball teams, many chose to abolish them. "They had to integrate," Piper Davis recalled, "any of 'em that had government contracts. Two or three cut their teams out because of integration. Stockham's team almost went altogether because of integration. The company felt it might have a little trouble, wouldn't get enough men to have a good club, enough whites who would play with blacks. Integration came out in the open, and whites didn't want to play." Stockham Valve and ACIPCO kept their industrial teams, but no whites would play on them. The two company-sponsored teams were the last to feed talent to the Black Barons, setting the stage for the final great era of Birmingham black ball.

No one did more to usher in that era than Abe Saperstein. Tom Hayes's partner in the ownership of the Black Barons, Saperstein was better known as the owner and coach of the Harlem Globetrotters, but he was a first-rate baseball man who took over the day-to-day operations of the Black Barons and had a sharp eye for new talent. Or, as in the case of Ted "Double Duty" Radcliffe, old talent. Saperstein recruited Radcliffe from the American Giants in Chicago, where he had been named the Most Valuable Player in the Negro American

League in 1943. Radcliffe, then forty-two years old, responded by helping the Black Barons win the Negro American League pennant in 1944.

Radcliffe, nicknamed Double Duty by Damon Runyon after seeing him catch the first game of a doubleheader and pitch the second, called Saperstein "my man. He was the greatest man for helping Negroes. He got 'em up [to professional ball]."[9] According to Satchel Paige and Cleveland Indians' owner Bill Veeck, Saperstein was instrumental in getting Paige up to the big leagues in 1948. Every black player who dealt with him lauded his honesty and integrity. "First and fifteenth," said Willie Patterson, a mainstay on the 1940s Black Barons, "they handed you that envelope. With Abe Saperstein, you didn't have to worry about no money."[10]

Saperstein had the clout to get the Black Barons booked where new owner Tom Hayes could not, including, on a couple of occasions, Yankee Stadium, where they played before as many as 30,000 fans. He also gave second jobs with the Globetrotters to many of the Black Barons who could play basketball, most notably Piper Davis.* Davis was perhaps the key player of the 1943 and 1944 Black Barons who won back-to-back Negro American League pennants. Their misfortune was that they had to play the Homestead Grays in the Negro League World Series those seasons. Named for a U.S. Steel company town near Pittsburgh, the Grays were not merely dominant in that period, but they were supreme, winning nine consecutive pennants from 1937 through 1945. The Barons were talented, but the Grays,

---

* Saperstein's efforts in behalf of black players was not limited to the South. In a Q&A session at the Yogi Berra Museum and Learning Center at Montclair State in New Jersey, Larry Doby, the first black player in the American League, told me that Abe had also worked hard to get him a connection with the Cleveland Indians.

with the great Josh Gibson at catcher, Buck Leonard at first base, and "Cool Papa" Bell in the outfield and later as coach, were practically their own Negro League All-Star team. The Black Barons tested them in 1943, extending the Series to the whole seven games,* but were swept in 1944, though their partisans were quick to point out that three of their best players—Leandy Young, Tommy Sampson, and the switch-hitting catcher Lloyd "Pepper" Bassett—were injured and out.

The Grays were to the Black Barons what the Atlanta Crackers were to the white Barons. Like the city's white fans, followers of the Black Barons soon developed a Brooklyn Dodgers mentality: "Wait till next year." They had no way of knowing that the "next years" were running out.

---

* According to the *Birmingham Reporter*, the sixth game, won by the Black Barons 1–0, was attended by Memphis' own W. C. Handy, Father of the Blues and composer of the immortal "St. Louis Blues."

JACKIE ROBINSON AND BEN CHAPMAN *at Shibe Park in May 1947. Chapman, the "Alabama Flash," hit .302 in fifteen major league seasons. As Phillies manager, he led merciless race-baiting of Robinson. In the interest of harmony, Commissioner Albert "Happy" Chandler, himself a southerner, ordered Chapman to smile with Robinson in public. Jackie also forced a smile. Robinson played in the first integrated baseball game in Birmingham in 1954. It was illegal, but city officials looked the other way.*

7

"WELL, I'M GOING TO THE BALLGAME"

I N THE SPRING OF 1948 Paul "Bear" Bryant was a rising star in college football, having turned the moribund University of Kentucky football program into a Southeastern Conference contender with a 15–6 record over the preceding two seasons. At that time he was a well-known figure in Alabama, having been an All-Conference selection on the Crimson Tide's 1934 national championship team, but he was nowhere near the colossus he would eventually become, not just to Alabama but to all of college football. Within twelve years Bryant would be one of the reasons that Alabama's baseball culture was almost forgotten by a new generation—ironically because Bryant's secret unfulfilled passion was to play baseball.

As a student at Alabama, he and Don Hutson, the great all-around athlete and future superstar of the Green Bay Packers, went

off to Texas during the summer of 1934 to play on a Texas oil company's baseball team (had the nascent NCAA had enough clout,
both would have been suspended from playing college football). At
any rate, Hutson was an ace at baseball, and Bryant, sadly, had to
admit that he lacked the experience and finesse to succeed at the
game he loved. In the 1970s he would renew a friendship with New
York Yankees owner George Steinbrenner, whom he had met two
decades earlier when both were members of the College Football
Coaches Association. The Yankees came to Tuscaloosa to play an
exhibition game, and Bryant, giddy as a schoolboy fan, had his picture taken with former Birmingham A's and current Yankees star
Reggie Jackson.

In 1948, though, Bear Bryant was just another fan in the all-
white right field section of Rickwood, sitting with his former coach
and mentor Frank Thomas, a fellow baseball fan. Bryant had come
down from Kentucky for a visit, and Coach Tommy, as he was affectionately called, treated him to a game at Rickwood. Thomas told
Bryant that he had to see this fantastic teenager who was playing left
field for the Black Barons. At Fairfield Industrial High School the
kid had been such a terrific quarterback that he had attracted the
attention of even the white papers. Wistfully, Bryant watched the
kid play. The idea of integrating SEC football had already crossed
his mind. He had scouted some black high school football players in
Kentucky, but had hit a brick wall with the school's administration.
But in 1948 he had no idea he would eventually be the coach of the
University of Alabama and that it would take twenty-three years
for him to bring the school its first black football player. On that
afternoon in Rickwood Field, Bear Bryant just sat back, watched the
game, and enjoyed his first look at Willie Mays.

• • •

· IN THE LATE 1940S southern baseball was faced with a dilemma. The pall of the Depression that had lingered over Birmingham for years was finally dispelled by the revival of industry during the war. With prosperity, though, came increasing racial tensions. Returning black GIs who had fought for their country were less and less inclined to accept segregation in any form. Section 597 of the 1944 code of Alabama hung over the city like a cloud:"It shall be unlawful to conduct a restaurant for the serving of food in the city, at which white and colored people are served in the same room, unless such white and colored persons are effectually separated by a solid partition extending from the floor upward to a distance of 7 ft. or higher and unless a separate entrance from the street is provided for each compartment." Also:"It shall be unlawful for a Negro and a white person to play together or in company with each other in any game of cards, dice, dominoes, checkers, baseball, softball, football, basketball, or similar game."

The law had little effect on young black boys such as Willie Mays, who was born in 1931 and had already been playing playground sports with white kids for years; in any event, Section 597 wasn't enforced on school grounds. Its purpose was to keep *organized* sports, particularly high school, college, and professional games, from being integrated. "I always enjoyed playing ball," Mays told a writer named Lou Sahadi in 1988,

and it didn't matter to me whether I played with white kids or black. I never understood why an issue was made of who I played with. . . . I never recall trouble. I believe I had a happy childhood. Besides playing school sports, we played football against the white kids. And we thought nothing of it, neither the blacks nor the whites. It was the grown-ups who got upset. If they saw black kids playing on the same team with white kids, they'd call the cops, and the cops would make us stop. I never got into a fight that was started because of racism. To me, it was the adults who caused the problems.[1]

Bob Veale, who was four years younger than Mays and would go on to win 120 games in thirteen seasons for the Pittsburgh Pirates and Boston Red Sox, has similar recollections about growing up in Birmingham. "We didn't know as kids we were breaking segregation laws. We just thought we were playing baseball. I had white friends, kids I played ball with all the time. We weren't thinking about integrating anything, we were just playing baseball."

Although neither Mays nor Veale perceived segregation as a major force in their lives when they were children, it put a huge burden on professional black ballplayers in Alabama. The Black Barons were always plagued by defections; long before Satchel Paige went north, black players knew they could never make the barnstorming bucks in segregated Alabama that they could in northern states, where they were allowed to play against white players. So the Birmingham Black Barons, despite their deep talent pool, could never quite overtake their great Negro League rivals, the Kansas City Monarchs and the Homestead Grays.

• • •

· BASEBALL HAD NEVER BEEN more popular than it was in the post–World War II South. In 1947 attendance exceeded an unprecedented two million in the Southern Association alone, and the number was even higher in 1948. Still, many franchises were in financial trouble, largely because the facilities had suffered during the cash-poor war years and needed repair and renovation. Frank Shaughnessy, a general manager for the Montreal Royals of the International League back in the 1930s, came up with an ingenious moneymaking solution, though it took several years for some minor leagues to understand its potential. Prior to Shaughnessy most teams simply played for a pennant; the team with the best record took the pennant, and that was it. The Southern Association and the Texas League made natural rivals for the Dixie World Series, but for most minor leagues, the end of the regular season was it—there was no postseason.

The Shaughnessy playoff system pitted the four teams with the best won-lost records in an elimination tournament. The first round paired the top-seeded team with the fourth seed, and the team with the second-best record with the one that had the third-best. The winners would then play each other for the championship. It was that simple.

At first International League teams played just a single playoff game per round; it didn't take long for league officials to understand that a series of games, say, best of three or even best of five, would draw more paying customers than one game. Almost overnight several leagues found that they had walked into a financial windfall.*

_____

* And not just professional baseball leagues: several football leagues such as the All-America Football Conference and even the National Hockey League adopted the

The Southern Association first used the Shaughnessy system in 1948, and it proved to be a boon for the Barons, who finished third behind Nashville and Memphis with an 89–64 record, 11 games out of first place. Under new manager Fred Walters, the Barons, with Boston-supplied prospects, caught fire and swept through the play-offs, whipping the first-place Nashville Vols, who had finished the regular season with a 95–58 record. They then went on to face the Fort Worth Panthers in the Dixie World Series. That the Barons were given the opportunity to beat Nashville in the playoffs isn't as unfair as it seems. Southern Association ballparks were a motley collection of styles and dimensions. For instance, in Ponce de Leon, the Atlanta Crackers' ballpark, there was a magnolia tree growing in center field that outfielders had to play around. The Little Rock Travelers' home field, Ray Winder Field, had a distinctive hump in left field that caused hard-hit balls to bounce right over an outfielder's head.

The Nashville Vols' park, Sulphur Dell, featured enough strange quirks and eccentricities to put a modern fan in mind of a miniature golf course. First base, for instance, was just 42 feet from the grandstand, and someone with a perverse sense of humor decided to build the left field grandstands just 26 feet from third base. That was nothing, however, to what the park's builders put out in right field. Right field was constructed as an incline that was barely perceptible ten or so feet in back of first base but which got steeper the deeper you went. About 230 feet from home plate the turf reached a 45-degree angle then leveled off to a 10-foot shelf, after which the incline began again, reaching another 45-degree angle at the right field fence. Most

---

Shaughnessy system. In time the ingenuity of the idea reached British and even French rugby leagues.

batters didn't have much trouble hitting fly balls over the right field fence, which was just 262 feet from home plate (left field was a bit longer but still under 300 feet). But if a drive fell short, it could be hell for a right fielder, who had immediately to choose between two options. He could play deep and come running down the slope to make the play, or he could hang out on the 10-foot plateau and take his chances that the ball would be hit in front of him, in which case he could make the play on the run, moving downhill.

At any rate, the park was what baseball people called a band box—a park that heavily favored hitters. Rickwood, under Eddie Glennon, had good dimensions for hitters, but nothing like Sulphur Dell, and the yawning space between home plate and the grandstands, which Connie Mack had walked off back in 1910, did a lot to counter the favorable outfield dimensions by keeping a great many foul pops from drifting into the stands and giving the hitters another chance. In Sulphur Dell the catcher and other fielders had little chance to catch anything before the ball went into the stands, and many a first or third baseman broke bones crashing into the fences before they learned the futility of chasing foul balls in the park.

Consequently every Nashville pitcher in 1948 had a high ERA.* The Vols' management loaded their batting order with left-handed pull hitters, and even some of the right-handed hitters were chosen for their ability to hit the ball to the opposite field. A left-handed-hitting outfielder named Charlie Workman, who had hit 25 home

---

* There was at least one pitching star on the 1948 Nashville Vols roster, Alva Lee "Bobo" Holloman from Thomaston, Georgia. Bobo was 7–2 for Nashville in 1948 despite an ERA of 5.27. He would win baseball immortality in his only shot at the big leagues in 1953 with the hapless St. Louis Browns when he pitched a no-hitter in his first major league start. He won only two other games for the Browns, finished the season with a 5.23 ERA, and never pitched in the major leagues again.

runs for the Boston Red Sox in 1945, found new life playing for the Vols, batting .353 with an unheard-of 52 home runs. Another outfielder, named Charlie Gilbert, who had played six years in the major leagues with just five home runs, hit 42 at Sulphur Dell in 1948 and was considered so dangerous that pitchers walked him a league-high 155 times. He scored an astonishing 178 runs.

There was at least one legitimate hitter on the Vols' roster: a catcher named Forrest "Smoky" Burgess, who would play eighteen years in the National League, make six All-Star teams, bat .295, and win a World Series ring with the 1960 Pittsburgh Pirates. Smoky hit a mere 22 home runs that season, but led the Southern Association in batting at .386.

Nashville's batting stats terrified most opponents, but Bob Scranton recalls, "The first time I saw the park I knew why their guys hit so well. I figured if they could hit like that there, our guys would hit even better." Scranton was right—the Barons scored 25 runs in two games at Sulphur Dell and finished off the Vols back at Rickwood to take the SA pennant. In the Dixie World Series the Barons swept the Fort Worth Panthers by a total of just five runs. Bob Scranton remembers 1948 as high times. "I was making $250 a month as traveling secretary," he says. "I got $250 more when we won the Southern Association pennant* and a full share, $1,600, when we won the Dixie World Series, which was really big money."

In some ways it was a high-water mark for the team. The Birmingham Barons, playing in a town with between 250,000 and 300,000 people in the metropolitan area, had sold nearly 446,000 tickets in 1948. Counting free admissions for Ladies Day and other

* Though old-timers refer to the Barons' 1948 championship as a pennant, it was not called that at the time, since the team finished third during the regular season.

promotions, Rickwood Field had probably admitted more than half a million.

Enthusiasm for baseball was citywide and crossed racial boundaries. The only tragedy was that the vast majority couldn't share that enthusiasm. A black preacher, the Reverend John W. Goodgame of the Sixth Avenue Baptist Church, spoke for whites and blacks when, after services every baseball Sunday, he told his congregation, "Well, I'm going to the ballgame."

• IN THE LATE SPRING OF 1945, the Kansas City Monarchs played the Black Barons in Birmingham. The Monarchs had a new shortstop who was learning the position at the advanced age of twenty-six, having given up a couple of years of his career to the U.S. Army. Jack Roosevelt Robinson was doing just fine for Kansas City; he would bat .387 in 47 games that year, but he didn't care for the grueling traveling and didn't approve of the lax standards that permitted betting on games by players and owners alike. Against the Black Barons he scored the go-ahead run on a sacrifice fly in a game that was later ruled a draw when Birmingham's manager, Piper Davis, filed a complaint of umpire interference. In August of that season Robinson met with Brooklyn Dodgers general manager Branch Rickey and set in motion the events that would integrate major league baseball and doom the Negro Leagues.

Some thought Robinson was prime major league material; others, such as Ben Chapman, "the Alabama Flash," did not. Chapman saw Robinson in two games at Rickwood and, in an interview with me in 1978, judged him to be "ordinary. He could maybe fill in as a bench player on some of the Yankee teams I was on, but he would never make it as a starter." In 1947, as manager of the Philadelphia Phillies, Chapman led his team in race-baiting of Robinson so vicious that some white southerners playing in the National League objected.*

Rickey, like all of major league management, was contemptuous of the Negro Leagues; he dismissed them as "rackets," almost certainly referring to Pittsburgh Crawford owner Gus Greenlee, who ran a gambling organization and had ties to organized crime. When baseball's "great experiment," as author Jules Tygiel called Robinson's entry into the major leagues, proved to be a success, the raid on the top Negro League players was swift and merciless. Black ball was shorn of its best young talent. In 1945, in an act of blatant hypocrisy, New York Yankees president Larry MacPhail openly urged black ball owners to apply to the National Association, which governed the minor leagues; the NA would, MacPhail was implying, accept Negro League teams as "official" minor league franchises—in other words, black farm teams for white baseball.

---

* Chapman, who died in 1993 in Hoover, Alabama, near my parents' old house, was a pretty good player, putting in fifteen years in the big leagues, seven of them with the Yankees (1930–36). He was a four-time All-Star who led the AL in stolen bases twice and hit .302 in 1,717 major league games. He was also, I thought at the time I interviewed him, one of the most virulent racists I'd ever met; in an interview I did with him in 1979, his incredible rationale for shouting "Nigger!" at Robinson was "Hell, yeah, we called him that. We'd say anything to get an edge on anybody. Hell, we called Joe DiMaggio 'Wop!' and Hank Greenberg 'Kike!'"

When Chapman said Robinson couldn't have cracked the lineup of the early 1930s Yankees team, he was saying, in effect, that he was a better player than Robinson, which, of course, was nonsense.

Art Clarkson, who was principal owner of the Barons from 1980 to 1990, tells me that Ben changed later in life: "He really was a different man in later years and acknowledged the error of his old ways. I told him once I was going to a school in a black neighborhood to talk to kids about baseball, and he volunteered to go along. Ben went, talked to them, and really enjoyed it. To tell you the truth, I don't think he'd ever had an opportunity like that before."

It was a lie, and everyone knew it. The Yankees, certainly, had no intention of doing any business with a black team, and in fact had no interest in signing any black players. The first black player to make the Yankees' major league team would be Kansas City Monarchs star Elston Howard, and that would not happen until 1955, by which time Howard was already twenty-six years old and had missed several of his prime years.[*]

The American and National Leagues had no intention of recognizing the legitimacy of the black leagues. Some—the Yankees and Red Sox stand out in retrospect as the most obvious—clearly didn't want to sign black players, and the clubs that did didn't want to deal with compensating the players' teams. The president of the Negro National League, the Reverend John J. Johnson, stated what everyone knew after the 1947 season when he said that the Negro American and National Leagues were denied membership to the National Association and that the invitation to join the National Association by MacPhail had been a sham. "The Negro Leagues," Johnson told reporters from black papers, "still possess no status, no voice, no rights, no relationship at all to the [white] major or minor leagues." MacPhail's breathtakingly candid statement summed up the entire association between the white major leagues and professional black ball up to that time.

After the euphoria of Robinson's signing by the Brooklyn Dodgers had passed with no overtures from the major leagues to the black

---

[*] Howard, against whom Mays would play in 1948, wanted to be the first black Yankee so much that he endured the blatant racism of the club's front office and even gave away a couple of seasons at catcher waiting for his good friend Yogi Berra to get old. As Yogi himself put it, "Elston could have been starting catcher for most major league teams, and if he'd started a couple of years earlier, he'd sure be in the Hall of Fame." In 1963, sixteen years after Robinson broke the color barrier, Howard became the American League's first black Most Valuable Player. He was thirty-three years old.

leagues, Johnson said that those who made a living from black ball now had to face the facts: 1947, he said, was "a disastrous season" for Negro League baseball.

The Reverend Johnson was correct, but historical fairness requires some balance. As Bill James wrote in *The New Bill James Historical Baseball Abstract*,

> Negro League historians are wont to rant that the white club owners did not respect the "contracts" of the Negro League teams in the period of the league's disintegration. They miss, it seems to me, an obvious point: these teams didn't respect one another's contracts, either. They operated on letters of agreement, which players and teams felt free to discard as soon as they became inconvenient. Why would we expect the white club owners to respect "contracts" that the Negro Leagues themselves didn't respect?[2]

• THE SON OF A COAL MINER, Lorenzo "Piper" Davis is probably—as a player, manager, oral historian—the most important man in the history of Alabama baseball. All of that would have been enough to secure his place in Alabama sports history, but there was one more very important accomplishment. He did for Willie Mays what he could not do for himself or many of his friends and teammates: groom him into a major league ballplayer. Davis grew up obsessed with baseball; he loved the game so much that he even followed the fortunes of the white Barons, listening to the popular radio broadcasts of Eugene "Bull" Connor. The bitter irony of that fact would not become apparent to young Piper for many years.

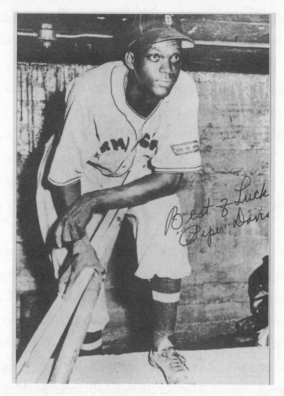

Lorenzo "Piper" Davis: *Black Baron player and manager, he may have been the most important man in the history of Birmingham and Alabama baseball.*

Baseball was baseball; his biggest thrill before his playing days, he said, was seeing the 1931 Dixie Series duel between Dizzy Dean and Ray Caldwell.

Most of what we know today about the Birmingham Black Barons in their golden era was passed on by Piper Davis. Most black baseball talent before 1950 came from the South; no state produced more than Alabama, and no city in Alabama more than Birmingham. The first-rate players who came out of black industrial ball from the 1920s through the 1940s could have filled out the roster of at least one major league team and perhaps put some extra plaques on the wall of the Hall of Fame: Artie Wilson (the last man in professional ball to bat over .400), Lester Lockett, Bill Powell, Jesse Mitchell, Willie Lee, Bill Greason, Jimmy Zapp, Leroy Morney, Willie Foster, Charlie Mason, Jimmy Newberry, Lyman Bostock, and Sam Hairston, to name just a few.*

Five players on the 1948 Black Barons—Artie Wilson, Sam Hairston, Bill Greason, Jehosie Heard, Davis, and Mays—were all signed by major league clubs. None but Mays was given a fair shot at the prize, and he became, perhaps, the greatest player in baseball.

Piper Davis graduated from Fairfield High School. Forged by the competition of the industrial leagues (where he played with, among numerous other fine ballplayers, Willie Howard "Cat" Mays, Willie's father), he came to the Black Barons in 1942, by which time he had already played industrial ball with most of his teammates. He played every infield position with style, hit with authority, and dazzled on the bases. He was a terrific all-around athlete who, in addition to excelling in baseball, was awarded a basketball scholarship to Alabama State and played with the Harlem Globetrotters until his legs got so sore that he was forced to give it up.†

---

* Lyman Bostock's son, Lyman Bostock Jr., made it to the major leagues in 1975 with the Minnesota Twins; he compiled a .311 batting average over four seasons. He was shot and killed in 1978 by a man who mistakenly thought Bostock was having an affair with his wife, a longtime friend of Bostock.

Sam Hairston made it to the big leagues for four games in 1951, by which time he was almost thirty-two years old. The Hairstons hold a major league record for producing the most big-league ballplayers: two of Sam's sons, Jerry Sr. and Johnny, and two grandsons, Scott and Jerry Jr., all played in the major leagues. Jerry Hairston Jr. won a World Series ring in 2009 with the New York Yankees.

† Bo Jackson, the Heisman Trophy–winning running back from Auburn, played pro football with the Oakland Raiders and, for eight seasons, major league baseball with the Kansas City Royals and Chicago White Sox. In 1990, at a Kansas City Royals games where

Superstars: Satchel Paige (*far left*), *jazz great Lionel Hampton, and Lorenzo "Piper" Davis. This photo was originally loaned to the author in 1987 for an interview for a Birmingham magazine. Davis could not recall when or where the photo was taken. Two good bets are during the break for the East–West All-Star game in Chicago, sometime after 1942, or perhaps in Birmingham at one of the numerous jazz clubs on or around Birmingham's Fourth Avenue District.*

In 1942 Black Barons manager Gus Welch offered him five dollars a game and seven and a half for doubleheaders. By his second season his pay was doubled. It's difficult to evaluate exactly how good a player Piper Davis really was in his prime. Some who saw him in later years after years of grind thought he was "ordinary," a typical white put-down for black players, but that still meant ordinary by big league standards. Others who saw him when he was

---

Piper Davis was being honored, Jackson said, "He warned me that my legs couldn't take the constant stress of playing two sports all year around. I should have listened to him. He was right. I think if I hadn't played football, I could have played baseball for another five–six years—maybe more."

younger, the *Birmingham News'* Alf Van Hoose and Bob Scranton, for instance, thought he would have definitely been All-Star or perhaps Hall of Fame material had he gotten his shot. Bob Veale, who saw all the National League stars of the 1950s, told me, "His natural position was shortstop, and that's what you have to judge him by. I thought he was as good as Pee Wee Reese and maybe a little better in the field than Ernie Banks. Ernie had more power, but that's about it. I'd say if Reese and Banks are in the Hall of Fame, Piper probably could have been, too." Bob Scranton agrees: "I saw Phil Rizzuto play at Rickwood, and if we're talking shortstops Rizzuto was probably a better fielder than Piper, but I think Piper was a better hitter. Let me add that I think Piper could have made the Hall of Fame playing second or third base, also."

He was good enough to be chosen in the East–West All-Star game at Chicago's Comiskey Park five years running, from 1945 to 1949.* But Piper did not play in the 1945 game, though he had received more votes than the Kansas City Monarchs' Jackie Robinson. Davis was suspended for an altercation in which he was said to have struck an umpire. Some said it was a punch; others said that Piper hit the ump accidentally while waving his arms in the course of arguing a call. Whatever happened, the incident probably scared off scouts sent by the Brooklyn Dodgers' Branch Rickey, who knew the first black man in the major leagues would have to be one who could control his temper.

---

* The East–West All-Star game was regarded by most black fans as a bigger event than the Negro League World Series. Players jumped from team to team with such frequency that it was hard for fans in different parts of the country to keep up with them, but the All-Star game brought the best players together in one glamorous showcase.

Both the St. Louis Browns and Boston Red Sox gave Davis a contract, but despite his excellent performance would never commit to bringing him up to the parent team. By 1948, with Jackie Robinson established with the Dodgers and Larry Doby breaking the color barrier in the American League with the Cleveland Indians, some black stars began to wonder whether they were in limbo. It looked as if the younger players like Willie Mays would get their chance, but older stars—meaning thirty or over—like Davis began to think the dream would never become real for them.

In 1948 Davis was thirty-one and had no more illusions. Offered a handsome $750 a month to play and manage the Barons, he accepted. In Chattanooga he saw Willie Mays for the first time. Piper knew all about him. He had played with Willie's father, Cat, or "Kitty Cat," as he was called for his reflexes, in the industrial leagues and had heard that Willie was attending Davis's old high school, Fairfield. Davis also knew that Cat's father, Willie's grandfather, had been a legendary local ballplayer. He had heard that Willie, in addition to being a terrific baseball and football player, was, as Davis had been, outstanding at basketball. (The *Birmingham World* had placed Mays on its All-County team, and he had led all Jefferson County scorers with 241 points.) Piper knew that other players called Willie "Buck" (slang for young black men and also, according to Bob Veale, he ran like a buck), "Duck" (because of his posterior and also, some said, because he walked like a duck), and "Buck Duck" for both (though Mays insisted well into adulthood that he never understood the nickname).

Davis knew one other thing: what Willie was doing in Chattanooga. He was so good even as a teenager that he could pick up some extra cash playing barnstorm ball. It was past midnight when

Davis saw him in the lobby of the team's hotel. Willie walked up to him and said hello. Davis admonished him—didn't Willie know that if it was found out he was playing ball for money he wouldn't be allowed to play high school sports? Willie laughed; he didn't care. When Davis got back to Birmingham, he called Cat Mays and told him about the situation. Cat said that if Willie wanted to play, he should be allowed to. Davis shrugged and told him to have Willie out at Rickwood the next day. Mays was there early.

The New York Yankees, taking their marching orders from their GM, Larry MacPhail, later claimed they didn't sign Mays because he "couldn't hit a curveball." They were right; no seventeen-year-old was ever particularly good at hitting curveballs thrown by professionals. But Mays could do everything else on a ball field like an adult, only better. He covered vast territory in the outfield; astonished opponents who watched him haul down their would-be doubles and triples swore that he moved toward the ball *before* it was even hit. He threw with astonishing power and accuracy and, just as important, released the ball quickly and unerringly to the right base. As for hitting, when he connected, the ball took off like a bazooka shot, even though he stood in the batter's box with a wide stance that was all wrong for his chunky 5' 10½" frame. The stance was copied from pictures and newsreels he had seen of his idol—not Josh Gibson or "Cool Papa" Bell or even his dad but Joe DiMaggio, who was two or three inches taller than he was. Mays always wanted to check the paper to see how DiMaggio had done. Some of his teammates, like Bill Greason, kidded him: Why do you care what that white guy does? But Willie cared. He wanted to be adored as DiMaggio was, not just by black fans but by white fans, too, and not just at Rickwood Field but all over the country. Willie wanted to play the same position, center field, and in the same town, New

York. So in the summer of 1948 he was learning to hit curveballs with almost terrifying swiftness.

That's how Willie Mays became a Black Baron before he was even out of high school. Some of the veterans resented his being given a starting position (left field at first), but Davis quickly let them know that dissension would not be tolerated. In very short time those same veterans became fired with Willie's enthusiasm, and when they saw he could hold up his end at bat—a respectable .262, with power—and play enough left field for two outfielders, they became fans.

WILLIE MAYS *became a Black Baron before he was even out of high school. By the time he was seventeen, Mays was a sensational all-around athlete, also starring in football and basketball at Fairfield Industrial High School. The New York Yankees would later claim they didn't sign Mays because "he couldn't hit a curveball."*

• • •

· THE BARONS MET the hated Monarchs in the 1948 Negro American League playoffs, taking two games in Birmingham before the elite black sporting crowd, which included Bob Savoy of Bob's Little Savoy Cafe. It would be overstating the case to say that Mays spurred the Black Barons on to the pennant and a victory, but he may have supplied the edge. In the final game in Kansas City, Bill Greason pitched magnificently with exceptional help from Mays, who ran down at least three potential extra-base hits. "Who is he?" asked Kansas City manager Buck O'Neil after the game. "Who is that boy? I tell you, he has a cannon for an arm."

In Greason's words, "You could feel the lift he gave us from his first day on the team. There was a little bit of sadness on the Black Barons that season. We could all sense that something was leaving the game, and a lot of the players who were honest knew that the Negro League wouldn't survive much longer. But Willie made us remember in every game he played why we wanted to play base-ball so much in the first place." After their victory, the Black Barons retired to a fabled black nightspot, Kingfish's Blue Room. They were not accompanied by their sensational young outfielder. Willie Mays was underage, and Piper Davis made him go back to the hotel after the game. After all, the World Series against the Homestead Grays still had to be played.

But not even Willie Mays could lift the Black Barons over the Homestead Grays, and they went down to an exciting and honor-able defeat. The Black Barons lost a hard-fought game one, 3–2, and then, back at Rickwood, suffered another tough loss, 5–3. In the third game, as bitterly contested as the first two, Willie Mays ripped a ninth-inning single to score Bill Greason for a 4–3 victory, but in

JOY IN MEMPHIS! *This famous photo of the 1948 Birmingham Black Barons celebrating a victory over the Kansas City Monarchs—a game played in Memphis, as the Negro League liked to spread their games around to please fans in different cities—is often said to be taken after the team won the Negro National League pennant. Actually, the photo was taken after game three, when Jimmy Zapp hit a game-winning home run to put Birmingham up three games to nothing over the Monarchs. The Black Barons would go on to win the pennant. This was only the second known time Willie Mays appeared in a photo (top row, center).*

the fourth and final game, played in New Orleans before a sell-out crowd, the Black Barons, emotionally spent, lost 14–1. "We wanted to win at least one game against the Grays in front of the home-town crowd," Greason recalls, "but it was not to be." The powerful Grays, led by future big leaguers Luke Easter (who would play for six years with the Cleveland Indians, hitting 27 or more home runs for three consecutive seasons in 1950–1952) and Hank Thompson (who would be Mays's teammate for seven years with the New York Giants), jumped out to an early 6–0 lead. The Barons thrilled the home crowd by coming back to tie it up. But the Grays scored four runs in the last two innings to win. It would prove to be the final Negro League World Series.

Exciting as the baseball was, black fans deserted the old leagues in droves, flocking to the big-league parks where they could see Robinson, Campanella, Doby, Don Newcombe, Monte Irvin, and other favorites.

Piper Davis stayed on with the Black Barons. The following season his young phenom, Willie Mays, batted .311, and in 1950 continued his swift rise to baseball immortality, batting .353 and .477 for two New York Giants minor league teams before joining the parent club in 1951. Jimmy Zapp left the Black Barons after the 1949 season, angry that for some unexplained reason he wasn't on the roster of the barnstormers who would travel with and play the Jackie Robinson All-Stars. He was suspended from the Negro American Leagues and never played again, proving that gross injustice in the treatment of players by management was not confined to white leagues. Artie Wilson was first signed by the Cleveland Indians and then given a halfhearted chance by the New York Giants; after 22 at-bats for the Giants in 1951 he settled in the Pacific Coast League—still regarded by many as the best minor league in the country—where he had a sensational career. In Oakland he got to play for a season with Piper Davis. He still lives in Portland. Bill Greason became a pastor at the Bethel Baptist Church, Berney Points, in west Birmingham, not far from Rickwood Field, and has been a strong community leader for over half a century.

Eddie Glennon used his connection with the Boston Red Sox

to try to persuade them to sign Willie Mays. They sent out sham signals but never made a serious offer. This, and not the sale of Babe Ruth to the Yankees in 1920, was the real curse of the Red Sox. In 1949 they lost a sensational pennant race to the New York Yankees; they would become the last team in major league baseball to integrate and would not win the World Series until 2004.

· IN OCTOBER OF 1948 there was an event at Rickwood that caused white baseball fans who missed it to gnash their teeth over segregation. Jackie Robinson and Roy Campanella, backed by New York Cubans owner Alex Pompez, brought Jackie Robinson's All-Stars to Birmingham. There was no real Black Barons team to challenge them: Piper Davis, Artie Wilson, and other veteran Black Barons had left for fall ball in Puerto Rico. Willie Mays, in his senior year at Fairfield High School, was available to play for Birmingham, as were Ed "Stainless" Steele, Jimmy "Schoolboy" Newberry, and Lyman Bostock. And so, on October 12, before a sold-out black crowd and a small but appreciative bleacher full of white fans, Willie Mays, age eighteen, played a game against Jackie Robinson for the first time.

Mays later told his biographer Charles Einstein that he played hooky from school to be ready for the game; if any of his teachers at Fairfield knew that he had played that night—and it's hard to believe that none of them knew about a game involving America's most famous black ballplayer—none of them admonished him. A crowd of more than 7,000 saw Mays smash a double in three at-bats and make a terrific catch and throw in the outfield. They also saw

Robinson steal home. Hometown hero "Schoolboy" Newberry gave the crowd some thrills by fanning both Robinson and Campanella, but Robinson's All-Stars prevailed, 3–0.

The *Birmingham World* reported that Mays and the other Birmingham players were rewarded with a hefty $105 in cash after the game. The next day Willie Mays was back in school at Fairfield High.

"It was a time that I would never want to see come again," says the Reverend Greason, "and yet it was a time I was very proud to have lived through. We lived with anger and we played with pride. It was a time when almost everyone I knew was a fan of the BBBs or a BDF. BBB stood for Birmingham Black Barons; BDF meant Brooklyn Dodgers Fan. That was for Jackie and Campy."

• IN THE SPRING OF 1949 an old man made a sentimental journey to Birmingham, still wearing his traditional straw boater, which had been out of fashion for nearly twenty years—Connie Mack was never known to wear a uniform while managing his team. He took a cab from the Tutwiler Hotel out to Rickwood Field. Mack was eighty-seven years old, and his Philadelphia A's would finish with an 81–73 record that year, his last winning season in the major leagues. Following a disastrous 52–102 record the next year, Mack retired from baseball after nearly fifty-seven years of playing and managing, marked by nine pennants and five World Series titles.

For the last time he walked the dimensions he had helped lay out for Rick Woodward nearly four decades earlier. In less than five years he would sell his remaining interest in his beloved A's, who would be moved to Kansas City and later to Oakland, where the owner, Charles Finley, would return minor league baseball to Bir-

mingham in the 1960s. Mack would die in 1956. The baseball palace he built in Philadelphia would be called Connie Mack Stadium
from 1953 until its demolition in 1976.

Sadly, his friend Rick Woodward, who had come to seek his
aid in 1909, was not there that day to see Mack's A's defeat the Barons, 3–2. "I always wondered why," says Bob Scranton. "As I recall, it
was because Rick was very ill." Poor health probably was the reason
Woodward was not there to see Mack; the following year he would
complain of ill health and send his oldest son, Joe, to represent the
family at the fortieth anniversary of Rickwood Field. Six months
later, Rick Woodward died at age seventy-four, the same age at
which his father died.

In more ways than one, an era was at an end.

RECALLING THE PAST: *Re-creations of billboards that appeared on Rickwood's right field fence in the 1920s, including, in the top row, advertisements for the Tutwiler Hotel, where many of the Barons from out of town and visiting players stayed, and Fatima Cigars, the favorite of Barons owner Rick Woodward.*

"THE BARONS WERE
A MEMORY"

B ASEBALL RULED in Alabama in the first half of the
twentieth century, and Birmingham was its capital. Baseball players were gods; they had no rivals for the public's affection.
Paul Hemphill, twenty years from writing the book that would
liberate him from Birmingham,* was in grade school, and on a trip
downtown to Blach's department store to buy his first suit, when
he "got a glimpse of Fred Hatfield, the Barons' nifty third baseman,
on his off-season job in the men's department."†1 The young Paul,

---

* *The Nashville Sound* (1970), the first thinking man's book about country music, sold more
than 70,000 copies.
† Not only wasn't it unusual for minor league ballplayers to have off-season jobs; it was
the norm for major leaguers. In 1951 Yogi Berra won the first of his three MVP awards
for the New York Yankees. In the off-season he worked in the boys section of a department store in Newark to help make ends meet. His colleagues were teammate Phil Riz-

A BARON AND A MONARCH: *Willie Lee, a pitcher for the Barons in 1956 and 1957, displays his baseball card from a later stint with the Kansas City Monarchs, the Barons' archrivals.*

Hemphill told me years later, was mesmerized: "The idea that you could go to so fabulous a place as Rickwood Field and see these men accomplish such amazing feats and then see them walking around town, doing what we did every day, was almost too much to imagine."

Hemphill had an intimate relationship with Hatfield, for Hemphill and his father usually sat along the third base line, where, during the 1949 and 1950 seasons, he saw the third baseman play so often that he could instantly recognize him in a department store. "I

zuto (winner of the 1950 American League MVP) and Philadelphia A's pitcher Bobby Shantz (who won the award in 1952).

don't think I could have recognized him as easily as I did if I'd only seen him play on television," he told me.[*]

And yet, a little something was lost in the relationship between Birmingham and its ballplayers every year through the 1950s, until, by the end of the decade, white minor league ball and black ball were practically dead. Numerous easy answers have been put forth as to why this happened, none of them, taken by themselves, providing a plausible explanation. The most popular explanation for the swift decline of the Barons and Black Barons was television—after all, it was said, how could you expect to sell something that's being given away for free? One need only look to baseball in the twenty-first century, where a dozen major league games can be found on the average satellite menu, to see the fallacy of this argument. Television, major league baseball owners would soon find out, created far more fans than it kept away.[†] And besides, televised big-league games weren't that common until the late 1950s, by which time not only the Barons and Black Barons but the Southern Association and minor leagues everywhere had taken a hard financial hit.

Some said it was the movement of major league teams around the country, encroaching on prime minor league territory. But looking back, one sees very little movement of major league teams in

---

[*] Hatfield, who was from the small town of Lanett, Alabama, was a pretty good high minor league player, hitting 25 home runs and driving in 101 runs for the Barons in 1949 and hitting 27 with 101 RBIs in 1950. Though he was never a star, he managed to have a nine-year career in the major leagues, mostly with the Red Sox and Tigers. Hemphill said that even into the late 1950s he found himself picking up the newspaper to check box scores and see how Hatfield was doing.

[†] Though, as Willie Morris once pointed out to me, "The combination of air-conditioning and television did keep a lot of people in the South from the ballparks during the summer."

the 1950s. The Boston Braves moved to Milwaukee in 1952, the St. Louis Browns moved to Baltimore, where they became the Orioles at the end of the 1953 season, the Philadelphia A's to Kansas City after the 1954 season, and, of course, the Brooklyn Dodgers to Los Angeles and the New York Giants to San Francisco after the 1958 season. The last two moves, it's true, struck a blow to the heart of the Pacific Coast League ("the third major league," some called it), but none of the relocations invaded the territory of minor league teams in the Far West, the Deep South, or Texas, most of whose franchises had begun to lose customers before any big-league team moved. (Besides, there was no major league team in the Deep South until the Braves moved to Atlanta in 1965, by which time the Crackers were long gone.)

The baby boomers grew up with college football, but though college football games have always been a major event in the South, the rise of college football had nothing to do with the decline of white minor league or black ball in Alabama or anywhere else in the South. By the time Alabama won its first national championship under Bryant, in 1961, the Southern Association and Negro Leagues were near collapse.

A simple explanation does not exist for the decline in popularity of southern professional ball or the minor leagues. It's true that fathers who had once taken their sons to see minor league baseball now spent more and more time on Little League fields. It's also true that many parks like Rickwood, located in lower-class urban areas, became increasingly unsafe, especially at night.

As for the decline in the Negro Leagues, by the beginning of the 1950s black fans had superstars on several big-league teams to root for, and that's where their fans' attention and money went. Yet that was only in the North, because there was no major league ball south of Washington, D.C.—the southernmost teams were the Washington Senators and the St. Louis Cardinals and Browns. Suddenly, though, with Jackie Robinson, Roy Campanella, and Don Newcombe playing for the Dodgers and Willie Mays, Monte Irvin, and Hank Thompson on the New York Giants, most black fans in the South were more interested in whether the Dodgers or Giants won than in whether or not the Black Barons could beat the Kansas City Monarchs.

Almost overnight the Negro Leagues became a de facto minor league system for the American and National Leagues, but one from which the big leagues took only a small quota. In 1952, five years after Jackie Robinson's debut with the Dodgers, only six of sixteen big-league teams had black players. The Negro Leagues lost their best talent, but unlike the white minor leagues they did not have the saving grace of an affiliation and the financial support of a parent club.

The lack of a relationship between the major leagues and the Negro Leagues had a hugely negative impact on black baseball at nearly every level. In the 1980s sportswriters would bemoan the relative dearth of African American baseball players—and by extension, fans—the assumption being that football and basketball were luring the best athletes.

The great wave, though, of young black football and basketball players didn't start until the late 1950s and early 1960s. Baseball's problem was what happened in the 1950s—or rather, what *didn't* happen. For decades the Negro Leagues had provided employment for thousands of great young athletes. Major league baseball, with its quota system, took only a few of the greatest players and let the Negro Leagues' talent pool dry up in their wake.

• • •

• WHATEVER THE REASONS for the swift decline of Birmingham baseball, there's no doubt that segregation was a major factor, and no one took a more active role in maintaining segregation
than Theophilus Eugene Connor. He came to be known as Bull
mainly because people couldn't pronounce, let alone spell, his real
first name, but also for his booming voice and his talent for shooting the bull between innings during his enormously popular radio
coverage of Barons games. Sadly, none of Connor's broadcasts survive, but those who remember them recall phrases like "Th'ow that
onion, boy, th'ow it!" and "Now you goin', chilluns, now you goin'!"
A short-to-second-to-first double play was described thusly: "Shine
threw to Billy, Billy threw to Piccolo Pete Susko, and now they all
OUUUUUT!"[2] Compared with Connor, Mel Allen, who had
broadcast University of Alabama football games before moving to
New York to do play-by-play for the Yankees, sounded like Edward
R. Murrow.

The Sporting News, the so-called bible of baseball, said that "he
was the most popular baseball announcer in the South" and that
he had "earned a following second to none throughout the Southern Association." According to his biographer, William A. Nunnelley, while in his early twenties, Bull went to Dallas, Texas, to attend
what was called a "baseball matinee: which featured a re-creation of
a game by an announcer using telegraphic reports. . . . [F]ans unable
to attend an actual game could follow the progress of their favorite
team at a matinee in a downtown storefront studio."[3]

According to the legend stroked by Connor himself, the regular
announcer was ill and couldn't go on, and Connor, with no previous
radio experience, stepped up and volunteered; he got five dollars for

dramatizing the accounts that came across the Western Union wire and won the crowd.

That, he would claim, was how he got started. By 1922 he was doing the Barons' broadcast on WKBC in Birmingham, and within a few years he was one of the best-known figures in the state. Connor always insisted that his move into politics, a run for a seat in the Alabama House of Representatives, was in response to fans urging him on, as if he needed any urging. (As he said to a Birmingham news reporter after the election, "I'm going to tell the truth ... I had no more idea of being elected than beating Lou Gehrig out for first base with the Yankees.")[4] The kicker is that, as a politician, Connor was, as Alabama politicians go, straight-arrow and honest. During his two-year stint as state representative, he fought against pay raises for legislators and for civil service reform. He supported the Workmen's Compensation Act.

In 1937 he was elected to one of the three city commissioner posts that, along with the mayor, ruled Birmingham. Having his choice of positions, he opted for public safety commissioner, a move that had ominous overtones for the future. Here, too, he proved to be a reformer, rooting out graft in the fire and police departments and eliminating kickbacks—at least open kickbacks—in city services.

While Bull wasn't the only high-profile racist in Birmingham from 1937 to the apocalyptic year of 1963, his popularity and public persona certainly contributed to the unwillingness of the city to follow the momentum created by Dr. King and the rest of the civil rights movement. "The black community of Birmingham," Paul Hemphill would write,

> could only stand by and watch helplessly as the reign of Bull Connor unfolded. Blacks formed nearly forty percent

of the city's population at this time, but because of poll taxes and other restrictions not five percent were registered to vote. They remained as always: a shadowy underclass of domestics and laborers scratching out an existence under utter segregation in the forgotten corners of the city. Since there was no visible leadership to speak in their behalf, they could only smolder and keep their grievances to themselves. Sporadic visits from the Klan were all it took to keep them in the place prescribed for them by the white man.[5]

By 1952 Bull Connor seemed on the verge of becoming a demagogue on a par with Louisiana's Huey Long (though Long was not nearly so rabid a segregationist as Connor) or even an earlier version of George Wallace.[*] In that year, though, Connor's career was derailed when he was caught with his secretary in a room at the Tutwiler Hotel. He escaped legal retribution when his trial resulted in a hopelessly deadlocked jury.[†] With no chance of being elected to public office in 1953, he wisely retired—for a while. He would be back, and there would be no uglier irony of the civil rights era than the fact that the battle against segregation in Birmingham would involve so much confrontation with Bull Connor, the man who represented the one thing in the city that united whites and blacks, baseball.

---

* Though Wallace would become the symbol for segregationists for his "Stand in the Schoolhouse Door," while a judge early in his career he had earned good marks from black lawyers for his fairness. Only after losing the Democratic nomination for governor to James Patterson in 1958 did he become an ardent segregationist.

† A city ordinance forbade persons of the opposite sex who were not husband and wife or parent and child from sharing a hotel room in Birmingham.

• • •

• THE 1950 BARONS—managed by future Red Sox Mike "Pinky" Higgins, who would manage the Red Sox from 1955 to 1965—finished second, four games behind the despised Atlanta Crackers, who had better talent, most notably a power-hitting third baseman from Texas named Eddie Mathews, as well as thirty-six-year-old "Fireman" Hugh Casey, who had saved 56 games in seven seasons with the Brooklyn Dodgers.

The next season the Barons—managed by former Washington Senators outfielder Red Marion, brother of the St. Louis Cardinals' great fielding shortstop Marty Marion—finished second to the Little Rock Travelers. The team is remembered today largely for two colorful personalities.

Louis Norman "Bobo" Newsom, from Hartsville, South Carolina, was forty-four years old and had pitched nineteen seasons in the majors, and by the time he became a Birmingham Baron he had won 205 games in an astounding fifteen different uniforms. His best three seasons were from 1938 to 1940 with the St. Louis Browns when he won at least 20 games in each season. He also lost 20 games in three different seasons, but each time pitching for truly bad teams. In 1934, pitching for a wretched Browns club, he threw a no-hitter against the Red Sox—and lost the game in the tenth inning on a bad-hop grounder. In 1947 he got a real break when, pitching for the lowly Senators, he was picked up on waivers by the New York Yankees midseason and won 7 games for them with a 2.80 ERA, including the opening game of the World Series against the Brooklyn Dodgers—which was bittersweet, for he later found out that his father had died of a heart attack in the stands.

After the Series, the Yankees voted him a 75 percent pay share. When he ordered his championship ring, he told the jeweler, "Just make it three-quarters size—that's my measure in this town."

Bobo was a hard-luck guy, the only pitcher whose career began in the twentieth century to win more than 200 games and still have a losing record (he finished 211–222). Despite the hard luck, though, Bobo was irrepressible. "There may have been a more traveled, more injured, more quotable or more entertaining pitcher than Bobo Newsom," wrote one baseball historian, "but it is hard to think of one offhand." It was said of him, "He was tough as shoe leather, as unlucky as an old maid, as colorful as a treeful of owls, and about the friendliest fellow you'd want to meet."[6] He was the Barons' best pitcher in 1950, winning 16 games with a 3.40 ERA, constantly supplying Birmingham sportswriters with lead stories by talking to himself in the clubhouse. Alf Van Hoose began one column on Newsom with this paragraph: "'I'll tell you, Bobo,' said the tremendous fellow, pulling off a sweatshirt he could have dried by pitching in a lake. 'Ole Bo didn't have his regular stuff out there tonight. . . . Four runs. I give up, Bobo. Why that's the most a team's got off Bo in two months.'"[7]

He often talked to himself while on the mound, too. Fans along the first and third base lines were apt to be silent so they could hear exchanges like "Now, Bobo, you're going to whiff this guy on a high fastball." And he often did.

With Bobo Newsom and Jim Piersall on the same team, the 1951 Birmingham Barons became one of the most quoted second-place teams in baseball history. Piersall was one of the young players the Boston Red Sox committed to seasoning up with the Barons. He had played six games for the parent team in 1950, and in 1951 wowed the city with his hitting—.346 with 15 home runs in 126 games—and spectacular fielding. Some sportswriters, after watching Piersall play just a couple of dozen games in center field, thought he might be as good as anyone they had ever seen at the position. Alf Van Hoose, who scored the Black Barons games and wrote about the white team, penned a column in the *Birmingham News* that caused a minor uproar:

> To those who contend Jim Piersall is the finest center fielder in Birmingham baseball history, a word of caution: Was he superior to the Willie Mays the New York Giants bought from the Black Barons in May, 1950?

> According to those who saw them both, Piersall and Mays were rated as equal in speed, as in the simple ability to run down a ball hit over one's head, and in range, the ability to cover ground all over the outfield. Piersall was rated slightly better at getting a fast break on a ball, while Mays had a slight edge in hustle, alertness, and throwing.

> Mays outthrow Piersall, you ask? Did you ever see Mays take a wall ball in right center and aim at third? Or retreat in center field for a fly ball and dare a runner on third to become ambitious? If you haven't, reserve judgment. . . .
>
> As regards Mays' throwing, it might be pointed out that before the Giants paid $15,000 for him (a record price for this league) scouts trailing him saw him clearest as a future pitcher. Bill Maughan, watching him in the interests of the Boston Braves, often said, "That guy is a pitcher. With his loose form he could throw all day. And hard."[*8]

---

* Piersall always insisted that he was as good in the field as Mays—see his comments in Appendix 3, "Voices of Rickwood." Their career numbers don't say that he wasn't. Piersall's

Most of the people who saw Piersall up close in Birmingham during the 1951 and 1952 seasons would have said that he was the one with the loose form—sometimes too loose. His verbal battles with umpires and occasional shouting matches with other players and with fans on the road filled newspaper columns. In 1952, while with the Red Sox before a game at Fenway Park, Piersall goaded Yankees second baseman Billy Martin by mocking his Roman nose with "Hey, Pinocchio!" Martin asked him to settle the issue under the stands; an experienced street brawler, Martin proceeded to break Piersall's nose, leaving his jersey smeared with blood.

Piersall was sent back down to Birmingham. Bob Scranton picked him up at the airport, in the rain, and Piersall changed into his uniform in the backseat of the car. The rain stopped, and just as the lights came on at Rickwood there came Piersall, to the astonishment of the crowd, swinging two bats and waving to them. In his first at-bat in the game, he hit a line drive off the top of the scoreboard; the left fielder for the Memphis Chicks picked up the ball and, assuming it was a home run, tossed it over the fence, thus making it a home run.

For the rest of the 1952 season Piersall hit just about as well as he had the year before (.339), but was in constant trouble, getting himself thrown out of four games in three weeks. In the most famous of these ejections, he climbed up on the roof at Rickwood and aimed a water pistol at the umpire. The trajectory fell short and

---

range factor—fly balls caught per game—was 2.68, slightly higher than Mays's 2.60, and his career fielding average was .990 to Willie's .981. A mitigating factor is that Mays played longer than Piersall, playing over 2,800 games to Piersall's 1,600-plus, and the average includes the statistics of Mays's declining years. Also, Mays averaged .69 assists per game, Piersall .59.

showered the crowd, providing welcome relief on a hot day. He then moved to the grandstand to heckle the home plate umpire.

Suspended for three days, Piersall sought treatment and was diagnosed with "nervous exhaustion"—at the time no one knew the term "bipolar." Though he would be plagued with emotional problems for years, he got himself under control and returned to the Red Sox later that year. In 1953 he finished ninth in the American League MVP voting and made the 1954 and 1956 All-Star teams.*

• WITH BULL CONNOR out of power, things began to progress in spite of the laws that were on the books. On April 1, 1954, the Chicago White Sox and St. Louis Cardinals simply got off the train at Birmingham Terminal on their way north and played the first integrated professional baseball game at Rickwood Field. Without fanfare Cardinals first baseman Tom Alston became the first black batter to face a white pitcher in Birmingham. Also on the field for the White Sox was Minnie Minoso, the first black Latin player to start in a big-league game. There were no demonstrations, no riots, no disturbances. In fact, the game is remembered more for a home run by Stan Musial, who posted his entry in the "Who Hit the Longest Home Run in the History of Rickwood?" sweepstakes. Old-time followers of the Black Barons used to insist that it had to be Mule Suttles, but nobody measured home runs back then. The lon-

---

* Years later, in his 1955 autobiography, *Fear Strikes Out*, Piersall wrote that "going nuts" worked to his advantage. "Whoever heard of Jimmy Piersall," he wrote, "until that happened?"

gest recorded blast was Walt Dropo's mammoth 479-foot shot in 1948. Reggie Jackson always insisted that no one could have hit a ball farther than he did on a couple of occasions in 1967.

Musial's bid during an exhibition game between the Cardinals and the Barons was a titanic shot over the right field bleachers—alas, still called the "Negro bleachers" at this late date. Alf Van Hoose always swore that he had overseen the measurement of Musial's homer and that it landed 486 feet from home plate, completely clearing the roof and outdistancing even Dropo's famous homer. While Dropo's home run was almost certainly a blast, its exact distance would have been impossible for Van Hoose to know, because he never saw the ball land. Also, though Musial might well have been the greatest hitter in National League history, he was not known for hitting for such long distance. Consistency was his trademark; he never hit more than 39 home runs in a season. Bob Scranton, who was there, estimates that the ball landed about 440 feet from home plate, still a pretty good shot.

A far more important piece of baseball history, though, was made the very next day.

· SECTION 597 of the Alabama code was tying Birmingham up in knots, and it wasn't doing baseball any good either.

Theoretically, the April 2, 1954, exhibition game between the Brooklyn Dodgers and Milwaukee Braves should never have happened. The Braves came to town with a lineup of sensational players, including future Hall of Fame third baseman Eddie Mathews (who would go on to lead the National League with 47 home runs that season) and left-handed pitcher Warren Spahn (also a future

HANK AARON *in a spring training game at Rickwood, 1974. He hit two home runs that day. One week later in Atlanta he would surpass Babe Ruth's career record of 714 home runs. Aaron had played in Rickwood as a shortstop for the Indianapolis Clowns and against the Brooklyn Dodgers in 1954 at the first integrated game in Birmingham. He would be the last Negro League star to become a major league star.*

Hall of Famer, who had led the NL the preceding year with 23 victories). The Dodgers, of course, had future Hall of Famers Jackie Robinson, Pee Wee Reese, and Duke Snider, who hit 42 home runs in 1953, and Roy Campanella, 1953's NL Most Valuable Player.

Birmingham baseball fans, black and white, were in a frenzy. Connie Mack's great Philadelphia A's team and the Ruth-Gehrig-DiMaggio era teams had played at Rickwood, along with, in 1922, the Ty Cobb–led Detroit Tigers and St. Louis Cardinals with Rogers Hornsby, who played against each other there. But at no time in the history of Rickwood Field had both dugouts been filled with such luminaries, including one of the least-heralded players who, within the next two decades, would shatter baseball's most treasured record. A slender rookie at the time, Henry Aaron had played short-stop at Rickwood with the visiting Indianapolis Clowns only one year earlier. That day, however, Aaron took the field for the Braves.

Why the game was allowed has never been explained, as it was in blatant violation of Section 597; one explanation is that blacks *and* whites were ready to break down the fences to see this game. Another, perhaps more likely, is that since the game involved the National League's best-known team, the Brooklyn Dodgers, the city fathers decided not to object, since the league might have boycot-ted Birmingham for future games. No doubt that was the case that Eddie Glennon made to Bull Connor and the other members of the city commission. Whatever the reason, on this night at least, the segregationists agreed to look the other way.

The Negro bleachers were packed, and thousands of black fans spilled over into the SRO areas down the foul lines, around the out-field fence, and even into the seating area that was designated for more than 9,600 whites. Thousands of whites, confronted for the first time with the issue of sitting next to blacks at a public event, chose to ask for their money back, thus missing a game that featured the defending National League champions and seven future Hall of Famers. Thousands more presumably just wanted to see the game and took their seats.

Hank Aaron would later remember being overcome by play-ing on the same field as the man who broke baseball's color barrier. "The crowd had been roaring as soon as Jackie left the dugout, and when he stepped up to the plate, it was hard for me to hold back tears." Aaron had a double and a walk that night and scored a run. His teammate Eddie Mathews hit a home run, as did the Dodgers' Snider and Carl Furillo. Robinson batted twice with two doubles, but the Dodgers were blasted 17–2. The Braves hammered two renowned Dodger hurlers, one white, Carl Erskine, and one black, Joe Black. (They also teed off on a scrub who would pitch just 56 innings in the big leagues before pursuing a career as a coach, and eventually a manager, Tom Lasorda.)

The next night the BDFs—Brooklyn Dodgers Fans—in the crowd got their satisfaction as the Dodgers beat the Braves and their ace, Warren Spahn, 9–1. This time thousands of white fans, including presumably some who had left the day before, decided that integrated ball games weren't so bad and returned to Rickwood. The April 3 Dodgers-Braves game drew more than twice as many fans as the first game.

Afterwards, no one knew quite what to make of this game or whether it indicated that 597 was a paper tiger. But it was still on the books, waiting for someone named Bull Connor to use it for his own purposes. On May 17, 1954, the Supreme Court made the landmark *Brown v. Board of Education* decision; almost in response, a citywide referendum a few days later reaffirmed 597.

• IN 1953 EDDIE GLENNON felt that the Barons' affiliation with the Boston Red Sox was doing his team no good. He decided to go for the big one, and in the winter of 1953 he flew to St. Petersburg to the Yankees' spring training headquarters to have dinner with general manager George Weiss and owner Dan Topping. He gave them the full Birmingham pitch: the Yankees would have a farm club playing in the South's largest industrial city and in a first-rate ballpark. Topping asked with a grin whether Alabama fans would mind being associated with a team called the Yankees; Glennon reminded him that the team had been playing exhibition games in Birmingham for years to enthusiastic crowds, who had packed Rickwood to the rafters to see Babe Ruth, Joe DiMaggio, Yogi Berra, and their young phenom Mickey Mantle. Topping and Weiss bit and made plans for an agreement at the dinner table. So the Birmingham Barons hooked up with the New York Yankees.

For the next few years the Yankees moved some of their best talent through Birmingham. In 1953 alone there were outfielder Bill Virdon, who would be the NL's 1955 Rookie of the Year with St. Louis and later a manager for the Pirates, Yankees, Astros, and Expos; first baseman Gus Triandos, who would become a four-time All-Star catcher with the Orioles; Tom Sturdivant, who would win 32 games on the Yankees' 1956 and 1957 pennant winners; and outfielder Norm Siebern, who won World Series rings with the Yankees in 1956 and 1958 and played in four All-Star games.* In 1955 the Barons' pitching staff included Ralph Terry, who would win 66 games for the Yankees' AL pennant winners from 1960 to 1963.†

Still, attendance at Barons games continued to drop all through the 1950s. Occasionally Glennon hit on a moneymaker like bringing the 1955 Southern Association All-Star game to Rickwood, showcasing the talents of Memphis shortstop and future Hall of Famer Luis Aparicio. The game drew the second-largest crowd in Rickwood history, more than 19,800, a gate that approached the 20,000-plus who had seen Dizzy Dean and Ray Caldwell battle in the Dixie Series of 1931.

---

* Siebern was traded to Kansas City in 1960 for Roger Maris.
† Terry would give up one of the most famous home runs in baseball history to Bill Mazeroski in the seventh game of the 1960 World Series. He was given a second chance two years later and got Willie McCovey to line out to end the 1962 World Series.

But in 1956 the hopelessness of trying to drag the Southern Association into the twentieth century was highlighted by the league's president, Sam Smith. The Kansas City A's and Pittsburgh Pirates were scheduled to play an exhibition game in Birmingham, and Bull Connor and his supporters, citing Section 597, threatened to shut the game down. At this point it would have been a small matter for the major league commissioner's office, for either team, or, for that matter, the Barons themselves to go to court and have 597 declared unconstitutional. The Dodgers and Braves, after all, had played a game with black and white players two years before. But no one, it seems, wanted to stir up the pot, so the Pirates and A's canceled. "Let's face it," Smith was quoted as saying, "there are folks down here who just don't want their kids growing up to admire a Negro ballplayer." At the time Smith made this remark, Jackie Robinson, Willie Mays, and Roy Campanella, all of whom had played at Rickwood Field, had won a total of five Most Valuable Player awards in the National League. At the end of the 1956 season, the Brooklyn Dodgers' Don Newcombe would stretch that number to six.

Professional baseball in Birmingham limped to a sorry close. In 1958 both the Barons and Black Barons won championships, but compared with those in their glory years, the cheers were faint and the fans few. When it came time for the Barons to face Corpus Christi, the champion of the Texas League, Section 597 was again invoked and Corpus Christi's black players were forbidden to enter Rickwood Field. Eddie Glennon, who had done more than any man to support black ball in Birmingham, was desperate to play the games and offered to let the Texans substitute any white players—even major leaguers— in the Rickwood games. The gesture on both Glennon's and Corpus Christi's part was shameful, and the Baron's ultimate victory proved to be hollow. Just 18,000 turned out for the six-game series, on average perhaps a third of the number who had witnessed the first game of the great 1931 series. It was to be the last Dixie Series.

The Black Barons won, too, but they seemed to be playing in a vacuum in a mockery of a league that had shrunk to four teams. For most fans, the *real* Black Barons had died in 1952 when Tom Hayes, disgusted at the major league's refusal to accommodate the Negro Leagues, had sold the team.

In 1957 the Dodgers, already preparing to move to Los Angeles and thinking of expanding their talent pool, made a surprising offer to the dying Negro American League. Owner Walter O'Malley wanted to subsidize the remaining teams as part of the Dodgers minor league system. Incredibly, NAL president J. D. Martin turned him down; Martin thought that major league commissioner Ford Frick would agree to subsidize the NAL so all major league teams could draw from them. Of course, Frick had no such intention. The Black Barons played their last game in 1960.

The owners of the Southern Association teams desperately tried to find a way around integration, but it was futile, and one by one the proud franchises died. In 1960 the New Orleans Pelicans folded, and at the end of the season the Memphis Chicks, averaging fewer than 600 fans a game, called it quits. After the 1961 season the remaining owners met in Tampa to discuss a survival strategy. The Barons' owner, Albert Belcher, who had bought the team from Gus Jebeles, asked Eddie Glennon to attend; he did so as a favor to Belcher, but Glennon had already resigned to take a job with the minor league team in Denver. At the meeting the owners decided to pull the plug on the dying league. "I'm convinced that they were all for integration," says Bob Scranton, "but none of them were prepared for the legal battles that they knew they'd have to face."

Belcher certainly knew what he was up against. Bull Connor had survived disgrace and reemerged as commissioner of public safety. His response to the federal government's orders to integrate Birmingham's city parks and recreational facilities was to fill the swimming pool at East Lake Park with dirt. "The Barons," recalled Paul Hemphill, who often swam at the pool when he was growing up, "were a memory, Rickwood Field like a graveyard."[9]

And so the Southern Association and the Negro Leagues died not only without a bang but without even a whimper.

· EDDIE GLENNON SPENT four years with Denver and then returned to the South in 1966. About thirty-five years after he had asked Connie Mack for a job in Philadelphia, he finally made it to the big leagues. The Braves moved to Atlanta and hired him as a community relations liaison. A large part of his job was promoting Hank Aaron, the man he had introduced to the first integrated baseball crowds in Birmingham twelve years earlier. His specialty was setting up community day/nights that brought thousands of fans to see the Braves play at home. He also started the annual Gameboree off-season banquet. According to former Braves PR director Bob Hope, "Eddie was well known and respected all over the South."

Glennon died of a heart attack in 1968 and is still fondly remembered by many in the Braves organization. The Eddie Glennon Gameboree has been held annually for forty-three years. Among the 2009 honorees was Hank Aaron.

Bear and Charlie O: *Paul "Bear" Bryant and Oakland and Birmingham A's owner Charlie Finley were close friends. The Bear attended many A's games at Rickwood Field.*

EVERYTHING DIES
BUT . . .

B Y 1963 there was no professional baseball in Birmingham, which was just as well, because baseball was not meant to be played in a maelstrom.

On Thursday, April 18, Martin Luther King completed the final draft of his "Letter from a Birmingham Jail," called by Diane McWhorter, in *Carry Me Home: The Climactic Battle of the Civil Rights Movement*, her Pulitzer Prize–winning account of the civil rights struggle in Birmingham, "a masterpiece, a triumph of tone as much as of exposition, *the* statement of purpose for the modern civil rights movement and probably the most eloquent treatment of the nexus between law and injustice since Henry David Thoreau's essay 'Civil Disobedience.' King had placed the black struggle into the archetypal American drama of religious persecution."[1]

On May 6 the Barons' old radio announcer Bull Connor turned

fire hoses and police dogs on peaceful demonstrators, many of them children, in Kelly Ingram Park in downtown Birmingham. That night Dr. King told an estimated crowd of a thousand, many of them parents of the kids who had been arrested, "Don't worry about your children who are in jail. The eyes of the world are on Birmingham. We're going on in spite of dogs and fire hoses. We've gone too far to turn back."

The city had already been given the ugly nickname of Bombingham by the rest of the nation when, after numerous bombings of black homes, a bomb went off on Sunday morning, September 15, at the Sixteenth Street Baptist Church in downtown Birmingham, killing four young black girls who were primping in the ladies room before the service. And, of course, on November 22 President John F. Kennedy was assassinated in Dallas, capping a year that seared the memory of anyone who lived through it.

In the spring of 1963, shortly after the bombing of the black-owned Gaston Hotel, Jackie Robinson, who had made so many memorable appearances at Rickwood Field, came back to Birmingham, accompanied by former heavyweight champion Floyd Patterson. A great many blacks were angry at Robinson for supporting Richard Nixon in the 1960 presidential race,[*] but all listened with rapt attention to his address at the Sixth Avenue Baptist Church.

Shouts of "Hallelujah!" and "Eyes on the prize!" spread through the sanctuary, but a hush fell on the crowd as Robinson spoke.

---

[*] According to Robinson's best biographer, Arnold Rampersad, in *Jackie Robinson: A Biography*, Nixon was genuinely inspired by Jackie, and Robinson believed that there should be a civil rights presence in both major parties. Robinson and Nixon later parted company, but it should be remembered that, as journalist and historian Garry Wills pointed out, more than 90 percent of American schools were integrated during Nixon's administration.

Many people in this world, which is made up of four-fifths colored people, are looking at you and admiring your courage. And I want to say to you that just looking at all of you out here, that the inspiration of your togetherness, your actions, your songs, you just don't know what it means to guys who have come down here from New York.

I just wish the same kind of enthusiasm that is shown right here in this church tonight could be shown to Negroes throughout America, because they would have a much deeper, much more sincere desire, to get involved in our struggle.

· **THINGS BEGAN TO CHANGE.** In November 1962 the campaign to strip Bull Connor of power—a move endorsed not only by blacks and white liberals but also by many businessmen who saw Birmingham's chance for growth literally going up in smoke*— succeeded when voters abolished the three-man commission

---

* Many regarded Birmingham's horrible national publicity as the principal reason that it failed to keep up with Atlanta. For his part, Paul Hemphill thought the idea that the two cities were ever in competition was an illusion: "Although Birminghamians these days still claim that their city was neck-and-neck with Atlanta in the race to be the dominant city of the South until the sixties, the war was lost long before that. During the fifties Atlanta's population grew by forty-seven percent while Birmingham's grew by less than five percent. The basic difference between the two neighboring cities, separated by only 150 miles, was that Atlanta was a diversified city looking to the future while Birmingham was a closed society clinging to the past" (*Leaving Birmingham*, pp. 113–14).

But even as Hemphill wrote this in 1993, Birmingham was well on its way to becoming one of the medical capitals in the country and thanks to physicians such as Dr. James Andrews, who did groundbreaking work on Bo Jackson's hip, could lay claim to being the sports medicine capital of the United States.

in favor of a mayor and nine-man council. Even though he was endorsed by the governor, Connor lost his bid for mayor, and on May 23 Bull Connor's twenty-three-year tenure as the all-powerful public safety commissioner was officially over, although he dragged the proceeding on a few months longer with various legal challenges. As Connor fought for his political life, Dr. King organized various protests aimed at logjamming the penal and legal systems with the volume of arrests, which only further enraged Connor to escalate his violence toward the demonstrators.

Bull Connor remained in office for another ten years, but his power base was almost gone. Perhaps his ugliest legacy, Section 597, would remain on the books for several more years, but by the spring of 1964 it was all but ignored. Glenn West, the Barons' general manager after Eddie Glennon, told the *Birmingham Post Herald* in 1997, "The ordinance was still on the books when Mr. Belcher announced that the Barons were back, but we just played our games anyway."

Barons' owner Albert Belcher removed the one hated feature of Rickwood Field—the chicken wire that separated the Negro bleachers from the rest of the park. Rickwood got a new paint job, and the neglect of two years was erased in a matter of weeks. Baseball was back in Rickwood. Not quite the way it had been before, but it was still baseball.

In 1963 old Southern Association teams in Nashville and Chattanooga had joined the South Atlantic League while Atlanta had made the jump to the International League. (The Crackers, however, would vanish forever when the Milwaukee Braves moved to Atlanta for the 1966 season.) But the new Southern League brought back many of the old rivals in a new integrated circuit with major league affiliations. On April 17, eight years after Jackie Robinson retired from the major leagues, the first legal integrated professional base-

ball game involving a Birmingham team was played at Rickwood as
the Barons hosted the Asheville Tourists.

"It was a skittish and tense situation. Blacks and whites never
had played together legally in Birmingham, or sat together at a sporting event where they weren't separated by chicken wire," recalled Bill
Lumpkin thirty-three years later. "There was not one single incident.
Nothing. Oh, there was a phone call. A bomb threat.

"'I was called out of the box seats and told,' Belcher said. 'I didn't
believe it. I had family and friends sitting with me. I went back, sat
down, and never said a word to anybody.' The significance of the
night did not occur to Belcher until just before the game when, 'It
hit me like a ton of bricks. Whites and blacks playing together for
the first time.'"

Something had happened the night before that Belcher did not
reveal until he told Lumpkin many years later. A few days before
the opening, someone knocked on his door. It was the local leader
of the Ku Klux Klan. He gave Belcher assurance there would be no
trouble from his organization at the game. "If it hadn't been for that
I would have been worried."[2] Belcher offered no explanation as to
why the Klan decided not to disrupt the game. The likeliest explanation is probably the right one: after the federal government's show
of power regarding integration of schools and colleges, there wasn't
much point in trying to stop a baseball game.

• THE 1964 BARONS, led by the great Bert Campaneris, were
contenders, missing the Southern League pennant by one game. A
native Cuban, "Campy" spoke precious little English and found his
way around Birmingham mostly through the good graces of Glen

West. After Birmingham, Campaneris went on to play for nineteen years, mostly with the Oakland A's, winning three World Series rings and making the All-Star team six times. Also, on one dazzling night, September 8, 1965, he played every position in the field.

In the spring of 1964 Campaneris was beaned hard. "When he was hit," West told writer Ben Cook, "I thought he had been shot. There was our top prospect lying on the ground. I called one of the top neurologists at UAB [University of Alabama at Birmingham] and asked where I could take him, and they told me to bring him to UAB." West told the doctor that Campaneris wasn't white; the doctor told him to bring him in anyway. He was nineteen, so West signed in as his guardian. "Me and Campy," he later recalled, "integrated UAB."[3]

• THE MAN WHO BROUGHT CAMPY to Birmingham and did more to shake up Birmingham baseball—and, later, all of major league baseball—was Charles O. Finley. "If I had to pick a single man," wrote Marvin Miller, the first executive director of the Players Association in his 1991 autobiography,* "as representing the transition for the old 'family' business baseball men to the newer corporate types who came into baseball after having made their fortunes elsewhere, that man would be Charlie Finley. . . . He was, without a doubt, the finest judge of baseball talent I ever saw at the head of a team."[4]

Finley—or "Charlie O," as he liked to be called—was born in

---

* I'm proud to say that I worked with Miller on *A Whole Different Ball Game: The Inside Story of Baseball's New Deal*, which contains the most detailed and account of how the players finally won the right to free agency.

1918 in Ensley, Alabama, the heart of steel mill country just outside Birmingham. His father, a low-level executive for a steel company, moved his family for a few years to Gary, Indiana, only to return in 1930, just in time for young Charlie to be a batboy for the Barons.* He went on to marry the daughter of an insurance salesman and made his fortune in medical insurance. In 1954 "Charlie O" tried unsuccessfully to buy the Philadelphia A's from Connie Mack, but six years later he succeeded in his lifelong ambition of owning a major league team when he bought a controlling interest in the A's, then located in Kansas City.

But before giving the Barons and Birmingham the major league connection they both so desperately wanted, Finley asked for a couple of concessions: one, that the team's name be changed to the A's to establish a clear relationship with the parent team and, two, that they wear the same distinctive green-and-gold uniforms as his Kansas City (and soon to become, after the 1967 season, Oakland) A's.†

Finley, with his own minor league team with major league affliliate, further increased his community standing in 1967 by hiring Bear Bryant's son, Paul Jr., as GM, and the first pitch on opening day was thrown out by onetime semipro baseball player Paul Sr. before a crowd of more than 5,100. The A's won 2–0 despite a line drive from an Evansville player that struck future Hall of Famer Rollie Fingers on the side of the face, breaking his jaw and shattering his cheekbone.

---

* Finley always claimed to have been at Rickwood for the great Ray Caldwell–Dizzy Dean pitching duel in the 1931 Dixie Series, but some suspected he made up the story to establish a mythical connection to the Barons.

† Conservative major leaguers were shocked at the A's new uniforms; some said they looked as if they had been stolen from a softball team. The Phillies' Larry Bowa, on seeing the A's take the field for the first time at a spring training game, asked, "Is this fast or slow pitch?"

Fingers recovered and with teammates Reggie Jackson, Joe Rudi, and Dave Duncan went on to win the Southern League pennant. They also, along with future Cy Young Award winner Vida Blue and catcher Gene Tenace of the 1969 Barons,* formed the nucleus of the 1972, 1973, and 1974 world championship Oakland A's. In his *Historical Baseball Abstract*, Bill James suggested that the 1967 A's might have been the greatest minor league team ever assembled.

Long before John McCain and Sarah Palin devalued the term, Charlie O. Finley was a maverick with his bright green-and-gold uniforms with white shoes, his live mule mascot, "Charlie O," and his Day-Glo orange baseballs.† Perhaps his most bizarre gimmick was a remote-controlled mechanical rabbit that popped from a hole behind home plate and delivered fresh baseballs to umpires. (Catchers hated it, because they feared stepping in the rabbit hole while chasing pop-ups.)

Marvin Miller thinks that Finley's biggest fault as a baseball executive was that he never understood the free market in a salary arbitration case:

> Charlie's method of presenting an arbitration case was to act like a movie version of a small-town lawyer. He was a spectacle to behold. He used no notes. He never sat down; he strolled all over the room, gesturing with his hands and

---

* This Oakland A's team was one of just two clubs since 1953 to win three straight titles; the other was the 1998-99-2000 New York Yankees.

† Finley tried the orange baseball out during spring training; his assumption was that the bright orange color would help the hitters pick up the ball better as it left the pitcher's hand. For some odd reason, they didn't do that, and batters complained that the initial spin of the ball blurred more than that of a white ball. Perhaps some physicist will someday explain this phenomenon.

REGGIE JACKSON, *the straw who would later stir the drink for George Stein-brenner's Yankees. In 1967 he stirred the Birmingham A's to a Southern League championship, along with Rollie Fingers, Dave Duncan, and Joe Rudi, the nucleus of the Oakland A's 1972–1974 world champions.*

talking. While he acted antsy, his speech was slow and deliberate, as if he were Perry Mason delivering a big courtroom speech. . . . He was the God of Baseball, sent down from Olympus to set confused mortals straight on all questions pertaining to baseball. It was a stellar performance. I love watching him.

He would say things like: "*Mister* Reggie Jackson and his representative maintain that he deserves this *princely* salary"—"princely" was delivered with scorn—"because he is"—he would pause deliberately—"a *superstar.*" He'd pause again before looking around the room and say, "Gentle-men, I ask you, *what is a superstar?*" We waited with bated breath for him to tell us precisely what, in his evaluation, a superstar was and why Reggie Jackson failed to meet those standards.

When Miller calmly refuted Finley's case by citing Jackson's sta-tistics, Finley retorted that Miller hadn't taken "intangibles" into account. "It didn't seem possible," Miller replied, "that a team that had just won two straight World Series could have players so lack-ing in intangibles." Jackson won his case.[5]

· IN 1972 AN INCREDIBLE EVENT occurred at Rickwood Field. The first 30-game winner since Dizzy Dean and the only professional ballplayer ever to be convicted of racketeering, former Detroit Tigers ace Denny McLain, appeared there. Tall and slen-der with a boyish charm and puckish grin, McLain, who had won an amazing 55 games in 1968 and 1969 and appeared on every TV show, from Ed Sullivan to the Smothers Brothers, had fallen on hard times. Shortly before the 1970 season, Commissioner Bowie Kuhn suspended him for half the season after a *Sports Illustrated* story linked him to professional gamblers. No sooner did he get back into uniform than the mischievous McLain dumped a bucket of water on a sports-writer who was asking him questions he did not wish to answer. It exacerbated his problems that he was found to be carrying a gun.

McLain went from winning 31 and 24 games the preceding two seasons to 3 in 1970. Pitching for Ted Williams and Washington in 1971, he lost 22 games. The Senators dumped him on Oakland,

DENNY McLAIN, *one of the strangest stories in baseball history. A two-time Cy Young Award winner, he won 108 games for the Detroit Tigers from 1965 to 1969, including 31 in 1968, and was the last 30-game winner in the major leagues. He was suspended by Commissioner Bowie Kuhn for half the 1970 season for associating with gamblers. By 1972 he was struggling to make it back to the majors, and Charlie Finley gave him a shot with the A's, hoping his name would sell tickets. It didn't work. In 1985 he served the first of two prison terms, the first for drug trafficking (cocaine), embezzlement, and racketeering, and the second for embezzlement and fraud. McLain served six years in total.*

and Finley thought it would be great publicity to give him a shot in Birmingham with the Barons as a springboard to a possible comeback. From a baseball perspective it was a disaster; McLain's ERA at Rickwood shot to over 6.00, more than twice what he had allowed at a major league level. From a business perspective, McLain's appearances were sensational; he regularly drew four or five times the gate of any other A's pitcher and was popular with Birmingham fans, with whom he routinely traded quips and shouted his predictions. Some were reminded of the second coming of Dizzy Dean, with a significant difference that Dean was on the upside of a fabulous career while McLain was in a downward spiral.

Ten years later the Tigers honored him with Denny McLain Day in 1982, and in 1985 he was convicted of extortion, racketeering, and drug possession.

· IN 1975 FINLEY sold the principal interest of the Birmingham A's to a family in Chattanooga, and the team moved to historic Engel Field for the 1976 season. The same year Rickwood's big brother, Shibe Park in Philadelphia (then called Connie Mack Stadium), was demolished, though for all intents and purposes it had been dead since a fire in 1971 partly destroyed it. The last game had been played there on October 1, 1970, when Phillies catcher Tim McCarver scored the winning run in a 2–1 victory over the Montreal Expos.

Finley continued to use the Chattanooga A's as a talent pipeline to his big-league club in Oakland. The magic, though, had gone out of his minor league franchise and thus the parent club. In a relatively small market such as the Bay Area, which he had to share with the National League's San Francisco Giants, Finley could no longer compete in the era of high-priced free agents.

Losing his ace Jim "Catfish" Hunter to George Steinbrenner's Yankees, Finley decided to hold a massive "estate sale" and tried to peddle Joe Rudi and Rollie Fingers to the highest bidders. Commissioner Bowie Kuhn blocked the sales "in the best interests of baseball." Furious, Finley responded by publicly humiliating Kuhn, calling him "the village idiot."

Over the next two years, the once glorious A's disintegrated into one of the worst teams in baseball. Finley tried to move the team to New Orleans, but the other major league owners, backed by Kuhn, and Oakland and Alameda County authorities, who didn't want to lose the team, stopped him. In 1981 he finally sold the A's to local buyers.

• CRIMSON TIDE RADIO ANNOUNCER John Forney, a partner in the advertising agency Lucky and Forney, was anxious to revive Birmingham's baseball fortunes. He had his eye on Jules "Art" Clarkson, who, as GM of the Memphis Chicks, had done a remarkable job putting fans in their ballpark, about reviving the Barons. Clarkson, an aficionado of sports history, drove to Birmingham on a hot July day, climbed the fence, walked onto the field, and was dazzled by Rickwood. Or at least by its history; by 1980 the ballpark was a bit rundown. "Man, I thought, when I walked around, it was like I could see the ghosts playing ball—Satchel Paige, Josh Gibson, Dizzy Dean, Ty Cobb, Babe Ruth, Oscar Charleston. They were all still there."

Born in Chicago and raised in Los Angeles, Clarkson, like Finley, made his money in the insurance business and had a flair for promotion. In his first season at Memphis, he drew more than 150,000 fans, the sixth-highest minor league attendance in the country, beating their preceding year's gate by more than 50,000. In his second year the Chicks drew more than a quarter of a million.

To Clarkson the old-fashionedness of Rickwood was precisely the selling point. He enjoyed walking in Connie Mack's footsteps, watching from Glennon's Gardens, and even tracked down a handful of seats that had been shipped to Rickwood from the Polo Grounds after the New York Mets had moved to Shea Stadium.* He spruced up the old ballpark without attempting to modernize it, with one major exception: he installed a new electronic scoreboard. (Clarkson insists, contrary to popular belief among Birmingham baseball fans, that he did not tear down the old scoreboard, which had already been taken down when he got there. The manual scoreboard would rise again thirteen years later.)

Clarkson put together a working group, including Bob Scranton, brought the Montgomery minor league franchise to Birmingham, and ended an old agreement with the Detroit Tigers and established a new affiliation with the Chicago White Sox. There was on important holdover, though, from Detroit, Howard Johnson, a switch-hitting third baseman who became the first player in the major leagues to have more than 30 home runs and 30 stolen bases in three seasons. Johnson earned a World Series ring with the 1986 New York Mets and in 1991 became just the second Met to win the National League home run title (the other was Darryl Strawberry in 1988).†

---

* For years fans and collectors would ask what happened to the old seats from the Polo Grounds with their distinctive "Y-over-an-N" logo. Apparently the seats, which had been in the Polo Ground since the time of John McGraw, had simply rotted or worn out by the 1970s and were removed and then destroyed. When I visited Clarkson at Rickwood in 1987, he had a few of the last surviving seats for visitors, so you could "sit in the seats and pretend you were watching Willie Mays make that catch off Vic Wertz in the '54 series."

† The affiliation with the White Sox produced at least two outstanding regulars. In 2002 while with the Seattle Mariners, Mike Cameron, a Baron in 1995 and 1996, joined Lou Gehrig, Willie Mays, and Mike Schmidt on the roster of the fifteen players in baseball history who hit four home runs in one game. The 1996 Baron Magglio Ordóñez has compiled a .312 batting average in thirteen seasons with the White Sox and Tigers. The Barons also seasoned Jack McDowell, a 1993 Cy Young Award winner, and later lead guitarist for the rock band Stickfigure.

Art Clarkson *brought baseball back to Rickwood in 1981 after a five-year absence when Charlie Finley moved the team.*

Clarkson put winners on the field and, to quote onetime Birmingham A's star Reggie Jackson, "meat in the seats." Opening day 1981 became a major event with former Barons Norman Zauchin and Ben Chapman and former Black Baron Piper Davis all throwing out the first pitches.* That season the gate topped 220,000, harking back to the golden age; in 1983 the Barons won the Southern League pennant and drew over 250,000. As Birmingham radio personality Courtney Hayden put it, "Rickwood reminds you of the line in the Bruce Springsteen song 'Atlantic City' about everything dying but coming back."

• Attendance dropped sharply during the 1985 season as reports of car break-ins were widely circulated. In addition, the

---

* I would love to know what Chapman thought of sharing the spotlight with a former Black Baron.

SOUVENIR PROGRAM — $1.00

team was perhaps Clarkson's worst, though it was managed by former New York Mets catcher Jerry Grote (of the '69 Miracle Mets). The season's biggest publicity came when a Huntsville outfielder named Jose Canseco hit three home runs at Rickwood, the last one a towering 450-foot shot off pitcher Jeff Robinson. In the locker room after the game, Robinson told Clarkson, "I swear to God, I threw him a good pitch." "Yeah," Clarkson replied. "It was a great pitch. It went all the way to Nineteenth Street."

The city of Birmingham would put up no money for more parking, and the lots surrounding Rickwood could accommodate no more than seven hundred cars. There was no public transportation to Rickwood for night games. Plumbing, electrical, and structural problems worsened with age. The simple act of watering the field became a nightmare; the crew had to go out to the main water valve in the street, turn it on, then return to shut it off when they were finished. There was no turning back the clock.

Clarkson signed a new agreement with the Chicago White Sox and proceeded with plans for a new stadium in Hoover. Thus Bo Jackson, recuperating from a hip injury, and Michael Jordan, trying to transform himself into a baseball player in 1994, missed playing at Rickwood Field. On August 30, 1987, the Barons beat Columbus 18–7, their final game in Birmingham before leaving for the suburbs. As Rickwood emptied and the lights were shut off, certificates were handed out to the fans who attended the final game.

Gene and Cindy Northington had been going to Rickwood since they were children; Gene had been a member of the booster club, the Birmingham B's, when he was a teenager. Just before they left the ballpark, they walked onto the field, scooped up a handful of dirt from the mound, and placed it in a glass jar. Then they stopped to take one last view of the old ballpark before walking out the front gate.

· **PAUL HEMPHILL** recalled,

> In the summer of 1991, having heard that the Barons were drawing nearly five thousand people per game to this wonderful new "facility," enough to have the new owners applying for a step up in classification to Triple A, I wanted to see it firsthand. On the drive over, I remembered Rickwood: its odd dimensions; the hand-operated scoreboard;

the determined urchins (I among them) outrunning old men for foul balls beneath the rickety bleachers; the steam engines chugging along just beyond the outfield fences; electrifying catches by Jimmy Piersall and orbital home-run shots by Walt Dropo; fans passing the hat for change and bills in appreciation of such daring deeds; umpire baiting from the roof by an ebullient Irish general manager named Eddie Glennon. But most of all I remembered the fans, men of Birmingham that was mostly gone now, callused workingmen reeking of Lava soap and Mennen's after-shave, out for a beer and something to cheer about, braying through the turnstiles for a night on the town before going back to the grind.[6]

· AFTER YEARS of being used for high school and local college baseball (and occasionally football games), in 1993 Rickwood finally caught a break from a former minor league ballplayer. Ron Shelton, a onetime infielder in the Orioles chain, had written and directed the finest films on baseball (*Bull Durham*) and basketball (*White Men Can't Jump*) and would later direct the best film on golf (*Tin Cup*). Shelton, a repository of baseball lore, couldn't resist the opportunity to shoot the baseball scenes for *Cobb*, his film biography of the Hall of Famer, at Rickwood Field—the last remaining ballpark in the South where Cobb had actually played.

Before filming could begin, though, the few modernizations Rickwood had undergone had to be removed. With assistance from the film crew, the manually operated drop-in scoreboard and gazebo press box were re-created along with the vintage signs on the out-field fences. Rickwood Field was again in its glory.*

In the scene I walked in on, Roger Clemens, then of the Boston Red Sox, was playing the fiery and pugnacious White Sox pitcher Ed Walsh,†while Tommy Lee Jones stood at the plate as Ty Cobb. Re-creating one of the numerous battles between Walsh and Cobb, Clemens would spout phrases like "Cobb, I hear you're from Roys-ton, where men are men and sheep are nervous." Jones walked to the plate carrying a pair of women's panties in his pocket, announcing to Walsh that his wife had left them with him last night. Clemens's first pitch looked to be around 80 or so miles per hour, and Jones, not wearing a batting helmet, shied off the plate. The two then shot more insults at each other; Clemens, seemingly as much into his character as Jones was into his, threw a pitch faster and more inside.

---

* Working on a story for *The Sporting News*, I walked though the tunnel and onto the field to see two native sons, former major leaguer Harry Walker and former Birmingham Black Baron Bob Veale, discussing baseball history. Harry (called "the Hat" for his nervous habit of tugging his cap while on the field), whom I had met through family friends, had a long history of baseball in the family, including a grandfather, father, and uncle who all played in organized ball. He and his brother Fred—"Dixie," to baseball fans in the 1930s and 1940s—are the only siblings to both win batting titles, Dixie in 1944 and Harry in 1947. Dixie was one of the nucleus of players who openly challenged Branch Rickey's decision to bring Jackie Robinson into the major leagues; Rickey stood firm and exiled Dixie to the Pittsburgh Pirates. Harry, playing with the Cardinals in 1947, supported his brother's stance but soon repented. (So, belatedly, did Dixie in 1972, admitting that Robinson had been a great ballplayer and that he should have welcomed him onto the team.)

Thus more than two decades after their major league careers ended, a movie being filmed at Rickwood Field brought Harry Walker side by side with Bob Veale, the two of them swapping jokes and stories, enjoying their stint as advisers for *Cobb*.

† Walsh, who pitched in a preseason game in Rickwood in 1914, isn't much remembered today, because he pitched "only" for fourteen years and won "only" 195 games in the big leagues, but he won 24 or more games in four seasons, and in 1908 led the major leagues with 40 victories.

TOMMY LEE JONES *as Ty Cobb in Ron Shelton's* Cobb *in 1994. The baseball scenes were filmed at Rickwood. In one scene, Jones's Cobb battled with pitcher Ed Walsh, played by Roger Clemens.*

Walker, eyebrows raised, leaned over to Veale and whispered, "88?" Veale replied, "89, maybe 90." A few feet away one of Shelton's assistants asked, "What if the next pitch is a few miles per hour faster and about six inches more up and in?" "Then," Shelton said calmly, "we're shooting the Ray Chapman story."*

The face-off between Roger Clemens and Tommy Lee Jones is the only known confrontation between Academy Award and Cy Young winners.

A 1996 television movie, *The Soul of the Game*, about the last

---

* In 1920 Cleveland shortstop Ray Chapman became the only major league player killed by a pitched ball, thrown by the Yankees' Carl Mays.

years of the Negro Leagues, with Edward Herrmann as Branch Rickey, Delroy Lindo as Satchel Paige, and Blair Underwood as Jackie Robinson, immortalized Rickwood Field on film again.

Unfortunately, a third film project involving Rickwood Field, a biography of Jackie Robinson, hasn't yet materialized. In 1997 director Spike Lee was in Birmingham shooting his award-winning documentary *4 Little Girls*, about the victims of the 1963 bombing of the Sixteenth Street Baptist Church. Lee visited Rickwood and snapped some photos in anticipation of a film based on the life of one of his heroes.* Lee didn't get the funding he wanted for the project and then got tied up with other films but says he intends to return to it someday.

• IT WASN'T HOLLYWOOD, though, that saved Rickwood Field; it was Birmingham baseball fans. Since 1992 the park has been managed by the Friends of Rickwood, a group of businessmen, civic leaders, and fans—including Tom Cosby, Terry Slaughter, A. H. "Rick" Woodward III (grandson of the man who built Rickwood), former Barons owner Jack Levin, former mayor Richard Arrington, and Bob Scranton.

By 2005 more than two million dollars had been spent restoring and maintaining Rickwood, and further restoration projects are underway as this book goes to press. Today there are still ghosts at Rickwood, but they have a lot of live company with high school and college baseball games, baseball camps, and tournaments year

---

* In his film *Do the Right Thing* (1989), Lee plays a character called Mookie wearing a Brooklyn Dodgers jersey with the number 42 in homage to Robinson.

round. ("Don't tell anyone in Birmingham that you can't play baseball in February," laughs David Brewer, executive director of Friends
of Rickwood.) And every spring the Barons return for the annual
Rickwood Classic.

Rickwood Field has been certified by the National Park Service's
Historic Building Survey as the nation's oldest baseball grandstand
on its original site; therefore it is officially America's oldest ballpark.
It has also been included in the National Trust's African American
Historic Places Initiative.

Everything dies, but maybe it comes back. The story of how
Rickwood was saved—and how your own local ballpark might be
preserved for future generations—can be found on the next page, in
Extra Innings.

GLORY DAYS *by Birmingham artist Warren Mullins.*

APPENDIX 1

. . .

THERE USED TO BE
A BALLPARK

The lyrics from the Sinatra classic "There Used to Be a Ball-park" reflect a sad reality for many of America's great old ballparks. But several of them are still left, and there's time to save many more. The blueprint for action was drawn by Birmingham's own Friends of Rickwood. The following paper by FOR's current executive director, David Brewer, for a National Park Service conference, is a step-by-step history of how Rickwood was saved and restored. Fans and supporters of many other classic minor league ball-parks across the country have turned to this plan, calling on Brewer and the Friends of Rickwood and visiting Birming-ham to see firsthand the success story of Rickwood Field.

· · ·

TAKE ME OUT TO THE BALLPARK:
THE RESTORATION AND REVITALIZATION
OF RICKWOOD FIELD

David M. Brewer
Executive Director
Friends of Rickwood
Birmingham, AL

Introduction

RECOGNIZED BY THE Historic American Building Survey
(HABS) as America's oldest baseball park, Rickwood Field served
as the home park of the Birmingham Barons from 1910 through
1987.[1] From 1920 to 1963, it also served as the home park of the
Birmingham Black Barons, and is today recognized by the Negro
Leagues Baseball Museum as one of only two remaining former
Negro League ballparks.[2] Rickwood also frequently hosted the
play of traveling and barnstorming teams from the heyday of
major league baseball, including more than fifty current members
of the Baseball Hall of Fame.[3]

Rickwood Field, however, is more than *just* baseball. It is a key
component of both local and national social fabric and collective
history. In the days of fewer entertainment options, going to your
local baseball park to support the hometown team constituted a
major social event, and provided a source of both community pride
and community identity. In broader terms, the opportunity to witness the play of American cultural icons brought Birmingham and

WILLIE LEE AND DAVID BREWER *at Rickwood on June 1, 2005, the day before the tenth annual Rickwood Classic. Willie was a Black Baron from 1956 to 1957, and David is the executive director of the Friends of Rickwood.*

regional residents into the national fold and reassured them that they, too, shared a stake in the "great American pastime."

Our nation and its game have, of course, changed dramatically in ninety-five years. Rickwood Field has witnessed and experienced many of these changes and remains today truly from another era, a bygone chapter in our nation's past. An unforgettable park experience highlights this and helps to remind us why historic preservation remains a worthwhile endeavor. On a rainy March evening just before dusk, as I walked through the tunnel and emerged onto the field, I suddenly became aware of an elderly gentleman sitting to my right, in the box seats behind first base. He had not spoken to me; I simply felt him sitting there. When our eyes met, he stood and adjusted the collar on his overcoat and, after pulling his hat down tight, walked laboriously down the steps onto the field and extended his hand in an unspoken greeting. And then in a tone rich with emotion, he said, "Son, this park is still just like I remember it."

At that moment, a gust of wind peeled back the corner of the tarp covering the pitcher's mound. When I had replaced the weight on the tarp and turned back around to face the dugout, he was no longer standing there. After making one more pass through the grandstands, I locked the gate and began my drive home. Later that evening, I thought more about what he had said—"this park is still just like I remember it." In those few heartfelt words, he had given value to everything that we are doing at Rickwood Field. Not the Friends of Rickwood alone, but the entire Birmingham community, and every visitor and ballplayer who steps through the gate. In a true labor of love, we are together keeping one of America's treasures alive.[4]

If the "why" of restoring and revitalizing an old ballpark seems obvious, the "how" remains a bit more elusive. By pursuing a multi-tiered strategy defined in the *Rickwood Master Plan*, Friends of Rickwood has established itself as an effective steward of this American treasure and has successfully completed more than a dozen renovation component projects, consisting of upgrades to the facility, field, and grounds.[5] Central to the comprehensive revitalization of the park is its continued role as a high-profile baseball venue, buttressed by the marketing of the park as a dynamic destination and living history museum.

It is my hope that information presented herein will illuminate both the "why" and the "how" of the equation, through an examination of the strategies and challenges integral to this ongoing project. This overview will also propose that the restoration and revitalization of Rickwood Field can serve as a model for similar endeavors, while not ignoring the notion that preservation success may be fleeting. And although we frequently talk in terms of "having saved" the park, in reality the project remains ongoing, with many challenges still ahead.

Okay, So Why Save an Old Baseball Park?

WHEN TALKING ABOUT any preservation project, the obvious place to start is with "Why?" and in the case of Rickwood Field, the question is specifically "Why invest in an old baseball park?" We think that there are a number of compelling reasons:

- the HABS status as America's oldest baseball park (there is only one "oldest" anything, and we believe that this NPS endorsement adds tremendous credibility to our project)
- the park's rich baseball history
- the park's role in community and national social fabric, including the civil rights story
- the park's architectural significance
- the park's potential role as a catalyst for community revitalization

In August 1993 the National Park Service's Historic American Building Survey completed its Rickwood Field documentation project and concluded that Rickwood Field is the nation's oldest baseball grandstand on its original site, thereby qualifying it as America's oldest baseball park.[6] There are, of course, many other great old parks, and not infrequently we receive comments about a particular park's being a challenger to this status. But, to date, no challenger's claims have been substantiated. In each case thus far, it has proven to be an earlier piece of real estate, occupied by a later grandstand.[7]

Rickwood's role as host for the play of the Barons and their Southern Association and later Southern League rivals, the Black Barons and their Negro League counterparts, and the frequent play of major league teams, supports further the preservation argument. The park's first six decades produced an impressive list of alumni, including baseball legends Babe Ruth, Ty Cobb, Jackie Robinson, Ted Williams, Willie Mays, Joe DiMaggio, Satchel Paige, Dizzy Dean, Hank Aaron, Honus Wagner, Rube Foster, Rogers Hornsby, Cool Papa Bell, Lou Gehrig, Stan Musial, Ernie Banks, Reggie Jackson, and many others.[8] And although the Black Barons concluded their last season in 1963, and the Barons left for the suburbs in 1987, baseball continues today to be alive and well at Rickwood, with approximately two hundred games played annually.

Paralleling the park's baseball legacy is its role in Birmingham and American social fabric. Erected in 1910, Rickwood Field exemplifies the enthusiasm and optimism of early twentieth-century America, a nation immersed in the transition from a rural agrarian society to that of an urban, industrialized society. A. H. "Rick" Woodward, son of a wealthy Birmingham industrialist, and builder of Rickwood Field, typified further the enthusiasm and boosterism of early twentieth-century America, and specifically the young city of Birmingham, the rising industrial center of the New South.[9] As industry established itself in Birmingham, neighborhoods and communities sprouted around the plants, mills, and mines of this blue-collar, working-class town.

The economic and social transition that accompanied this growth, however, brought profound changes to everyday life. The new industrial worker found himself faced with a much more regimented and much less autonomous lifestyle, including a growing domination by the company and the time clock. As industrial life became more arduous, employers instituted programs designed to boost both morale and productivity. The introduction of company-sponsored recreation programs, including baseball teams, became commonplace, with Birmingham companies, large and small alike, fielding competitive baseball squads. Baseball in general, and Rickwood Field specifically, became a core component of Birmingham's working-class industrial identity.

The high caliber of play among many of these company-sponsored teams set the precedent for professional baseball in Birmingham. Ultimately, both the Barons and the Black Barons tracked and recruited local talent from this rich pool. As this talent-feeder system developed, fan loyalty toward individual company squads soon evolved into a passionate following for Birmingham's professional baseball teams.

In this broader view of Birmingham civic pride, Rickwood became the focal point of community identity. And although segregation statutes prevented black and white fans from socializing together at Rickwood Field, both races packed the grandstands to cheer on their respective teams and heroes. Moreover, owing to the Barons' and the Black Barons' shared use of the park, Rickwood occupies a place in our community's and nation's civil rights story, and it recently achieved inclusion in the National Trust's "African American Historic Places Initiative."[10]

In architectural terms, Rickwood Field represents classic early twentieth-century ballpark design and is considered to be the first minor league stadium built of concrete and steel.[11] The grandstand, coupled with a 1928 mission-style entryway and 1936 field light towers, forms the core of America's oldest baseball park. While researching ballpark design, Rick Woodward enlisted the assistance of legendary baseball icon Connie Mack in the building of Rickwood, resulting in a park fashioned after Pittsburgh's Forbes Field and Philadelphia's Shibe Park, and referred to at the time as "the South's Finest Ball Park."[12] Today Rickwood remains a prime example of second-generation American ballpark design, a style that replaced the earlier wooden grandstands. This era of ballparks offered greater fan comfort and amenities while retaining the human scale lost in the later generation of larger, more grandiose modern baseball stadiums.

Reflecting this combination of sports history, social history, and the history of the built environment, *Baseball America* magazine ranked Rickwood Field as one of the top five minor league ballparks of the twentieth century in terms of "significance beyond their cities." And in a subsequent analysis of ballparks old and new, *Baseball America* editors wrote that "the history of Rickwood Field . . . speaks for itself," with the park's significance continuing "to stand the test of time."[13] Ultimately, however, the preservation case must be made not only in cultural-historical terms but also in economic terms.

To that end, we cite the approximately 20,000 annual visitors to Rickwood, many of whom stay the night in Birmingham and spend their money at local hotels, restaurants, and entertainment venues. Moreover, a revitalized Rickwood Field is serving as a catalyst for the reinvestment and redevelopment not only of the neighborhood surrounding the park but also of Birmingham's larger West End community. National media exposure for the park, including Rickwood's portrayal as only one of Birmingham's numerous cultural and historic attractions, has direct economic implications for the city's heritage tourism and entertainment industries.[14] As we continue to make the pitch for Rickwood's ongoing revitalization, the bottom line remains, however, "how do we go about achieving our objective of comprehensive revitalization of the park?"

A brief examination of agency background sheds light on this central challenge. The Friends of Rickwood, a 501 (c) 3 nonprofit organization formed in 1992, is a true grassroots organization, with one full-time employee, a board of directors, and roughly five hundred members. The group's diverse board and membership, consisting of preservationists, baseball purists, and community members, is committed to keeping alive this unique piece of Americana. To date approximately two million dollars in renovation to the park has been completed, highlighting the wide support for the project and the tenacity of the Friends organization, including its ability to establish goals and to see these goals to fruition.[15]

The Strategy

THE TOTAL REVITALIZATION of Rickwood Field includes the ongoing marketing of the park as a competitive baseball venue. Our game schedule has averaged approximately two hundred baseball games per year over the past eight years, including the play of the Birmingham Board of Education's high school baseball program, the Birmingham Police Athletic League, numerous men's amateur leagues, college and junior college ball, and the hosting of tournaments and showcase events. This level of activity highlights the park's role in providing recreational opportunities across a broad demographic range. The Rickwood Classic, our annual turn-back-the-clock high-profile fund-raising event, also continues to bring the

Birmingham Barons back to their old home park, generating both significant revenue and invaluable media exposure.

The marketing of the park as a key component of the local and regional historic site community, as well as a living-history tourist destination, is also ongoing. Toward this end, the Friends have in the past several years more aggressively pursued an educational and tourism path through a combination of means, among them the launching of the revised Rickwood Field website, the design and production of a new multipage marketing brochure, as well as a new "rack" brochure, funded in part by the Alabama Bureau of Tourism and Travel, that is now available to the traveling public through the state's brochure distribution program.[16] The city of Birmingham, the Birmingham Regional Chamber of Commerce, and the Birmingham Convention and Visitor's Bureau have also been instrumental in our marketing efforts. Inclusion in several recently published travel guides, as well as a presence on numerous ballpark and heritage travel websites, highlights our tourism and educational marketing efforts.[17] On-site efforts include the creation of the "Rickwood Self-Guided Tour," designed to address "walk-up" visitors to the park. Moreover, we continue to host fieldtrips and student groups of all ages, highlighting further Rickwood's role as an educational site. This multitiered marketing approach has proven successful; for example, Rickwood Field was recently listed by *USA Today* newspaper as one of the "10 great places to touch base with the best."[18] Despite this success, funding remains the key ingredient, bringing us to the core of the "how" component.

Fortunately, our revenue stream originates from several sources, including a mix of public and private funds, leaving us not solely dependent upon a single revenue source. Rickwood Field is currently a line item in the city of Birmingham's annual budget, but it is not funded fully by the city, in the same manner as other city of

Birmingham–owned sites. Our line-item status notwithstanding, the city's role, both financial and emotional, is invaluable. Other public funds have come through grants from the state of Alabama, including the Alabama Historical Commission, the Alabama Bureau of Tourism and Travel, the Alabama Department of Community Affairs, and the Alabama State Park's Joint Study Committee.

Private sources also continue to account for a significant portion of our funding, including the crucial support of the foundation community. The Birmingham business community has been extremely supportive as well; our 1993 corporate campaign raised considerable funds. In addition to cash pledges, other Birmingham business and firms have contributed generously with in-kind services and expertise.

Facility rentals also generate essential revenue, along with a modest addition generated from merchandise sales. Individual contributions remain an invaluable funding source, as does the annual Rickwood Classic, which continues to produce a profit each year. The Friends organization has also been successful in marketing the park as a ready-made vintage baseball set for photo shoots, commercials, and movies, all of which generate revenue as well as increased visibility.[19]

But despite our success to date, many challenges lie ahead, with funding remaining our biggest issue. Our status in the city's budget is precarious at best; it requires a renewal of the relationship each fiscal year. Grant funds and corporate support are also becoming increasingly competitive. Recruiting "new blood" into the organization and project is a further ongoing challenge, as is developing a relationship with the younger generation, the generation that will have to "take over the reins" at the end of our watch. Moreover, keeping the project in the media spotlight continues to be a formidable task. At the core of all of these challenges, however, is the realization that a ninety-five-year-old facility requires almost constant attention and care. The park's mechanical systems are old and outdated, and will necessitate extensive upgrades in the near future. Because exposure to weather and climate is taking its toll on the physical structure, the need for extensive stabilization and repair to the concrete is becoming more acute.

Hand in hand with mounting challenges, however, is the growing relevance of saving the park, including Rickwood's role as a potential model for similar efforts in other cities. Preservation and revitalization endeavors are being considered or ongoing in various stages at numerous other historic baseball parks, several of them involving grassroots "friends" type of organizations, with community members mobilizing to "save" local parks.[20] Other communities have pursued for-profit paths and view minor league and independent league baseball and the modernization of their facilities as salvation. The growing trend toward building new parks with a vintage look and feel further reinforces the relevance of preserving and revitalizing the classic ball yards of yesterday.

Whatever the case, it is our hope that the revitalization of Rickwood Field may in some way assist other communities in their baseball park preservation and restoration projects. Our approach is, of course, not fail-proof, nor does it fit every case, and each day presents new challenges. The success enjoyed to date by Friends of Rickwood certainly does not provide all of the answers, but we hope it helps reveal some of the questions.

In conclusion, I'd like to quote briefly a true friend of Rickwood Field, Donnie Harris, former Black Baron center fielder.

In response to a question concerning Rickwood's relevance in the new-park-versus-old-park argument, Donnie replied simply, "You can have those new fields with artificial turf and sky boxes. This IS a BALLPARK. You need the sun and wind in your face. To me, Rickwood is a one-of-a-kind place." We concur—and look forward to many more years of baseball and community pride at Rickwood Field.

APPENDIX 2

• • •

THE BARON OF RICKWOOD

DESPITE NEARLY FORTY YEARS of consciousness-raising on the subject of the Negro Leagues, we still leave off the names of dozens of great old-time black ballplayers when we play games like "Who are the best players not in the Hall of Fame?" Everyone says Shoeless Joe Jackson or Pete Rose or Gil Hodges, but Lorenzo "Piper" Davis could have played on teams with any of them and been a standout.

In 1987 Piper sat down with me at Rickwood Field and, later, at Ted's Restaurant on Fourth Avenue South, about five miles from Rickwood, with Barons owner Art Clarkson. He recollected his life and career for me and a small paper called *Fun and Stuff*, which would later evolve into *Birmingham Weekly*. Here's his story.

The name Lorenzo Davis is unknown even to many longtime Birmingham baseball fans—let's call him by the name by which he's better known, Piper. He was a great player and a great manager— Willie Mays has acknowledged as much on several occasions—and a heck of a basketball player, too, as the Washington Generals can readily testify. (Piper played with the Globetrotters four winters before returning to Negro League Baseball.)

He had one shot at the bigs, and the deck was stacked against him: in 1950, at age thirty-three, after twelve bona fide seasons as

Piper Davis (center) *greets Black Barons (left to right) Reverend Bill Greason, Tommy Sampson, Jimmy Zapp, Alonzo Perry, Bill Powell (who was also Piper's brother-in-law), and Rufus Gibson at a 1994 reunion to "roast" Piper.*

an All-Star in the Negro Leagues, he was given the opportunity to try out for the Boston Red Sox. He was the first black player signed by major league baseball's most racist organization. He was cut a short time later for what the Red Sox deemed "economic reasons" and never got a single at-bat in the majors.

The experience would have soured most players, but Davis, though often sharp-edged and occasionally sharp-tongued on the subject of professional baseball, never lost his enthusiasm for the game. Married for forty-nine years to the former Laura Perry, he looks as fit in person as he did in photos of his Negro League prime, and doesn't hesitate to jump out of a chair and do an imitation of Willie Mays lunging at pitchers or Satchel Paige delivering his "hesitation" pitch.

• I got my name from the town where I was born, in 1917, Piper, Alabama—you don't know where that is, do you? Well, if you hadn't been there, I don't think you would know. I don't think you would find it on a map even today. It was a little coal-mining town.* There weren't but a couple hundred people there after World War I, and I'll bet there aren't many more than that now.

When did I start playing ball? At such an early age that I can't remember. I can tell you that I already felt like a ballplayer by the time I was in grade school. I remember that in the heart of the Depression, about 1935, we were living in Fairfield—that's real close to where Willie Mays grew up, if you recall—and I played with an industrial team, TCI, a pipe and valve company. You don't hear much about this today, but the company teams had a lot to do with baseball back then.

There weren't any Little League or Babe Ruth teams, and most of us—not just the black boys but most of the white boys, too— learned to play organized ball on company teams. Willie did, and when I met Mickey Mantle in Birmingham in 1967 when the Yankees came down for an exhibition game, he told me he learned his ball on a company team, too, for a mining company.

Back in the thirties, Birmingham was one of the best places for the Negro Leagues to find talent because of all the industry and all the company teams. ACIPCO [Alabama Cast Iron and Pipe Company] and Stockham Valve were two companies that always had good teams. Right after Pearl Harbor I worked at and played for the team at ACIPCO, and I played with two men, Sam Hairston and Bobby Wilson, who both made it to the major leagues. Most of the other guys on our team played professional ball of one kind or another, most of them in the Negro Leagues.

---

* Piper is on the map today, about fifty miles southwest of Birmingham.

I was with the Omaha Tigers in 1936, and that's just about the time a baby named Bob Gibson was born in Omaha, and if I had known about it, I would have gone and looked for him and tried to sign him when he was little, cause he not only became a great baseball player but also a terrific basketball player with the Harlem Globetrotters—just like I was. Did you know that?

In Alabama my father had borrowed some money and wanted to send me to Alabama State. Things were really hard back then in Birmingham, but I got a partial scholarship, so he tried to raise the money to pay for the rest. I felt bad about him doing that. I decided that I couldn't put the burden on him and I'd try to earn a living as a professional ballplayer. My mother gave me some money—it couldn't have been more than twenty-five dollars—and just before I left, she told me to be sure to keep some no matter what for bus fare back home. It was good advice, and I always tried to do that.

In 1937 I broke my leg in a collision at second base, and that ended my playing with Omaha. The next year I tried to play some ball for the Yakima [Washington] Browns—that's where Willie Jones ended his career, by the way. But there wasn't any money in that, and I came back home to Birmingham and got by playing company ball for ACIPCO. You could make a living doing that if you also worked at doing something else, so I worked for the company and played baseball. I remember we got about $3.50 a day during the week, and $7.50 a game on weekends. Sometimes there'd be a doubleheader, and we got $10—we both loved that and hated it, because we needed the extra money, but playing two games in that heat could really be grueling, and, besides, some of us felt a little cheated that we didn't get $15.

You have to remember that these industrial teams were where most of the great players in the Negro Leagues in the South came from. The company teams were like farm teams, though we didn't use that word back them. Of course, there was a lot of discrimination at that time, but baseball in the industrial leagues was one of the few places where a black man could get a square deal. There was a lot of good teams in Birmingham back then, one from Sloss Furnace and TCI and one from a company called Perfection Mattress. We made jokes about them—you know, on days when they weren't playin' good you'd say, "You couldn't have got much sleep on that Perfection Mattress." But they usually had a good team.

I would have to say that, on the whole, black players in the industrial leagues got a pretty good deal. It seemed to us that we got just about everything that the white guys did. The companies paid for all the equipment except for our gloves, and they paid expenses when you had to travel. I'll say it this way: the company teams treated you better than the Negro traveling teams. It was a better deal.

It was during the war, 1943, when I was approached by the Birmingham Barons. I'm not bragging, but I was as good as any ballplayer around, I mean black or white. I wouldn't say this when he was alive, but I think I was even better than "Kitty Cat" Mays, and if he was around, I think he'd be honest and back me up on that. But Cat didn't actually play on the Barons. I'd better explain that. He played a few games with the Black Barons under a different name when the team needed an extra player, but he wasn't a regular Black Baron.

Anyway, the Barons offered me a pretty good contract—$350 a month and $2 a day for meal money. I was only making about $3.30 a day, but I had two kids to feed, and, believe me, there wasn't any money left over, so leaving the company team to play for the Barons was a big thing.

That's also how I came to play for the Harlem Globetrotters.

When I went down to sign my contract with the Barons, I met a man named Welch—I don't recall his first name, but he worked for Abe Saperstein, who had hands in different sports. He did promotion for the Black Barons, but he also owned the Globetrotters. When I went down to sign, a friend of mine said to Mr. Welch that I was a heck of a basketball player, and Welch was interested and called Mr. Saperstein. So Mr. Saperstein told him over the phone, "Offer him fifty dollars more and sign him for the Globetrotters, too." I can tell you that was a terrific day. I went home and took my wife and my boys and two cousins out to a big dinner to celebrate.

For the next three years I played with the Birmingham Black Barons and the Harlem Globetrotters. After that, I decided to devote myself entirely to baseball, partly because it could be pretty tiring to play both sports, but also because by then we were making more money barnstorming with baseball teams than playing basketball with the Globetrotters. That's when I got to meet most of the great stars in what you might call the last era of the Negro Leagues.

I knew Don Newcombe very well. A lot of people thought Jackie Robinson regarded himself as coming from a higher position than most of the black southern players, I guess because Jackie grew up in California. But I recall him as a very respectful man, and I'm glad I got to play with him.

You want to know about Satchel Paige? Well, I saw a great many pitchers in my time, black and white, but I never saw a greater pitcher than Satchel Paige. Yes, he could throw a great fastball, but there were faster than him, white guys and black guys. One time— 1948, I think it was—the New York Yankees played two games at Rickwood Field, and I got to see this big Indian pitcher they had, Allie Reynolds. I think he threw about the meanest fastball that I ever saw. I mean, it was *mean*.

I don't mean it was the fastest fastball—it wasn't faster than Bob Feller's—but he threw a heavy ball—you know what I mean? It reminded me a lot of the kind of fastball Bob Gibson had. I also got to see this little catcher they had who everybody knew later as Yogi Berra, but I don't remember if they called him by that name then. I think I would have remembered that. I think he was playing outfield in Birmingham, and he was very quick—a little awkward but with a pretty good arm. He had a big wide swing, and damn if he didn't swing at *everything* they'd throw at him. And damn if he didn't hit nearly everything they threw at him. He hit one line drive that almost tore down a soda pop sign on the outfield wall. He was a very nice man. Some of the white ballplayers didn't take much notice of us, but Yogi and Allie Reynolds went out of their way to shake hands and be nice.

Anyway, I should stop for a moment and tell you a little bit about Satchel Paige and what the pitching was like back then. What I was going to say about Old Satch was that it wasn't so much his speed as where he could put the ball; he had tremendous control. But the main difference between the black teams I played and managed on and the ones I saw and the white teams, I mean the white Barons as well as the big-league teams I'd see when they'd play exhibitions at Rickwood, was that, on the whole, the white teams usually had better pitching, which means they had more good pitchers. Some of them even had coaches that would help the pitchers. They didn't have what you'd call pitching coaches back then, but there was always coaches around who had experience and could help the young pitchers.

That was a difference. Black teams didn't have the money and couldn't afford as many coaches. We were better than the white Barons, but they always had more pitchers, sometimes older guys who had pitched in the major leagues and knew a lot, sometimes young guys with strong arms that they could bring in for the late innings. Most black teams had to rely on only one pitcher to get through a game, and it got very tiring. Remember that when Satchel went out there, he was always thinking that he'd have to finish his own game.

I'll tell you a couple of other great pitchers that were just about as good. Did you ever hear of Willie Foster? He was one of the greatest left-handed pitchers I ever saw, one of the greatest pitchers I ever saw left- *or* right-handed. He had a fastball that sunk and seemed to be gaining weight on the way down. If you didn't get good wood on it, it hurt your hands. If you didn't hit that pitch just right, guys would say, it was like hittin' a bowling ball with a broomstick.

I remember in the sixties watchin' Sandy Koufax in the World Series, and I swear to you that's who Willie reminded me of. He had similar kinds of pitches. Man, he could have been a great pitcher in white folks ball if they had let him. You know what he ended up doing? He went back to college, graduated, and became a dean and also coach of the baseball team at Alcorn State. I know that Willie didn't regret his life, but I know he would have loved to have had a chance to pitch in the big leagues.

And I'm going to mention another great pitcher, and this will surprise you: his name was Dizzy Dean. You won't believe me, but I was at that game in 1931 when he pitched that great game in the Dixie World Series. I was fourteen, and I was sitting in what they called the "Negro bleachers" out in right field. What surprised me about the way Dizzy pitched in that game is that he seldom used that great fastball that you hear so much about. Most pitchers use a curveball as a first pitch, to get ahead on the count, but that day Diz was using a fastball on his first pitch. Then he'd get the batter out with a curve ball that most of the Barons batters couldn't hit real good. They'd reach out and slap it to second base or to shortstop or sometimes back to the mound.

I saw Dizzy a couple of times, and I would have to say from what I saw that he was about as good as Satchel. Now, you have to remember that Satch pitched for a much longer time, but when Dizzy was good, he was as good as Satchel. I'll say something else for his memory, too—he was respectful of the Negro Leaguers, and I guess that came from his relationship with Satch. You never heard black players call Diz "a cracker." If all the guys in white folks ball been like Diz, we'd all have been better off.

In 1948 I was thirty-one years old, and I thought it was time to do more than just play, so I became a Black Barons coach. We didn't use the term "manager," but that's really what I was. That's why I was around to watch when the Yankees and other major league teams came through Birmingham to play at Rickwood Field.

My rules were pretty simple. I wanted my players to use their intelligence, to be alert and play heads-up kind of baseball. I wanted my players to show respect for their teammates. If I heard someone say, "Oh, man, he should have caught that ball," I'd get on him right away. "You're sittin' here on the bench," I'd say. "You can't see how the wind is blowin' out there or whether the sun got in his eyes."

I didn't let any of my players disrespect any of their teammates or, for that matter, the players on the other team.

All the time, I kept on playing. I was about the best double play man in our league, and that's a fact anyone who was around then would agree with. Sometimes I'd give myself a rest and play another position, then switch with a guy I had put at shortstop. You know, if there was a couple of runners on base. If we got a double play, I'd switch back to, say, left field. No one cared about making rules against things like that back then.

You want me to tell you about Willie Mays? You know, you'll hear a lot about great ballplayers from the days of the Negro Leagues, but I think Willie was as great as any of them. I saw him mostly when he was young, but you could see his greatness then. I first coached Willie in 1948 when he was just seventeen. I'd already heard about him from the guys who had played with him and against him in pickup ballgames. It was in Chattanooga that I met him, and he was still in high school. I told him, "Son, if they find out you're playin' ball up here, that's gonna be the end of your playin' high school baseball." He laughed and shrugged and said, "So what? I don't care."

I figured there was nothing wrong with that attitude, because I had had it myself—if you want to play, you should play. I told him, "Well, hell, if you don't care what your high school principal thinks, you give me a call after school is out and I'll get you to play for the Barons."

I would call Willie the best natural ballplayer I ever saw. He could do everything right from the start, and experience just helped him to do it better. He was so good in the outfield that our other outfielders kind of got lazy. They would let him take anything that he could get to. I thought that was great, but I also thought that it was going to make some white outfielders a little bit angry when he played in the big leagues, because older white guys weren't going to like some brash black kid taking some balls that they maybe feel they could reach.

Anyway, I had to keep my outfielders sharp when Willie was in center or they'd get lazy. One time at the end of an inning, I said to my right and left fielders, "Man, you let him catch balls that were just a few feet from you. Now, if that's as hard as you're gonna try, I may as well put anybody out there, right?" They got the message. I didn't want Willie to try less hard; I just wanted the other outfielders to try hard, too. Willie still caught as many balls hit to their positions, but at least they were there to back him up.

One thing I want you to think about. When you look out to the outfield at Rickwood Field, remember that Willie Mays didn't just play center field there. He played *all* the outfield there.

By the end of the 1948 and 1949 seasons, there were big-league scouts everywhere, especially in the South, looking for black talent. The Boston Red Sox were scouting Junior Gilliam, or at least they said they were. He was playing then with the Baltimore Elite Giants.

The Barons were playing the Giants in Baltimore on a Saturday night, and I got four hits in four times at bat. I stole a base and helped make two double plays at shortstop and threw a runner out at home on a relay from the outfield. I know that sounds like I'm recalling it to make myself sound good, but that is what happened.

The next day, on Sunday, we played a doubleheader. That's three games in twenty-four hours, and, believe me, that wasn't all that unusual back then. In the Sunday doubleheaders—you're not gonna believe this, but it's gospel truth—I go three for four in the first game and four for four in the second, and one of those hits was a home run. So I get eleven hits in the three games, and I drove in, I don't know, must have been ten runs, maybe twelve, and all with the Boston Red Sox man looking at me. We also won the first two games and lost the third one 5–4 in the last inning.

The Red Sox man turns out to be their secretary, and he came down to see me in the clubhouse Sunday night to tell me that they're interested. He says they want me to go to Boston so we can talk about a contract. I had one problem, and it's that the Black Barons' owner, Tom Hayes, who lived up in Memphis, had me under contract. Now, you've heard stories about some Negro League stars not being under contract—you might have heard that that was the case with Willie Mays when the Giants tried to sign him.

But remember that I was the coach, actually the manager of the team, and so they had to have me under contract. I was anxious to see this was done right, so I'm careful to set up a talk between Mr. Hayes and the Boston Red Sox. As I recall it, Mr. Hayes got $7,500 up front and $7,500 more if I'm accepted to the team roster and am still there by May of the following year. What did I get? $200 up front, but on the rest I would split 50–50 with Mr. Hayes.

It was September, and our season was almost over, so the Red Sox said they wanted me to finish my season with the Barons and start the next season with them up in Scranton, Pennsylvania. That was one of their minor league teams.

Then, in the winter of 1950, they tell me to come down to their spring training camp in Cocoa, Florida. I thought that was kind of strange because this was the South, and I was the only black player on the team. Every time I go out to take batting practice or do some warming up, you know, running sprints and stuff, I hear some snicker or some kind of insult from the fans. I just shut my ears to it because this was the best chance for me to support my family.

Anyway, I got off to a great start in Scranton, and after the first few weeks I was leading the team in just about everything—I had the most home runs, runs batted in, stolen bases, and I was hittin' over .330. It was a little humiliating for me 'cause I'm leading the team in everything and we're playing in a northern town, but I'm still being treated like it's Florida.

At the team hotel in Scranton, I was sleeping in the waiters quarters. But then one of the sportswriters gets wind of that and starts asking around. So Mr. Welch came down from Boston and talked to the waiters at the hotel and paid one of them to let me stay in his home. That way the sportswriters couldn't find me to interview me.

Before you know it, it's May 13, and I'm playing really good ball, and all I'm thinking about is making that May 15 deadline and getting my half of that $7,500. After we get back from a road trip, two days before the deadline, I get a call that they want to see me at the main office. I figure this is it, I finally made it.

The plan, the way I understood it, was to send me to Louisville, which was a higher level of ball than Scranton, a Triple-A team. Anyway, when I get to the office, the general manager is waiting for me with the manager, Jack Burns, a man who had treated me pretty good. The general manager says to me, "Piper, I'm afraid we have to let you go." Man, I almost fell down right there. "Why?" I say. "I'm one of the best players on this team."

I really was about the best player on that team, but I didn't want to say it that way. The reason that they gave me was "economic conditions." I didn't know what to say or do. I felt numb. I knew it was a lie because everyone said that the Red Sox owner, Tom Yawkey, was one of the richest men in baseball. Everyone talked about how the Red Sox, who had lost the pennant to the Yankees in 1949 in a really exciting race, had practically set an attendance record. So how could they not keep me in their organization because of "economic conditions"?

I just mumbled, "Okay," shook my head, and walked away. I walked into the clubhouse still feeling stunned, and I'll never forget, Jack Burns followed me there. "Piper," he said, "Anything you want to take in here, you can have." The team had given each player their own brush and comb, so I took those and I took my cap and I left.

That's the only thing that ever happened to me in baseball that I had bad dreams about later. Sometimes late at night I'd just lie in bed and play that whole scene over and over in my head, trying to make it come out different than it did.

I can tell you one thing. I learned the truth of what I'd heard from some black players who had spent time up North and said it was harder to get along in the North than in the South. In the South, at least, you knew where you stood, and there were signs everywhere to tell you where to go or where not to drink water from. I mean, it angered you when you'd see that in Birmingham, but you knew where you were. In the North they didn't have any signs, and you didn't know where you were allowed to drink water.

In the South you knew not to go into a restaurant where they only served white people. In the North you'd walk into a restaurant not knowing, and the waitress would follow you and then walk up to you as you sat down and say something like, "I'm sorry but we can't serve you here."

Can I say something else? I never had any trouble with my teammates at Scranton. Some of the fans, yes, but my teammates were always good to me.

I didn't want to go down to a lower level, so I had a chance to play Triple-A level ball in Oakland. I took it, and I played professional ball and supported my family for five and a half years.

By the way, it wasn't always a picnic out there with some of the fans. They would tell you that in California it was better than either the North or the South. It was, but it wasn't no picnic.

The competition was pretty good in Oakland. I think in three of my five seasons I hit over .300. When I tell people that, they're surprised that I didn't hit better, but remember I was in my mid-thirties when I was playing for Oakland. I was there till 1956, and then I played for another California team, in Los Angeles, then in the Texas League and even in South America, in Venezuela. Two years later I came back to the Black Barons, in 1958. But it wasn't a happy time.

I had been gone more than eight years, and the Negro Leagues were practically dead. The fans, especially the black fans, didn't want to come see us any more. By then, Willie was the biggest star in baseball, and Hank Aaron and others were burning up the National League, so why would they want to come see us in what they thought was the minor leagues? Anyway, that's the way people thought. If they didn't go to the games, they could watch them for free on television, so why did they need us?

In 1959, it broke my heart, but the Black Barons folded. The last game we played at Rickwood I don't think we had two hundred people there. The first couple of years after Jackie Robinson integrated the major leagues, we'd draw even more fans than the white Barons. I don't just mean black people—white people would come out to see us, too.

What was so sad in that final year was that Rickwood Field was so much bigger than it had been when I played and coached there. I don't know how many seats they had there, but it sure looked like you could get twenty thousand people seated in the ballpark. What was so sad was when someone hit a home run, and kids would take off from around the third base line and run out to look for the ball. Sometimes it would take them five, ten minutes to find it.

In the 1960s I had a new experience, a really great one. I ended up scouting for Montreal, the Expos. I did that until I was in my seventies, and I guess I quit—that would be in 1986—because I woke up one day and said to myself that a man in his seventies shouldn't be out there on a baseball field.

Who was the best player that I scouted? Well, you've heard of Andre Dawson, haven't you?

People say to me, "What's the biggest different between the players you played with and coached and the ones today?" I'd say the biggest difference is that, black and white, it's hard to teach them anything. They're all making so much money that they're reluctant to listen to a guy like me or just about anybody else about the game's fine points.

I've got nothing against the players making all the money they can. I wish I'd had the kind of chance to make that kind of money, and a lot of the guys I knew wish they had that chance, too. Not just black guys, but white guys, too. But I have to say hits: money seems to take a lot of players' minds off the game.

I'm retired now, and I'm enjoying it. I guess that I was in baseball so long, almost sixty years, really, that I'm not missing it as much as I thought I would. I work with a group at the Hunter Street Baptist Church, and we carry senior citizens and people who can't get around easily to doctors and other places. It's a job that gives you a lot of satisfaction because every day you know you've helped someone.

The funny thing, with all the talk now about the Negro Leagues, I'm getting more attention from young fans than ever before. I get a lot of mail—sets of cards with pictures of Negro League greats that people send to me and ask me to autograph them and mail them back. I got one guy, a white guy, who must have sent me a dozen cards, and he sent me a nice letter and said he loves to give them away to people in his office. But I've got a suspicion that he's selling them for a profit. [Laughs out loud.] I think I'm going to write that boy a letter.

Right now, my daughter has a good job with the city, and I've got a nice house and my family is doing very well. My work is satisfying, and I feel like I'm doing something for the community. Birmingham? I know about all the troubles we've had, but it's a good city. I thought once or twice about moving to California, but when I came back in 1958, even when the worst part of the civil rights movement was growing, I knew that I would never live anywhere else.

Do I have any regrets? Well, of course, I've got a couple. Till the day I die I'll be dreamin' about what it would have been like to get to play in the major leagues.

The Hall of Fame? Yes, that would have been nice. I think I belonged with some of those guys from the Negro Leagues who finally made it in. Maybe someday some people will remember me, and I'll make it. But I'm afraid that by then most of the people that saw me play will be gone.

One thing that I think about every time I go to a baseball game here. That new stadium they're building out in Hoover sure may look nice, but it will never have all the memories that you'll find at Rickwood Field. It'll never have the history that Rickwood has. Believe me, no ballpark ever will. They'll never accomplish that kind of history anywhere else.

APPENDIX 3

. . .

VOICES OF RICKWOOD

An Oral History

THAT RICKETY LADDER TO THE PRESS BOX

as told by Don Keith

I NEVER CONSIDERED that being the PA announcer for the Birmingham Barons Double-A team at historic Rickwood Field could be hazardous duty. Truth is, I was only the relief PA announcer, filling in for Bob Sterling, the regular guy, when he needed to take a day or two off. That meant I could never get my chops, learn the players and their numbers, know how the various between-innings promotions worked, or really get into a groove.

The most hazardous part of the job was getting to the press box. We had to climb a rickety, open ladder from the top row of seats beneath the overhang up through a constricted opening to the roof, then walk a narrow, dark path to the small shack that served as the press box, the boards bending and squeaking beneath our feet. On hot, humid nights, the newspaper-beat writers sat on folding chairs out on the roof trying to catch a breeze, smoking cigars, drinking sodas (I think), and swatting bugs that fell from the lights overhead. One of the scribes, Steve Martin from the *Birmingham News*, was also the official scorekeeper. On a questionable play, I had to put down the microphone, lean out the front of the press box, and see whether Steve—mostly hidden in the dark—was scoring it a hit or an error. I had to relay the call to the scoreboard operator. With that huge control box in front of him, he couldn't lean out to see for himself.

For some reason, Sterling often felt the need to be off for Sunday afternoon games. It would be well over a hundred degrees inside that press box. The Barons' owner Art Clarkson was notoriously cheap. He allowed the PA guy and the scoreboard operator to order from the concession stand a free soda and one food item per game. But on those steamy Sunday afternoons, he generously allowed us to get one ice cream treat, too. Even *he* felt sorry for us.

I did get to see and hear my voice reverberate back to me the names of some great ballplayers, like Robin Ventura making play after play from the hot corner and Frank Thomas going yard time after time. But it was also comical to see Thomas at first base, tossing the ball around between innings. He would often heave it over the second baseman's head into left field, further confirming he was passing through Birmingham and on the way to the White Sox for his bat and not his arm.

Don Keith is the Birmingham-based author of seventeen books, most recently The Ice Diaries, *the story of the USS* Nautilus *and its historic trip to the North Pole in 1958.*

• • •

TALKING BASEBALL IN HEAVEN

as told by Tim Orton

THE FIRST BASEBALL GAME I ever saw in person was at Rickwood. When I was five or six years old, my mom took me to see the East–West All-Star game at Rickwood. I remember seeing the guys who represented the state team in pinstripe uniforms and thinking they looked like the New York Yankees. . . .

I remember being one of a mob of kids who would stand in the area near the Dugout Restaurant scuffling for foul balls. . . .

I remember being jealous of Bill Burch, one of my Ensley High schoolmates, who got to be the kid who put the numbers in the windows of the big scoreboard in left field. . . .

I remember the man who for years sold scorecards at the games. What was so memorable about him was his voice and the way he yelled SCORECARDS with his gravelly voice.

Directly behind home plate in the seats left of the walkway sat five older black gentlemen. I don't think I ever went to a game that those five gentlemen were not there. They discussed the situation on every pitch. I believe there is a heaven, and I hope those guys are still getting to hang out together and watch baseball.

Tim Orton is a graduate of Ensley High School, class of '64, and was a Birmingham area high school coach from 1969 through 1982. He has been a Birmingham Barons and A's fan since 1956 and does not expect he will ever quit rooting for either.

• • •

PROUD MEMBER OF THE KNOTHOLE GANG

as told by George Draper

MY FATHER OFTEN TALKED TO ME about his last days at Rickwood, and that was a long time ago. He was in the standing room–only crowd for the pitching duel between Ray Caldwell and Dizzy Dean [the 1931 Dixie Series]. In his later years he had forsaken all events that had crowds, but he always remembered that day and that game. My mother took me to Rickwood Field when I was in the first grade. It was Ladies Day.... I'll never forget how excited I was.

My cousin sent me a book on the story of Rickwood with a postcard. I see from the postcard there have been some changes in the stadium since the 1930s and 1940s.... Two spots in the stands were important to me in those days: one, the place in the right field stands well down the right field foul line where the Knothole Gang sat. I was a proud member of the Knothole Gang. We didn't go through the main entrance as I remember, but through a gate along side the right field line. The other spot was the bleachers down the left field line. On Sundays I would leave after church at West End Baptist, and after a hop, skip, and jump to Rickwood I would be at the park for the doubleheaders, two games for the price of one. The only thing that my folks required was that I be back at church for the night service....

After I left for the army the summer of 1946, I didn't get any word on the Barons except for items sent by Mom from the sports pages. The first thing I did after I returned in 1948 was to go out to the game, and I saw Walt Dropo. Except for a few games played in the afternoon after that when I walked from the campus at Birmingham Southern to the park, my days at Rickwood were gone. But I listened on the radio as much as I could until I left for graduate school. One thing I do remember about Barons baseball back then is that the announcer for the Barons was Bull Connor. He had a most unusual way of calling the game. A little too folksy, you might say. It was almost like he was getting ready to sell you a car.

George C. Draper Jr. grew up close enough to Rickwood Field to walk to the game and then walk home. He graduated from Birmingham Southern University and now lives in Alice, Texas. His mother took him to Rickwood on Ladies Day seventy-five years ago.

• • •

I SAW WALT DROPO'S TREMENDOUS HOME RUN

as told by Harvey Lux

HAVING BEEN BORN and raised in Birmingham, I have some vivid memories of Rickwood. My family had season tickets in the box seats along the third base line for many years. I remember the outfield being roped off on many occasions to accommodate the overflow crowds. I was there the night Walt Dropo hit his tremendous home run over the left field fence.

In 1948 we went to Fort Worth for the final games of the Dixie Series. In fact, we got to know many of the players very well, and on the night of the last game, Al LaMacchia, the Barons pitcher, promised me the game ball if he won. He did. He threw the ball up to me in the stands, and I caught it. I still have it—quite a prize for an eleven-year-old! I also have a ball autographed by all the players on that team as well as a scrapbook with newspaper articles and photographs.

Harvey A. Lux is retired from the steel fabrication business and lives in Spartanburg, South Carolina. He was seventy-two years old when he wrote this.

• • •

WATCHING THE BARONS FROM THE
HARDWARE STORE

as told by Ed Cherry

MY EARLIEST RICKWOOD memories are seeing the games on television in Birmingham. I lived in Fairview when television came along. Our first television experiences were at the hardware store window at Five Points West and in the sitting room of the Fairview fire station. I think it was 1948 or 1949. They both showed the first live broadcasts of Birmingham Baron baseball from Rickwood. I can remember the large crowds pushing and shoving at both the fire station and hardware store to get a better view of the small black and white screen. I guess that was another symbol of how well black and white work together to bring baseball pleasure to Birmingham.

Ed Cherry is a longtime Barons fan who now lives in Maryville, Tennessee. He often brings a busload of baseball fans to Rickwood and acts as the official Rickwood historian on the trip down to Birmingham.

• • •

I THINK BABE DID HIT THE LONGEST HOME RUN
BALL AT RICKWOOD

as told by Roger Dubois

BROOKLYN-BORN AND -RAISED, I grew up in the 1950s a diehard Dodgers fan. Although a rival player, Willie Mays, was the greatest I ever saw play.

My entire life I was led to believe that Babe Ruth hit the longest unofficial home run when he hit one during an exhibition game at Rickwood when it cleared the stadium, landed in a boxcar, and went to Nashville. Someday I was going to see where it was hit.

On March 23, 2000, I drove all night from my home in Minneapolis to Birmingham. I set foot for the first time on the field where Ruth hit his mighty blow and the home of the "Say Hey" Kid. Time stopped.

The next day I came back. I stood on the pitcher's mound, stepped into the batter's box, and walked out on the outfield warning track. Most thrilling of all, I located the tracks beyond the stadium wall where the Babe might have landed his shot into a boxcar. I felt the spirit of Ruth.

Roger Dubois is retired from the computer business and lives in Minneapolis. He was sixty-four in 2009.

• • •

I MISSED THE FIRST GAME OF THE
1931 DIXIE SERIES

as told by Jim Fitzpatrick

DURING EARLY 1931 in grade five, I wrote an "essay" about baseball. It was published in the *Birmingham News* and was one of the winners in a contest for elementary school students.

In the summer of that year, my friends and I began to walk from our homes in West End to Rickwood for games. This was early in the Great Depression, and our families had no cars and little money. The games were almost always played in the afternoon with an occasional morning game on a holiday. We left our homes before noon since we needed to arrive at the park early to find a way to gain free admission.

There were several ways to do this: (1) turn admission gates (they were not automatic), (2) return a ball that had been hit out of the park (it *was* the Great Depression), (3) wait for the exit gates to be opened during the seventh inning, (4) sell refreshment items in the stands, and (5) climb the outfield fence when the security people were not looking. Each of these had its advantages and disadvantages. . . . We preferred one of the first three.

One game we missed, and we always regretted it, was the first game of the 1931 Dixie Series in which forty-three-year-old Ray Caldwell (a former New York Yankee) outpitched twenty-one-year-old Dizzy Dean. This game is widely regarded as the greatest ever played at Rickwood. We listened to the radio broadcast on the front porch of my family home on Fifteenth Place SW. . . .

During these same early Depression years, the New York Yan-

kees stopped in Birmingham for four days each spring while traveling north from spring training in Florida. They arrived by rail at
the old Louisville & Nashville Station in midtown on a Wednesday
evening. Thursday and Friday they worked out at Rickwood, and
then on Saturday and Sunday they played exhibition games against
the Barons.

Our teachers learned not to expect us at school on those Thurs-
days and Fridays, and we always found a way to attend those exhibition games. Since this was long before Curt Flood and free agency,
the same basic squad returned over the three or four years we were
there. We saw such Yankees greats as Lou Gehrig, Tony Lazzeri,
Frank Crosetti, Joe Sewell, Babe Ruth, Earle Combs, Ben Chapman, Bill Dickey, Lefty Gomez, Red Ruffing, Herb Pennock, and
George Pipgras.

How could one not become a Yankees fan?

*Jim Fitzpatrick is a retired teacher (York Technical College) who grew up in
Birmingham and now lives in Charlotte, North Carolina. He was eighty-
nine when I spoke to him about his memories of Rickwood.*

• • •

RICKWOOD FIELD

by Debra S. Robertson

1910, Rickwood Field—
Coal barons, Black Barons, Barons—
History, sportsmanship and just plain fun,
It's here for everyone.

I walk to the bleacher
And sit in my spot,
My seat behind third base
Where I sat decades before
Watching Barons baseball.

My black and white reality
Fades to gray memories,
Some I remember well,
They belong to me,
yet, most I have never known.

The smells of Barons baseball
Waft through the stands to my nose—
Fresh peanuts, popcorn and hot dogs
Mingle with smoke and grass and sweat.

A vendor's voice above applause,
Crying, "Hot dogs, get your hot dogs here,"
Makes my stomach growl in anticipation—
And I look—but he isn't there.

I still hear the silence of the crowd,
The spinning ball across the plate,
Splatting against the catcher's mitt—
Third strike, third out,
And the Barons take the field.

The field seems different now—
Yet familiar like coming home.
The scorecard stands patiently by
For the keeper's hand to drop the inning's number
Or the game's final score.

The old ads are there no more,
Gone from the boards along the fence—
"Dollars for hitting this sign" not there,
And "Free suits for home runs" ceased to be.

I never saw Ty Cobb play,
Or Babe Ruth running to home,
And Burleigh Grimes' spitball pitches
Never crossed before my eyes.

I wasn't there for that famous game
Dizzy Dean pitched and lost—
To Birmingham's forty-three-year-old pitcher,
But the home crowd must have been wild.

And when the pigeon gave his life
In sacrifice for the game,
When the line drive whirled through the infield
I was not there to see.

And Jimmy Piersall, temper flaring,
Threw a tantrum, so I've been told,
Climbed to the roof, water gun in hand,
And soaked the crowd below.

Willie Mays, that shining star,
Skipped school to play ball here.
At sixteen, could he have dreamed
Of the man he would someday be?

Pie Traynor, Walt Dropo,
And "Stan the Man" Musial,
"Satchel" Paige, "Piper" Davis,
And George "Mule" Suttles
Kept Rickwood's diamond shining on.

Championships were played.
Championships were won and lost
By players now in the Hall of Fame
And those who were heroes at home.

The sounds and smells are only memories,
But the thrill of the game is real—
With the passage of time and Barons' baseball
Played here at Rickwood Field.

                              (Sent to Friends of Rickwood in 1999)

Debra S. Robertson has spent most of her fifty-plus years in the Birmingham area and now lives in Mt. Olive. She is fascinated with the historical aspects of the city and has written many poems on this subject.

                              • • •

ORANGE BASEBALLS, CHARLIE FINLEY, AND MY DAD

as told by Charles Stewart

OF ALL THE BARONS ITEMS in my collection, it is the 1964 program that connects me to Rickwood Field. I look at the cover, and I have no problem remembering that night I spent with my dad at the ballpark. Now that I think about it, it is not only my connection with Rickwood, but it also reminds me of some of the best nights I spent with my dad as a kid. That night was, and still is, my favorite time at a ballpark anywhere.

I can remember walking through the turnstiles ahead of my dad, and up to the concession stand with the smell of popcorn and onions. I remember the way the cool wind came whipping around the corner from the grandstand ramps and the noise that only a baseball field creates—the crowd, the announcer, and the sounds of the ball hitting the mitts and bats like the sound a great symphony makes while it is warming up for a concert.

We didn't sit behind the Barons' dugout this night, because the Barons were playing Charlie O. Finley's Kansas City A's, and we wanted to see the major leaguers up close. We sat several rows behind the on-deck circle, near the visitors' dugout. We had our Cokes and peanuts; my dad was a peanut man. He had his program and started to point out the different ballplayers and coaches to me. I didn't know half the players he named, and it really wasn't until I got older that I realized whom we had seen that night. My dad always carried a Cross pen with him, and he told me to go get the players' autographs before the game started. I took his program and went to the railing next to the entrance to the A's dugout and asked the different players coming out for their autographs.

The only player I knew was Rocky Colavito, whom I had gotten to sign a ball during spring training in 1962. I came back with Babe Dahlgren, who had been the player to replace Lou Gehrig at first base for the Yankees the day that Gehrig sat down. I got Jimmie Dykes, who had spent over forty years in the major leagues as both a player and a manager. And Jim Gentile, who had in 1961 come in third in home runs in the American League behind Maris and Mantle. I remember Gentile talking and laughing with the fans during the game while in the on-deck circle, so very different from today's players.

As much fun as it was meeting the players, the real fun that night was the experimental use of the orange baseball. This was one of Charlie Finley's ideas that he had convinced major league baseball to allow him to try. Finley argued that the orange ball would be easier to see at night, and therefore easier to hit and field. I remember watching the ball being hit high into the outfield night, and asking my dad if he thought it was easier to see. He shook his head no, like it was a crazy idea. I agreed with him that a white ball was much better.

The Barons ended up beating the A's that night 7–4, on the strong arm of Johnny "Blue Moon" Odom. But before we left the park, my dad sent me up to get the autograph of a gentleman sitting several rows behind us, Charlie O. Finley. After the game, on the way home, we talked about whom we had seen and met. My dad told me to take care of that program and not to lose it, and I assured him that I wouldn't. And here it is forty-three years later, and I still have that program and I'm still taking care of it.

Thanks, Dad, for a wonderful night at Rickwood.

Charles Stewart was born and raised in Birmingham (Woodlawn High School, class of '71). His favorite sport is college football, but he is renowned among Birmingham baseball fans for his extensive Barons/Rickwood collection. He lives near Auburn with his wife and seven children.

• • •

I COULD HAVE HAD A SATCHEL PAIGE BALL

as told by Rick Bernstein

I WAS TWELVE OR THIRTEEN when I got a job selling Cokes at
Rickwood Field. It was a terrific job, except that I was no good at it
and was always spilling Cokes on fans and on myself. Before long, I
graduated to peanuts—peanuts were easier.

I loved the games and hearing the stories about Rickwood's
glory years, but it always seemed a little sad to me that there weren't
more people at the ballpark. Sometimes an old-timer would say,
"Man, you should have seen what it was like back in 1950," or
something like that. But getting into a live sports event and earning
a few bucks on the side—that seemed like the greatest job in the
world to me.

In a glass case in my office I have about seventy-five autographed
baseballs, but I never look at the case without a tinge of regret. In
1967, I think it was, the Atlanta Braves had a promotional event
at Temple Emanuel on Highland Avenue to sell season tickets. I
remember that their announcer, Milo Hamilton, was there—he was
the one who later called the game the night Hank Aaron passed
up Ruth's record. There was a tall, slender elderly black gentleman
there, and I was vaguely aware he had something to do with the proceedings, but I didn't know exactly what.

My father kept saying, "Go get his autograph. Someday you'll
wish you had it." But I was too shy. As we were leaving, someone
said, "That's Satchel Paige." I'd heard the name before, but it didn't

mean that much to me at the time. Now I look at my glass case and all the autographed baseballs, and I remember that I could have had a Satchel Paige ball, but I was too shy.

Rick Bernstein is an executive producer at HBO Sports and a graduate of my old high school, Mountain Brook, class of '75.

• • •

GETTING PAID PEANUTS

as told by Bob Veale

WHEN I WAS THIRTEEN years old, I wanted to play for the Black Barons. I really thought I was good enough. When I was thirteen, I could throw as hard as a lot of the guys playing out there. Later I played for the Twenty-fourth Street Red Sox, an independent industrial-league team.

I was a batboy for the Black Barons. I didn't get paid much for that either: just peanuts. I mean that—I got paid in peanuts. But it was a lot of fun, and I got to meet everyone who was playing ball back then. I mean everyone—the white Barons and the Black Barons. I pitched batting practice and got to meet Jim Piersall and Walt Dropo, who were very fine men. I shagged fly balls before games for the white Barons, and then I'd come back and do the same for the Black Barons, so I got to see everybody.

I worked concessions at Rickwood—Cokes, peanuts, everything. Bob Scranton said I was the fastest man with a Coke he ever saw. I could handle three machines all at one time.

Of course, the most exciting player I saw at Rickwood was Willie Mays. He was as exciting as a Black Baron as he was in the major leagues, maybe more because he was even more reckless taking the extra base or diving for a ball. I was four years younger than Willie and often tried to play like him.

Here's something I remember: with the Black Barons, sometimes you could look out into the right field bleachers and you'd see some white people there. Not a lot, but some. There were white people who appreciated the Black Barons' brand of baseball.

A lot of people are in awe of Rickwood Field. I'm not one of them. I was born near Rickwood and spent so much time there that to me it's just home.

Born in Birmingham in 1935 near Rickwood Field, Bob Veale pitched for St. Benedict's College in Kansas, the Black Barons, and thirteen seasons in the major leagues, winning 120 games in ten years with the Pittsburgh Pirates and three with the Boston Red Sox. From 1964 through 1967 he won 67 games, all while wearing his trademark heavy dark glasses.

• • •

I DIDN'T KNOW I WAS PLAYING IN
AN ALL-WHITE LEAGUE

as told by Paul Seitz

I PLAYED WITH Rollie Fingers at Rickwood and against Jim Bouton when he was at Greensboro, North Carolina, in 1960. I don't know when he played at Rickwood. Most ballplayers don't care when it comes to race or color. The players are either your teammate or your opponent. I played in 1961 at Shreveport, Louisiana, in the Southern Association, a segregated league. I was there all year, twenty-one years old, and did not realize the league was all white. I found out in 1964 when I was named the opening-day pitcher, for the first integrated game at Rickwood. Even though I just said black or white was not an issue, the crowd was large for those days, and there was electricity in the air. I think Asheville won, I think 5–2.

For over thirty years, former minor league pitcher Paul Seitz has been the proprietor of the Little Professor bookstore in Homewood, Alabama, about a baseball's throw or two from the statue of Vulcan on Red Mountain.

• • •

NEVER DID *THAT* AT YANKEE STADIUM

as told by Jim Bouton

I SAW RICKWOOD FIELD for the first time in 2006 when ESPN staged a 1940s-era baseball game. I managed the Bristol Barnstormers and played a team of guys from Birmingham who were dressed in Black Barons uniforms. I had been active in trying to save Wahconah Park near my home in Massachusetts, so I was very interested in the fact that they had been able to save Rickwood Field, which was even older than Wahconah.

It was a thrill walking around the park. It's a real time capsule—it was like walking into an old scrapbook. At first I thought the billboards on the outfield walls were from the 1920s or something. I didn't realize they were reproductions until I touched them.

Seeing Rickwood brought back memories from more than forty years. I pitched in an exhibition game in Forbes Field in Pittsburgh—I think it was Bob Veale who I pitched against. I loved Forbes Field, and Rickwood reminds me of it—the big space behind home plate and the horseshoe curve on the top roof.

Rickwood also reminded me a lot of Shibe Park, though they might have been calling it Connie Mack Stadium by the time I saw it, around 1959, I think it was. I was approached by a scout, Tony Lucadello [the man who later discovered Hall of Famers Ferguson Jenkins and Mike Schmidt], after I pitched in the National Amateur Baseball Championships, and they flew me down to Philadelphia for a tryout. It rained, so I never got the tryout, but I had a nice tour of the stadium and got to see Richie Ashburn, Del Ennis, and other Phillies sitting around the clubhouse in their baseball under-

DANCING ON THE DUGOUT: *Former Yankees ace, best-selling author (Ball Four), film actor, and entrepreneur (Big League Chew) Jim Bouton dances on the dugout roof with an unidentified partner during the 2006 ESPN Classic at Rickwood. For this Classic, Bouton managed a 1940s-era team, the Bristol Barnstormers, in a throwback game against the Black Barons at Rickwood.*

wear smoking cigars, drinking beer, and playing poker. So I got a nice preview of life in the big leagues.

I had a ball in Birmingham. They have a big ceremony and hired some actresses to lend some atmosphere to the event. One of them was dancing on our dugout, and for some reason her partner jumped off. You can't let a lady dance by herself—so I jumped up there and joined her. Never did *that* at Yankee Stadium.

Famous for his high kick and losing his hat as he came off the mound, New-ark, New Jersey, native Jim Bouton won 39 games for the Yankees in 1963 and 1964. In two World Series, he was 2–1 with an ERA of 1.48. Then he blew out his arm, tried to make a comeback as a knuckleball reliever, and went on to write perhaps the most explosive and best-selling baseball book of all time, Ball Four, which revealed for the first time the off-field life of major league players—their desperation, their fears, and their after-hours antics. Ball Four *still ranks in sportswriter and fan polls as one of the best baseball books ever written. Since* Ball Four, *Bouton has written several other books (including* Ball Foul *in 2003, about his unsuccessful attempt to save historic Wahconah Park near Pittsfield, Massachusetts), started a personalized baseball card company, created Big League Chew bubble gum, was a delegate to the 1972 Democratic National Convention, and costarred in Robert Altman's cult classic* The Long Goodbye *with Elliott Gould. In the 2006 ESPN Classic, he managed a 1940s-era team, the fictitious Bristol Barnstormers, in a throwback game against the Black Barons at Rickwood.*

• • •

BOUTON WAS A HIT!

as told by Lamar Smith

THE WEATHER WAS terribly cold, particularly for the local team not accustomed to extreme temperatures and not experienced with playing baseball in late February, even if in Birmingham, Alabama. The visiting barnstormers from Connecticut were managed by Yankee great Jim Bouton in a special ESPN production at historic Rickwood Field. The local opponent, a team crafted from current collegians and former minor leaguers, was managed by former standout professional George Scott.

Action started quickly for the visitors as they jumped to an immediate lead. At the end of the first inning as part of the game's entertainment, a trio of local dancers began jitterbugging on the Barnstormers' dugout to the delight of the crowd. A couple of talented dancers were teamed with an additional young lady, all in period outfits that were not particularly suited for the nasty weather. As the dancers descended from the visitors' dugout, Bouton observed the imbalance in the number of performers. The situation was resolved at the conclusion of the second inning as the visitor from New England climbed into the stands and onto the green concrete surface, taking one young lady's hand to form a second dance team. Maybe not quite as polished as his 90-plus mile per hour fastball, Bouton's jitterbug acumen was very appreciated by all in attendance.

As the game progressed, each inning was concluded with Bouton and his three partners performing as if auditioning for *Dancing with the Stars*. And after the game at a meal at the nation's oldest ballpark, Bouton visited with each player on the opposing team as well as Rickwood Field volunteers and ESPN staff. His visiting team's lead was overcome by the locals in the late innings, but Bouton won over the fans on that cold Alabama night.

Lamar Smith has been attending the annual Rickwood Classic game for a decade and has been a member of the board of directors of the Friends of Rickwood for most of that time. He became a Yankee fan in the late 1950s and 1960s when the Yankees' games were the primary ones broadcast on Birmingham TV stations. In 2007 he visited the Yogi Berra Museum and Learning Center in Montclair, New Jersey, to watch the fourth game of the World Series with Yogi.

• • •

YOU COULDN'T BUILD A MOVIE SET THAT GOOD

as told by Ron Shelton

FILMING THE BASEBALL SCENES for *Cobb* at Rickwood Field was an easy choice. It's not only a beautiful old park; it carries more history than any park still standing. I never played there—I think maybe they weren't playing ball at Rickwood when I was in the minors. As a filmmaker who is a former ballplayer, how could I resist the lure of filming on the same field where Pie Traynor, Satchel Paige, Dizzy Dean, Willie Mays, and, of course, Ty Cobb once played? I'd look into the camera sometimes and feel like I was seeing ghosts whizzing by.

I loved the overhang and that old scoreboard, but I was surprised at some of the problems we had while shooting there— things we hadn't anticipated. For instance, we had to use long lenses to compress the space between home plate and the stands. Very few professional ballparks have that kind of space anymore.

The biggest problem, though, and this was really awkward for us, was in finding enough white people to show up for the crowd scenes. I mean, you just couldn't advertise, "Drop in this afternoon and appear in a crowd scene for a movie." The crowds were segregated back then, and we couldn't very well advertise, "White people only." We hit on a great solution—Jimmy Buffett was a friend, and he wanted to do a cameo in the film, so we gave him the part of the amputee who was heckling Cobb so bad that Cobb went into the stands after him. That's Jimmy Buffett in that scene, though it's hard to recognize him. Jimmy agreed to give a concert, and I don't know how to say this, but we figured he wasn't going to draw too many

RON SHELTON, *former minor league infielder in the Orioles chain, wrote and directed* Bull Durham, Tin Cup, *and* Cobb. *The baseball scenes for* Cobb *were shot at Rickwood Field.*

black people. We asked the crowd who showed up to come back as extras in the baseball scenes. And it worked.

How good a ballpark is Rickwood? Put it this way—you couldn't build a movie set that authentic, or one that looks that good.

Ron Shelton is the writer/director who made the best baseball movie, Bull Durham, *the best basketball movie,* White Men Can't Jump, *and the best golf movie,* Tin Cup, *ever made, and several other movies besides. He is also a former minor league ballplayer who, while in the Orioles chain, played in Durham Athletic Park, which he immortalized in* Bull Durham. *In the summer of 1993 he filmed the baseball scenes for* Cobb, *his film biography of Ty Cobb with Tommy Lee Jones, at Rickwood Field.*

• • •

I COULDN'T WAIT TO GET THERE

as told by Jim Piersall

RICKWOOD FIELD turned my life around. I was moved to the Barons from Louisville in 1951, and I considered it a demotion. I was very resentful. But when I got to Birmingham I liked it, and I loved Rickwood immediately.

I could really hit there—I hit .346 with 15 home runs and 30 doubles in about 120 games, and scored 100 runs. I could see the ball well; you could even see the ball really well at night. I was pretty good at hitting into the gaps, and it restored my confidence. There were some big leaguers on the team, including Bobo Newsom, who pitched really well for the Barons that year, winning 16 games.

We had a good team in 1951, though we finished second, 10½ games in back of Little Rock. We didn't have a very good team in 1952, though there were some very good players on the team like Ken Aspromonte. Mostly, people said, because the Yankees were in charge, and they were moving players up and down through the system. I only got to play about twenty games in 1952, and I was hitting about .340, but then they moved me out.

I couldn't wait to get to the park, I loved playing there. But one thing I didn't love—there was no air-conditioning in the clubhouse. We sat outside in front of a big fan to cool off. I heard that the center field fence was about 450–470 before I got there, but that wasn't realistic to test a hitter's home run power, but it was moved in to about 400 feet by the time I got there.

The Birmingham fans were terrific. I mean the white fans and

JIM PIERSALL (*left*) *played for the Barons in 1951 and 1952, batting .346 and .339, respectively. He was such a good outfielder that many who saw both Piersall and Willie Mays insisted that he was as good or better defensively than Mays. He played for seventeen years in the major leagues, a career marred by emotional breakdowns chronicled in his autobiography,* Fear Strikes Out, *which was made into a movie with Anthony Perkins as Piersall.*

the black fans, too. They would put the black fans out in the right field bleacher area. They were great fans. They came to see the Black Barons and white Barons, too, and they got to know me—they cheered me on when I made a good play. I loved that.

There were all these signs—Blach's department store and others—where you could win free stuff if you hit the ball over the sign. You could win a free pair of pants, a suit, a jacket, even Fruit of the Loom underwear. It was like having a built-in bonus. I won several things from Blach's. I got to know the family and kept in touch with them after I left Birmingham.

Sometimes we'd drive out to Bessemer, about ten miles southwest of Birmingham. They had a big railroad car plant there—I don't know if it's there any more—but there was some good home cooking kind of restaurants. My favorite was the Bright Star, which I think is still there. It was run by a Greek family, I can't remember their name,* and you could have a really great, big lunch before a night game.

Our manager was Red Marion, the brother of Marty Marion, the great fielding shortstop of the St. Louis Cardinals. Speaking of fielding, I got to know a lot of the Black Barons while I was there. They usually only played on Sundays when we weren't in town, but sometimes the schedules overlapped. It was great to talk baseball with them. A couple of them told me, "You're almost as good as Willie Mays in the outfield." Well, that was a terrific compliment. That was something people liked to argue about in Birmingham, since Willie had been there playing with the Black Barons just a couple of years before me. But I'm going to say this: I'm not ashamed of my fielding statistics compared to Willie's. If you look us up, you'll see what I'm talking about.†

I always enjoyed seeing Willie. In 1954 the Giants came to Boston when I was playing for the Red Sox, and we had an exhibition game for the Jimmy Fund, which, as you know, was Ted Williams's favorite charity. They staged a special fielding and throwing contest

---

* It is still there, and still run by the Koikos family.

† Mays's career fielding percentage was .981, and he averaged 2.60 putouts per game to Piersall's .990 with 2.68 putouts per game.

for us before the game. My memory of it is that I won, but maybe I just want to remember it that way. Willie said something about me that I'll never forget: "He may be goofy, but he comes to play."

Jim Piersall played for two seasons with the Birmingham Barons and spent seventeen seasons in the major leagues, finishing with a batting average of .272 in 1,734 games. A two-time All-Star, he led the American League in fielding average three times. When he broke into the big leagues in 1953, Casey Stengel called him "the best right fielder I have ever seen," and many believed the same was true after he moved to center field.

To many, though, he was better known for his book, Fear Strikes Out, *and the fine film made from it starring Anthony Perkins, about his struggles with mental and emotional problems. As his entry in* Baseball: The Biographical Encyclopedia *puts it, "At a time when psychiatric disorders were rarely talked about, Piersall showed that they can indeed be conquered." Following baseball, he had a long career as a broadcaster for the Chicago White Sox and Texas Rangers, and in 1999 he served as a roving instructor for the Cubs system.*

• • •

TRADING A FREE PASS FOR A FOUL BALL

as told by Jimmy Nelson

FROM THE DAY I WAS BORN in 1926 until I signed a minor league contract, I lived within a few blocks of Rickwood. Rickwood was the place all of my friends and I wanted to be. When we were very young and did not have the price of admission, some of us would get on the outside of the fence of the first base side and the others would get on the third base side, hoping to get a foul ball. We always had balls to play with. About the seventh inning they would open the gates, and we would rush in to see what was left of the game. We always hoped that the team that was behind would tie it up so they would play extra innings.

We could watch more baseball with the Barons winning. We all hated the Atlanta Crackers, and I still have trouble pulling for the Braves.

The Barons started a Knothole Club. If you joined, you got a free cap on certain days, and we would get in to see the game. We all sat together way down the first base line. Later on, there were teams formed within the Knothole Club. We called our team Woodrow Wilson, after the grammar school we attended, and we won. I have a picture of Sunny Jim Downey presenting us with the championship trophy of the first Knothole Tournament.

The next baseball season was the greatest yet. My friends and I all got jobs as either ball boys or batboys. Our main job was to get as many foul balls back into the game as possible. We also had to go downtown to get scorecards. We would start with eighteen balls, and usually had twelve to fifteen when the game was over. The

Barons used these for practice. If a foul ball went into the stands, we would run up and try to get it back. Crowds were small in the late 1930s and early 1940s. If a fan wanted to keep the ball, we would offer a free pass to a future game—that usually got us the ball back.

Uncle Bud Clancy, Kirby Highbe, Hank Bauer, Chief Wood Arkeketa, Nick Polly, Clyde Shoun, Ray Lamanno, Art Luce, Fred Tauby, Gar Del Savio, Hank Madjeski, Dutch Mele, Howie Fox— these guys and many more meant as much to me as the Yankees to kids who grew up in New York.

I still live in Birmingham, but in the other end of town. When I get a chance, if I am near Rickwood, I stop by and, if it's open, I go in and look around. What great memories. I wish every kid could experience Rickwood as I knew it.

Jimmy Nelson played semipro baseball for the Rock Hill Owls. He is retired from Stockham Valve and Fittings. He was eighty-two when we spoke to him.

• • •

I GOT A HIT OFF SATCH

as told by Glenny Brock

ONE DAY IN THE SUMMER of 2001, during one of my trips to my old neighborhood in West End, I stopped at Rickwood Field. The park was open for maintenance, but I didn't see any people at all, and it appeared I had the baseball field all to myself. It suddenly occurred to me that I was alone on the same field that Babe Ruth, Ty Cobb, Satchel Paige, Dizzy Dean, Willie Mays, and Reggie Jackson had all played on.

I walked out to the diamond and mimed a turn at bat. I hit an imaginary home run—I can't remember who I hit it off of, but it might have been Satchel Paige. I was rounding the bases and had just reached second when I realized that a bunch of guys who worked at the park were watching me. I was embarrassed and began to slow down until I realized they were cheering. When I reached home plate, we were all laughing and laughing. One of them told me I was one of the greats.

Glenny Brock is the editor of the Birmingham Weekly *newspaper. She grew up in West End, a few miles from Rickwood Field, and graduated from John Carroll High School in Birmingham in 1995.*

• • •

OH WHERE, OH WHERE IS MY REGGIE BALL?

as told by Rob Studin

MY FIRST MEMORY of Rickwood Field was in 1960—I was eight—shortly after we moved to Birmingham and I had started playing Little League. My grandfather and father took me to my first professional game. I don't remember anything about the teams or the game. I do remember that my grandfather had somehow gotten box seats near the first base dugout, and I spent the whole game hanging on the rail.

I have a vivid memory of my grandfather leaning back and smoking one of his cigars while my dad and I split a bag of peanuts. My father was always working and was intense all of the time. I remember how relaxed and comfortable he was and how happy that made me feel.

Rickwood was the biggest ballpark I had ever seen, and when we walked in from the tunnel, I was in awe. I remember thinking how vivid the green of the field was and how brown and smooth the dirt in the base paths was. Birmingham had rocky "red clay" on all of the baseball fields I had ever seen. The field just seemed perfect to me.

I also remember a bad experience. A foul ball rolled over to the rail, and I leaned over and picked it up. An usher came down and took the ball away from me. He said I wasn't allowed to reach onto the field for a ball, and I had to give it back. I don't think he meant to, but he scared me and I started crying.

I don't remember going to games for a few years after that, but I developed a love for baseball and played it every chance I got. If it were just a game of "hit the bat" on Forest Avenue, some 3-3-3 over at the Jewish Community Center, a game of catch with a friend, or just throwing pop-ups to myself, I really loved baseball and still do. My passion for baseball was again renewed when the Braves moved to Atlanta in 1966, and I started going to games at Rickwood again.

In 1967 I was fifteen and hadn't discovered girls yet. I went to a lot of games that year. As I said, I was really in love with baseball; there was not a lot to do in Birmingham for fifteen-year-olds on a weeknight in the summer, and Birmingham had a great team. I remember reading about a new player who was supposed to be the next Willie Mays. You could tell Reggie Jackson was a great athlete just by looking at him. He looked very young to be a professional player. He was so strong. We used to go early to catch batting practice. He would frequently hit it over the right field grandstand roof. That team also had Joe Rudi, Dave Duncan, and Rollie Fingers. I obviously didn't know how great they were going to be, but you could tell they were going to make it to the big leagues. We would go down to the rail and say hi to the players before the game. They were pretty good guys and would talk to us if they had time.

I am not sure how many minor league and major league games I have been to in my lifetime, but other than the foul ball they made me give back, the only other ball I ever got at a game was in 1967. We were far down the right field side when Reggie hit a towering shot down the line. I can't remember whether it hit the top of the grandstand, the light standard, or something else, but I do remember it bounced back in my direction and I made a very nice catch. I held it up and got a round of applause, a hero for ten seconds. I sure wish I had kept that ball, but I probably ended up playing catch with it the next day!

Rob Studin and I lived across the street from each other in Mountain Brook, a Birmingham suburb, during our high school years. His father took me to my first football game, Alabama–Auburn in 1966, and my first Birmingham A's game. What Rob neglects to mention in his account is that he pushed me aside to grab the Reggie ball that he wishes he had now. As executive director of financial advisory services for Lincoln Financial, he has a direct tie to the Philadelphia Eagles. He and his wife, Joy, regularly attend University of Alabama football and basketball games, and he finds it "very frustrating that the only sport [he] can play is golf."

· · ·

THE BARONS WERE A MEMORY, RICKWOOD FIELD
LIKE A GRAVEYARD

by Paul Hemphill

MAINLY, I REMEMBER my first suit: a coarse wool double-breasted
number bought on a trip downtown to Blach's department store,
where I got a glimpse of Fred Hatfield, the Barons' nifty third baseman, on his off-season job in the men's department. . . .

In 1954 my beloved Birmingham Barons began to wear a Rebel
flag, like a chevron, on their uniform shirts. In '55 a black teenager
named Emmett Till was lynched in Mississippi for allegedly allowing
his eyes to linger too long on a white woman; a black domestic named
Rosa Parks refused to move to the rear of a city bus in Montgomery,
Alabama; and explosions began to rend the night air in Birmingham as
black churches and homes were dynamited (the total came to thirty-
one during the decade). A full-fledged bus boycott was under way in
Montgomery; riots erupted when a black woman named Autherine
Lucy tried to enroll at the University of Alabama, bad enough to
bring in the National Guard; Birmingham unilaterally outlawed the
National Association for the Advancement of Colored People, even
made it against the law for whites and blacks to gather together; and
civic "leaders" uncomfortable with the Klan's violent image formed the
White Citizens' Council to "protect states' rights." . . .

In November [of 1961] it was abruptly announced that the
entire system of city parks would be closed rather than integrated;
and that included Rickwood Field, home of the Barons, since some
teams in the Southern Association intended to have black players
during the '62 season. In the wake of the Freedom Riders and the

closing of the parks and a black boycott of downtown stores, there was a movement led by the relatively progressive Young Men's Business Club to change Birmingham's form of government from the three-man commission to a mayor and council—meaning, Get Bull [Connor] out of there. . . .

The final rounds of golf on public courses had been played on the last day of '61, and Connor's response to Washington's orders to integrate the city parks had been to fill with dirt the pool at East Lake Park where I had learned to swim. Connor, in a particularly spiteful move, had tried to shut down Jefferson County's surplus food program, whose ten thousand recipients were ninety percent black. The Barons were a memory, Rickwood Field like a graveyard.

Paul Hemphill, who died in 2009, was one of the finest journalists ever to come out of Birmingham. His 1970 book on country music, The Nashville Sound, *was a major best-seller, and in 1987 his baseball novel,* Long Gone, *was made into a fine film starring William Petersen and Virginia Madsen. I was lucky enough to share a couple of afternoons at Rickwood with Paul, who was a treasure-house of fact and lore about Rickwood Field, the Barons, and the Black Barons. These excerpts are from his 1993 memoir,* Leaving Birmingham: Notes of a Native Son.

• • •

SAYING GOODBYE TO RICKWOOD (1987)

by Alf Van Hoose

I always thought my mother's flowers presented extra beauty because she nurtured them with so much love.

Old Rickwood, though degenerating dowdily through cracked cosmetics in recent years, is a special rose, of sorts, to me. Maybe because I love that place.

It has provided such a grand enrichment site for us through years that have flown so swiftly.

Ah, the friendships bonded there for me on relaxed spring and summer afternoons....

Cowboy Rogers, genuine character, was up there, too, before Western Union was trumped by fancy computers....

So many Rickwood player-alumni surface to memory, Willie Mays leading off. I was official scorer for Tom Hayes' Black Barons when this unmatched talent was known only to a handful of voting Birmingham citizens....

Walt Dropo, the Big Moose from Moosup, who could forget him? Or George Wilson, the bragging slugger, or Bobo Newsom, the fat, foxy pitcher winning a few as he traveled down the dark side of a colorful career....

Flag-year 1967 was significant by explosion of talent, future Hall of Famers Reggie Jackson and Rollie Fingers, plus Dave Duncan and a better big-league prospect than Fingers, George Lauzerique. Lauzerique squandered God-given talents.

Duty didn't call me to Rickwood Tuesday night. Nostalgia did.

Rico Petrocelli's[*] blazing Barons made more big-league plays in a 10–0 frolic over Charlotte than in any game I recall. . . .

It was another entertaining Rickwood drama. There have been thousands. There could be a rousing final tonight.

I won't be there. I waved goodbye to pro baseball at Rickwood Field Tuesday night. There were no tears—only, silently, "Thanks, ancient friend, for all the memories."

Alf Van Hoose, born in 1920, was a journalist and sportswriter for forty-three years, including sports editor of the Birmingham News for twenty-one years, and a regular columnist ten years before that. He was one of the good guys. He covered all sports and wrote about the Black Barons at a time when Bull Connor didn't approve. In fact, many white fans got their first knowledge of Birmingham's black baseball heroes from Van Hoose's columns. He died in 1997, at the age of seventy-six. These excerpts are from the Birmingham News, *September 17, 1987.*

• • •

---

[*] Rico Petrocelli was a slugging shortstop from Brooklyn who put in twelve years in the big leagues, all with the Boston Red Sox, for whom he played 1,553 games at shortstop and third base, hitting 210 home runs, including 40 in 1969. He managed the Barons in 1987 and 1988.

REGGIE SMILED FOR ME

as told by Buddy Coker

My favorite Rickwood memories:

Camera Day, Birmingham A's, 1967. As a twelve-year-old, I took my Kodak Instamatic out to Rickwood expecting a large crowd to get photos of the Birmingham A's. The A's were getting publicity for having some big-time prospects in Joe Rudi, Dave Duncan, Reggie Jackson, and George Lauzerique.* I was surprised at the sparse turnout, even though sparse turnouts were the norm during the A's years in Rickwood. I was able to wander all around the field and take snapshots (all black and white—I'm assuming color film was available but probably too expensive). I remember strolling out to right field and taking Reggie's photo. There was no one else around; he was not garnering any of the attention he would be receiving in a few years, and he seemed pleased to take a minute for the photo op. The smile in the photo still seems genuine.

Reggie remains a favorite player of mine. I recall the photo of him with the Bear when the Yankees visited Tuscaloosa—two of my sports heroes.† I had hoped through the years to be able to get Reggie's autograph on my picture in person at a card show or some other opportunity. I recently had that accomplished by mail order.

---

* All four would become stars with the A's in the major leagues except Lauzerique, who had boundless talent but burned out after playing just thirty-four big league games in four seasons.
† See page 297.

Atlanta Braves vs. Southern League All-Stars, August 17, 1970. Me and my autograph-hound buddies went early for batting practice. These were pre–cable TV, pre-TBS days, so the chance to see our favorite team, the Braves, in person was a must (thanks to caring and accommodating parents). I was starved to see major league baseball. Even though the Braves had been in Atlanta for a few years, Atlanta did not seem as close to Birmingham as it does now. Hank Aaron was our favorite Brave, and my favorite major leaguer, now that Mickey Mantle had retired. We were able to get Hank's autograph during batting practice; he was very cooperative about signing for young fans. The next day, my brother and I were shown in a photo in the *Birmingham Post-Herald* getting Hank's autograph with the caption "Big Moment." It certainly was.

In 1982 the Braves played another exhibition game. As a twenty-seven-year-old, I'm still in the autograph game. We went around to the Braves locker room and stood by the door. There was no security. Suddenly someone flings the door open from the inside, obviously not expecting a crowd outside. There are players and coaches in various stages of dress or undress. Pitching coach Bob Gibson, who is in a stage of complete undress, angrily shouts for someone to "shut that damn door."

Exhibition games with major league teams—Braves, Yankees, Senators, Red Sox, and Orioles all make appearances at Rickwood in the early 1970s.

The 1971 game featured the Yankees versus the Red Sox (I think). My mom chatted with fellow Kansan, Yankee manager Ralph Houk. I got autographs from Thurman Munson, Elston Howard, and my favorite Yankees of that day, Mel Stottlemyre and Bobby Murcer (who was also from Kansas). That same year, the Washington Senators, who were managed by Ted Williams, played the Braves in an exhibition game at Rickwood. Big Frank Howard of the Senators hit a massive home run. It seemed to start out as a line drive that continued to rise as it soared over the left center field wall. Powerful!

In 1972 Denny McLain tried a heavily publicized comeback at Rickwood. As I remember, there was a big crowd to see the last 30-game winner but he never did really make it back to the big time. It was exciting to see him, though.

I believe Dr. Robert Day of Birmingham played a big role in bringing the major league exhibition games to Birmingham. I think Dr. Day worked at Jefferson State Junior College with my dad. We always had great seats at these games. Dr. Day also arranged for me to get a seat behind home plate at the 1972 All-Star game played in Atlanta—another big thrill.

Buddy Coker, Vestavia High School, class of '73, grew up in Birmingham and graduated from the University of Alabama in 1977, going on to a sales and marketing career in industrial chemicals. Buddy LOVES baseball and has been going to Rickwood games for over forty years. He has been an avid card collector and Strat-O-Matic enthusiast since he was a teenager.

. . .

WILLIE KNEW WE MOVED THE SCOREBOARD
TWENTY-FOUR FEET

as told by Coke Matthews

FIRST AND FOREMOST, like so many, my touchstone memory of Rickwood begins with my father. Though a huge baseball fan, he was certainly the type of man who would have blended perfectly into the black-and-white photographs of baseball fans of the day— white starched shirt, pants high, thin belt, tie loosened. My first memory of Rickwood, besides getting into games free by wearing my Little League uniform, was Reggie Jackson and the A's of 1967. I was twelve, and when my Cleveland Indian/Rocky Colavito–loving grandfather came down to visit, my father retorted, "We have Reggie Jackson."

To Rickwood we went—and though I remember the game itself because of the buzz that Campy Campaneris was getting and those ceiling fans inside of Rickwood—what scorched my senses was Reggie Jackson taking batting practice. He was so much bigger than everybody else—with those A's sleeveless shirts accentuating his massive arms. And the balls just flew off his bat, one after another, up onto the right field roof or over the fence and out of sight. It was mind-boggling. It was better than the state fair. The game was almost anticlimactic. Charlie-O the Mule, Rollie Fingers sans mustache, and orange baseballs were also part of the Rickwood scene, but I only remember the details of Reggie.

The "restoration" story—and one that has played out over and over again—is the deep satisfaction each member of the Friends of Rickwood gets when we have the pleasure of hosting a veteran ballplayer or fan who is returning to the old ballpark for the first time since his playing days. My personal experiences include "wow" moments with the likes of pitcher Tommy Lasorda, Don Newcombe, Vida Blue, and Walt Dropo, all of whom told the fans, "It hasn't changed a bit" or "It is just how I remembered it." This, of course, is music to the ears of the group who had a hard time explaining to skeptics why it was important to replace the "modern" electronic scoreboard with a hand-operated scoreboard, right out of the collective memory of many generations of baseball fans and players alike.

The ultimate moment for this baseball fan came when Willie Mays, fellow Birmingham native and object of the baseball card–collecting frenzy of my youth, returned to Rickwood for the first time in several decades. He walked slowly out to home plate, glasses on top of his head, looking out to center field the whole way, not talking. I couldn't stand it; I had to ask, "So, first time here in a while . . . ?" His reply was "You moved the scoreboard." It wasn't a complaint or even an accusation. It was a fact: when we rebuilt it, it was about 24 feet off the original foundation. He knew exactly where it was supposed to be. Exactly. He ruled that ballpark briefly in his youth, and to many Rickwood will always bear his imprint.

Coke Matthews lives within a mile of the house he grew up in, in the Birmingham neighborhood of Crestline. He graduated from Mountain Brook High School in 1973 and has enjoyed careers as an attorney, as advertising executive, and, currently, as head of development for Children's Hospital, a job he loves. He considers himself a utility infielder.

• • •

"COACH BRYANT, WOULD YOU PLEASE SIGN THIS?"

as told by Joe DeLeonard

IN 1967 MY FATHER, an uncle, a cousin, and I went to see a baseball game at Rickwood Field. *Live*, not on television, but actually *at* the game.

My first Rickwood memorable moment occurred even before I set foot in the stadium. While waiting to get tickets, I found myself staring at a tall man who was also in line. This man seemed huge to me. To a seven-year-old, he was a giant, the biggest man I had ever seen. I had a hard time looking up, he was so tall. There was something familiar about him, though I couldn't quite say where I knew him from.

There was some kind of problem; I didn't know what it was, but his tickets weren't at the window. The tall man was grumbling at someone in the box office window. My dad looked over at the commotion, grabbed my program from me, held it out to the giant, and said, "Coach Bryant, would you please sign this?" The tall man forgot momentarily his problem and graciously signed.

My dad and uncle both chuckled—now they had a story to tell when they got home. I suddenly realized it was the same man I had seen on TV on the *Bear Bryant Show* every Sunday afternoon. My father told me my eyes got big as saucers.

Once inside the stadium, a whole new world appeared. Indeed, I had watched baseball on TV, with an announcer describing the action, but now inside the stadium it was totally different. My seven-year-old eyes could not follow all the action, and I often had to ask my father what had happened. Between the action and excitement, there was just too much to absorb at one time.

The highlight came when the A's won the game in the last inning on a home run. I thought the outfielder for the visiting team caught the ball, but was puzzled because the hometown crowd was clapping and cheering. My uncle told me it wasn't an out but a grand slam home run and we had won 7–6. I was baffled because I had never heard the words "grand slam" before.

I asked, "Who hit this home run?"

The reply was "Let's see? Jackson. Hmm, his name is Reggie Jackson."

Jackson's home run that night spoke volumes to me over the years. Reggie could run his mouth all he wanted to about how mistreated he had been in Birmingham during his brief stay or what it was like to grow up black in America in the 1960's and not make a dent with me. However, his home run made me think about "opportunity" and how everyone should have the right to succeed or fail on his own terms. His home run was far louder than his mouth! I didn't care that he was black. As a seven-year-old, I just knew he won the game for Birmingham.

I had no way of knowing this player would have a flair for the dramatic his whole career! The baseball fans in Birmingham were privileged to see a sample of greatness a couple of years before the rest of the nation. And on top of that I got to meet Bear Bryant! I became a fan for life!

Joe DeLeonard graduated from Vestavia Hills High School in 1969 and from the University of Alabama in Birmingham. Though he is an accountant by trade, his passionate hobby is collecting sports memorabilia.

· · ·

A GREAT-LOOKING TOWN

as told by Walt Dropo

I REMEMBER BIRMINGHAM as a great-looking town, wonderful to drive through. Here were nice-looking parks almost everywhere. Rickwood was a perfect miniature of major league parks that were still around in the early fifties. I'd say it was a combination of Shibe Park in Philadelphia and Forbes Field in Pittsburgh.

A lot of people called it a pitcher's park because of the space between home and the grandstand, which ate up all those pop flies. But I heard that Willie Mays and Jimmy Piersall thought it was a

ON MAY 21, 1948, *Walt Dropo made headlines around the country with a 467-foot blast. General manager Eddie Glennon marked the spot where the ball cleared the scoreboard with an X.*

hitter's park—and I'm with them. The visibility was great because of the background. When the pitcher released the ball, you could get a good look at it coming out of his hand. In that way it reminded me of Fenway Park in Boston.

My favorite landmark? I'd say the Tutwiler Hotel, an old-fashioned, elegant place to stay in the downtown area.*

Walt Dropo is a thirteen-year major league veteran, having played with the Boston Red Sox, Detroit Tigers, Chicago White Sox, Cincinnati Reds, and Baltimore Orioles from 1949 to 1961. In 1950 he hit .322 with 34 home runs and led the American League with 144 runs batted in to win the Rookie of the Year Award. He lives with his family in Beverly, Massachusetts, and his page on baseball-reference.com is sponsored by his grandchildren.

• • •

---

* The Tutwiler, which opened in 1913, was built to accommodate meetings of the American Iron and Steel Institute; developers hoped the grand hotel would encourage more steel interests to locate in Birmingham. Noted for its unusual design—it had no interior rooms and featured balconies overlooking the grand lobby—the Tutwiler was for years "the" place to stay and have a party in Birmingham. Among notable events were a press conference for Charles Lindbergh and a wedding party for actress Tallulah Bankhead. The original Tutwiler was demolished in 1974 to make way for a new bank building, but the name and the prosperity it symbolized lived on. In 1985 funding was secured to convert a period apartment building into the new Tutwiler, which is open today on Twentieth Street near the courthouse.

THE OLD WARRIOR IS HAUNTED

as told by Bill Lumpkin

EXCEPT FOR THREE YEARS in the Korean War and three years working on an Augusta, Georgia, newspaper, I've always lived in walking distance of Rickwood Field. I'll be eighty-two on my next birthday, and, oh, how many times did I walk as a youth to cheer the Barons, and, oh, how many times later did I sit in the Rickwood pressbox when covering games as a sportswriter, or drop by and sit in the stands to watch the last few innings when getting off from work early at night.

Even today, since the Barons deserted their original home and moved over the mountain to a more affluent white neighborhood, I'll drive by on the way to a doctor's appointment or to Walmart, stop, and remember.

The Old Warrior has changed. The fences have been re-commercialized to present a Ty Cobb–era appearance for the filming of the movie *Cobb*. As a kid, there was never a Bull Durham sign on an outer wall. There is now. I hated it when Birmingham reentered baseball in 1964 after a three-year baseball abstention, signed a working agreement with Kansas City Athletics owner Charlie Finley, who contended to be a former (1931) Baron batboy, and who later changed the name from Barons to Athletics and disgraced the Old Warrior by painting it a disgusting Kelly green and Fort Knox gold. The players looked like Bozos wearing those colors.

But that's not what I remember. . . . The Old Warrior is haunted. It has its ghosts, and when I walk into that empty old ball yard today I see them and, if I listen, I can hear them. . . . I'm one of the boys of summer once again.... The sun's sticky hot, hotter than four hundred hells, Uncle Ernest used to say; the red bricks on Ensley Avenue were steaming.

We're on our way to Rickwood. The Barons are playing. We'd skip and jump, kick rocks, take off our tennis shoes and tie them around our neck and go barefooted. Up the gravel trolley bed, past Burger Joe's, and rest at Wood's Pharmacy. Milk shakes were only a nickel. It didn't cost me or my brother a cent. Daddy let us charge them. His monthly bill was $3 once, all milk shakes, and I remember him telling us his bill was too high and to cut back or he'd cut us off.

The best place to walk was on the trolley bed, which divided Ensley Avenue. You didn't have to worry. Traffic was nil, and it was no problem getting off when you heard old No. 5 rumbling down the rails to Fairfield, or headed in the other direction to within a block of Rickwood on its way downtown. I don't remember any of us ever riding the trolley to Rickwood, but a lot of fans sure did.

There was a trolley spur that ran down Twelfth Street and dead-ended right at the right field side entrance. But the tracks have long since been removed.

This was a typical Birmingham June, July, or August, before and after World War II. The Barons were in town, and Rickwood was the place a kid on the West Side had to be. This was the big league in this world of Birmingham youth. The greatest players played at Rickwood. Has there ever been a better hitter than Charley Workman, although he did play for those dreaded Nashville Vols, who always had a lineup full of southpaw batters. But if there is a better hitter than the Barons' Dutch Mele, well, I haven't seen him.

We were walking to see the Barons ... Chuck Aleno, Jodie Beeler, Eddie Lyons, Ed Heusser, Johnny Conway, Rocky Stone,

Jake Daniel (he sure struck out a lot), Nick Polly, Mike Dejan, and what about Bill Thaxton (1943) and Ben Catchings (1944), who jumped right from a Birmingham amateur baseball league into the Barons' starting lineup. Ben sure stole a lot of bases. Hank Sauer still might be the greatest long ball hitter the Barons have ever had. He once hit a home run over the left field scoreboard when it was against the outer cement wall. I read where his ball traveled 405 feet before clearing the 33-foot scoreboard. (The scoreboard had been moved in 65 feet closer when Dropo's drive cleared it.)

Once Mrs. Minnie Little brought a real-life, breathing Baron named Gene Bradley to visit us. Mrs. Little was a good friend of my mom. Her husband, Frank, ran the Shell service station, a block from Rickwood, on the corner of Twelfth and Bessemer Road. Many of the Barons would stop in there for a Coke after games.

Bradley went out in the street and hit fungoes with us. What a treat that was. Surely, someday, he'd make the big leagues.

Like a snake making its way over hot coals, we'd slowly make our way along Bessemer Road (Third Avenue), pick up a stick and drag it across the wooden fence that kept kids out of the fairgrounds when the state fair was in town. Well, it didn't keep us out. We could climb it, or sneak in on the back side where there was no fence.

We'd take a shortcut thought Rising Station, a Negro neighborhood, maybe stop and chat. In those days, nobody had air-conditioning and everybody sat on the front porch or out in the yard. When the Barons returned in 1964 and integrated, the Barons would open the gates after the seventh inning, and many blacks sitting in their yards would come in and sit in the grandstand and watch the last few innings.

Now the challenge. Most of us belonged to the Knothole Gang. All we had to do was wear our cap and show our Knothole member-

ship card and get in free to sit in the left field bleachers, which was a
great place, because the left fielder was close enough to talk to.

But there was just something about walking through the gate.
We'd put on our shoes and stand across the street from the right
field grandstand and close to the house where Bill Walker, the caretaker, lived. We'd wait until the crowd thinned and watch for Mr.
Walker. He'd throw us out if he caught us. Then, as if by signal, we'd
break for the chain-link fence, up and over, and we were inside. We
had done it again.

We could have gone around to the back where it was easier to
slip in. There was a hole in the barbed wire when the chain-link
fence met the concrete wall. The only people who could see us there
were boys working the scoreboard, and we went to school with them.
Heck, you had to sit in the bleachers if we slipped in there.

I do remember times when we did walk in free as Knotholers.
Those days were in 1943 and 1944 when Pete Gray played for the
Memphis Chicks, and he played leftfield, not a stone's throw from
where we sat in the front row.

Pete Gray had only one arm, and he later went to the big leagues
and played for the St. Louis Browns. We kids were awestruck. Pete
would catch a fly ball, throw the ball up in the air, stick his glove
under right nub, catch the ball, and make his throw. Time after time,
he did this to cheers from the left field bleachers. Pete was so good
that he was selected as the Southern Association's Player of the Year
in 1933.

An ironic twist to this is that in those same two seasons a one-
arm outfielder was playing for the Chicks at Rickwood, the Barons
played an outfielder named Dick Sipek. He was a deaf mute and the
Barons' MVP.

Rickwood also has its romances. James Sutton was one of us

boys of summer. We played softball together. He never slipped in. He always went with his parents and sat in the grandstand, where he met Faye Guy. They later married.

And there was first baseman Norm Zauchin, who met his wife when chasing a foul ball and fell into her lap in the grandstand.

Bill Lumpkin grew up in Ensley, a suburb of Birmingham near Rickwood Field, and has followed the Barons since he was a boy. He started at the Birmingham Post (later the Post Herald) as an office boy and was sports editor from 1959 until his retirement in 1994.

• • •

THAT OLD-TIME BASEBALL ATMOSPHERE

as told by Reggie Jackson

MY BEST MEMORY of playing in Birmingham was hitting a home run near the light tower in right field. I think it went more than halfway up—they put an X to mark the spot. I think you can still see my X today. They told me at the time that no one had ever hit a ball up there. I don't know if anyone has since. I don't know if it was the longest home run ever hit at Rickwood Field, but I bet it was one of the longest.

I didn't get around much while I was in Birmingham. This was after the height of the civil rights era, and while it wasn't anything like what I was told it was like in the early 1960s, it was no picnic for a black man—at least for one who didn't know his way around. When I first got there, I stayed with two guys I later played with on the Oakland A's, Dave Duncan and Joe Rudi. For the first few days I slept on their couch. Then Joe told me that their landlord was going to evict them if I didn't leave. Man, this was in 1967. Joe got indignant and said that he was going to move out, but I told him not to do that, I'd find my own place. I moved to the Bankhead, which was named after the Bankhead family—you know, Tallulah Bankhead, the actress. It was one of the few places in the downtown area that would rent apartments to black people.

I was voted Southern League Player of the Year for the 1967 season, and we won the Dixie World Series. The baseball was good, and, of course, we were a great team. I got on fine with all the white guys on the team, and, of course, we later won championships

TWO HALL OF FAMERS: *Paul "Bear" Bryant, winner of six national football championships at the University of Alabama, listens intently as Reggie Jackson describes one of his prodigious home runs. Bryant, an enthusiastic baseball fan, was a close friend of Yankees owner George Steinbrenner, who brought the team to Alabama in 1978 for an exhibition game. Bryant had seen Jackson play at Rickwood in 1967, as well as Willie Mays in 1948.*

together at Oakland. But some of the sportswriters thought I was a little bit too cocky, especially after I hit a long home run. I really didn't care much what they thought, but there was a couple of the old guys who were pretty good. [Alf] Van Hoose and [Bill] Lumpkin were good to talk to.

Rickwood was a great park. I didn't see much of the old National League parks before they tore them down, but Rickwood Field reminded me a lot of Fenway in Boston—you know, that old-time baseball atmosphere.

Reginald Martinez Jackson was born in Wyncote, Pennsylvania, attended college at Arizona State University, and played in the major leagues for twenty-two seasons, earning three World Series rings with the Oakland A's and two with the New York Yankees. He hit 563 home runs during his career, was the American League's Most Valuable Player in 1973, and was chosen for fourteen All-Star teams. He retired after the 1987 season and was inducted into the Hall of Fame in 1993.

• • •

I WISH I HAD LEFT MY *X* THERE

as told by Ernie Banks

I BELIEVE I WAS ONE of the last players to come out of the Negro Leagues and into the major leagues. I began playing professional baseball a year after I graduated from high school. In 1950 "Cool Papa" Bell, who was the manager of the Kansas City Monarchs, asked me to barnstorm with him. Jackie Robinson was on that team. I was too shy to talk to him very much and felt lucky that he sometimes talked to me. He was very encouraging to me and said he thought I could make it in the big leagues.

I was in the Army in 1951 and 1952, and was lucky enough to play some ball while I was there and keep in shape. When I got out of the Army, I went back to the Monarchs. Buck O'Neil was the manager. I had an ankle injury and really got discouraged, but Buck talked me into coming back, and I was glad he did. Everyone knew that the Negro Leagues were fading. There was too much interest in the major leagues and which black players would be going up.

We played the Barons in Birmingham, and everyone talked about the fierce rivalry the Barons and the Monarchs had had just a few years earlier. Attendance wasn't great when I was there, but there was still some of that spirit of the rivalry. It was just a beautiful park with scoreboards and clock and all. I was happy in later years that I got to play in a ballpark like Wrigley Field that had the same kind of neighborhood feel, and though there was a lot of racial hostility around at the time, the white fans that came out to see us were very appreciative of our baseball.

They had *X*'s around the park to mark some of the long home runs that had been hit there. I always wanted to leave my X there, but I never did. I regret that. Sometimes over the years I thought about maybe going back so I could leave my X.

Ernest "Ernie" Banks, aka Mr. Cub, was born in Dallas, Texas, in 1931. He played eighteen full seasons in the major leagues. He hit 512 home runs, led the National League in home runs twice and RBIs twice, and won back-to-back Most Valuable Player Awards in 1958 and 1959. He was elected to the Hall of Fame in 1977.

• • •

A HOME RUN FIRST TIME UP

as told by Willie Mays

I GUESS YOU COULD SAY I was discovered by Piper Davis when
I was playing high school baseball. I remember my first at-bat at
Rickwood Field—I hit a home run. I can't remember now where I
hit it, but I think it was an opposite-field home run to right, where
the fences were a little shorter. The next time I got up to bat, I got
knocked down by a pitch. I mean, *knocked down*. The pitch hit me.
I don't think that's what the pitcher intended to do; I think he was
just throwing close, and I didn't know how to get out of the way. You
might call it a fast education. Piper came running out and talked to
me while I was still down. He said, "Can you get up and go to first?"
I said, "Yes." He said, "Good. When you get there, you steal second.
That will show them that they didn't scare you."

We had such a great team that year, in 1948. Bill Greason was a
fine pitcher, and Artie Wilson and Jimmy Zapp were such fine players. The moment I got back in Rickwood Field and looked around,
I noticed where the scoreboard was. I noticed they brought in the
fence—center field was deeper when I played. To tell you the truth,
I wish it hadn't been quite so deep when I played. It was a little scary
being seventeen years old and having to cover all that territory.

I live in San Francisco now, but I love to come home. I like
to talk to kids around here about baseball. I think I can make a
difference. We're losing so many good athletes to football and basketball. I want to try and get kids to stick with baseball. It's the
greatest game.

The "Say Hey" Kid, Willie Howard Mays, was born in Westfield, Alabama, just outside Birmingham, in 1931. As a teenager he was a sensation at football, basketball, and baseball and at seventeen starred on the Birmingham Black Barons Negro National League champions. In 1951 he was Rookie of the Year for the pennant-winning New York Giants. Over a twenty-two-year career he hit .302 with 660 home runs and 338 stolen bases while winning two Most Valuable Player awards. He is regarded by many as the greatest all-around player in baseball history.

Author's note: Paul Hemphill and I interviewed Mr. Mays on February 26, 2006, at the ESPN Classic at Rickwood Field.

• • •

BASEBALL IS A GAME FOR FATHERS
AND SONS

as told by Courtney Haden

EVERY STUDENT OF BASEBALL, from Abner Doubleday's kid down, has observed that baseball is a game for fathers and sons, and I concur. I cite my own father, a brilliant physician out of Blount County who took no passing interest in athletic competition of any sort. Nevertheless, when I reached a certain age, he called us a cab (he was no driver) and took us out to spend evenings at Rickwood Field.

It was vivid and green in a particular hue, and it shows up in my dreams periodically. I still have the fragments of a felt pennant I bought at Rickwood that season; unaccountably I remember Cal Ermer was the manager. I have a ball scrawled with names of yore: Grzenda, Limmer, Regan. I cannot remember a single play from any particular game.

Years later, able to find Rickwood by myself, I came out to watch the baseball circus that Charlie Finley had brought to town. Of all the stars to be, the one I noticed always was Bert Campaneris, lithe and weightless at short. I remembered every play he made. I was reading Heinlein that summer and thought of Campy as the Stranger in a Strange Land.

I'm scouting a young recruit now. She's only four, but she rocks a ball cap, and one of these years we'll roll out to Rickwood to catch nine innings. Who knows, maybe we'll take a cab for auld lang syne.

Courtney Haden is a Birmingham native whose local prominence crested during stints on FM radio during the 1980s and 1990s. Having survived celebrity's savage undertow, he writes for area publications even as he toils at the legendary Boutwell Recording Studios.

• • •

THE NIGHT "WICKI WOOD" FELL OFF
THE DUGOUT

as told by Sherry Northington

ONE NIGHT IN THE OUTFIELD, there was a burst of pitchers from the bullpen. There apparently was a couch in the bullpen and we do not know how it caught on fire, but the pitchers luckily got out without harm.

Pam and Sherry remember sitting in the two seats in front of the bats where the players would come to collect their bats before going on deck. We would sit and tell each one Good Luck.

One night it was frigidly cold, and Art Clarkson, who was not known for giving away free items, gave out free hot chocolate, but there were only ten people in the crowd. This was the reason he decided to splurge on the fans.

One night "Wicki Wood"—the team mascot, who can best be described as resembling an anteater—fell off the dugout because he was dancing backwards and then got stuck between the fence and dugout opening and he could not get out. He did not mean to fall off, which we think he wanted us to believe. The players were laughing along with the crowd.

On the way to the Barons game at Rickwood, Gene Northington, a Birmingham firefighter, heard on his fire radio about a fire on the way to the ballpark. His two daughters, Pam and Sherry, were in the car and didn't want to be late to the game. He arrived there before any assistance did; he managed to break a window and save a man from the burning building. He received Firefighter of the Year that year because of this.

Sherry Northington and her sister, Pam, were raised on the Birmingham Barons. Their father, Gene, belonged to the Birmingham Bees when he was a teenager.

• • •

SNEAKING OUT TO RICKWOOD

as told by David Wininger

I WAS ACTUALLY a pretty good kid, and never was in any serious trouble. I was also not particularly adventuresome until, at age twelve, I really wanted to go to a Barons game but had no one to take me. My best friend, Bill Smith, and I devised a plan to get out to Rickwood on our own. We walked from the Southside of Birmingham to the downtown area, which was maybe three or four miles. Then we caught a bus that went out to the western part of town where Rickwood is located. We did not sneak in but actually paid the quarter it cost for a kid. And there we were, sitting in our own seats at the grand old stadium to enjoy the night game. One of the distinctive things I remember about that night is the sound that the high pop foul makes when the ball bangs down upon the roof. The grandstands are covered from beyond third base to beyond first base. The roof has the most distinctive sound in all of organized baseball. (I can say that today because I have been to a lot of major league parks.)

We had a great time and gave little thought as to how we would get home. Instead of sitting, we watched the game walking completely around the stadium from the right field line to the left field line and back again several times. Along about the third inning, we were headed from left field back toward home plate. I looked up and, to my astonishment, saw my dad, D. B. Wininger, and Bill's dad, Wayne C. Smith, coming toward us. Thrilled to see my father, I exclaimed, "Hi there, what are you guys doing here?"

It was about at that point when it occurred to me what the

fathers were doing there. The glints in the eyes of both dads were evidence that they had come looking for us. We knew we were in a bit of trouble as we were grabbed by the napes of our neck and ushered out of the ballpark. We are both lawyers in Birmingham and still agree that this was one of the worst things we ever did as kids, but it was worth it. We had a great time. I still go to Rickwood at least once a month year round, and I always think of Bill's father, who was one hundred years old on November 2, 2009, just shortly before the hundredth anniversary of the ballpark. Rickwood will always have that memory for me.

David Wininger is a trial lawyer and real estate developer in Birmingham, Alabama. He is a major collector of New York Yankees and Alabama Crimson Tide memorabilia and has been actively involved in the restoration of Rickwood Field as a board member of the Friends of Rickwood.

· · ·

I DON'T REMEMBER A THING

as told by Rollie Fingers

You want my memories of Rickwood and the A's? I'm afraid you're out of luck. I can tell you about Reggie. He was very quiet and kept to himself a lot in Birmingham. He was a lot more outgoing in Oakland. That's when he became a colorful character.

I remember that after all the bad stuff that happened in Birmingham during the civil rights era how calm everything seemed in 1967. I was pleasantly surprised. The city was very nice, the parks and all, though on some days there was a haze from the factories that made me cough a little, and sometimes made my eyes itch.

The first time I saw Rickwood I thought I had stepped back in time. There were still a lot of old parks then, but when you saw Rickwood you could almost see guys like Shoeless Joe Jackson and Satchel Paige running around in it.

But I really can't tell you much more. The first time I pitched there—it might have been the first pitch I threw, I don't remember[*]—the ball came right back and smashed me in the face. Broke my cheekbone, gave me a huge black eye, really knocked me out. I spent a lot of time in the hospital, and when I got out I pitched pretty well—or so they tell me. I swear, I don't remember a thing, not a damn thing . . .

---

[*] According to the account in the *Birmingham News*, Fingers was hit by the line drive in the fourth inning.

Roland Glen Fingers was born in Steubenville, Ohio, in 1946, pitched in American Legion ball, and was a mediocre starting pitcher for Charlie Finley's Oakland A's before becoming a relief pitcher. Voted to seven All-Star teams, he led the American League in saves three times and picked up three World Series rings with the A's. He was elected to the Hall of Fame in 1992. He also picked up a championship ring with the 1967 Birmingham A's.

• • •

EVERY DAY I GOT TO SEE RICKWOOD FIELD
WAS A GOOD DAY

as told by Bob Scranton

EDDIE GLENNON was from Philadelphia. We were a couple of Yankees, and when we first went south to work for the New Orleans team after World War II, I guess people had some problems with our attitudes. It was very much of culture shock, but we loved the South and I loved working with Eddie on the Barons. Every day I got to see Rickwood Field was a good day.

Eddie was the first person connected with the Barons who had a really good relationship with the Black Barons, and I was proud to be part of that. Sometimes it was just the simple things he did—like finally letting the Black Barons use the some facilities as the white players. That seems obvious now, but it wasn't then.

I tell you, I really loved the food in Louisiana and in Alabama, too. I had never even *heard* of barbecue back then. My job was called "traveling secretary," but that's just because they had to call me something. There were so many things to do. In Double-A ball you didn't need a traveling secretary, because they only traveled on buses. We traveled by bus to some cities, train to others, and to a few, planes— I think Little Rock, Arkansas, was the first city we flew to, and we flew when we played the teams in the Texas Leagues. It was a bus ride to Atlanta, but we always took a train to New Orleans; it was a beautiful train ride down there.

When we were home, I worked like hell from nine in the morning till midnight. On the road, my job was mostly taking care of the players, dealing with emergencies. Most of the emergencies involved money, as when someone had to send money home in a hurry or something like that. It was fun to seek out the really good restaurants wherever we were. I tell you one of the things that I loved so much about the job was meeting all those young guys who were going to become big-league ballplayers and following their careers in the major leagues. I also loved the opportunity to meet managers and players of big-league teams when they came down to Rickwood.

Who do I remember best? Oh, I don't know, but I sure remember meeting a funny-looking guy named Yogi Berra in 1948. He was very friendly, very open, and seemed very happy to be in Alabama.

I had a great career. I have nine beautiful children, and I got to work in baseball almost my whole life. What more can you ask?

Bob Scranton was born in Connecticut in 1923. In 1946, he was hired by the New Orleans Pelicans of the Southern Association. In the next season, he came north to Birmingham with Eddie Glennon. The next twenty-two years he served as the Barons' traveling secretary. In 1979 he was working with the Memphis Chicks with Art Clarkson, who in 1980 became principal owner of the Barons and brought Scranton back to Birmingham with him as a part owner. Retired now, he lives in Mapletown, a suburb of Atlanta. His pride and joy is his granddaughter, Caroline Harkins.

• • •

TO THINK I WAS A PART OF IT FOR TEN YEARS
IS A GREAT HONOR

as told by Art Clarkson

I WAS AN EX-FOOTBALL PLAYER—I played arena league—and once sold tickets for the Southern California Suns of the World Football League. I never expected to make a lot of money, but working in sports was something I loved. I later worked for the Memphis Grizzlies of the WFL. We had several name players—Larry Csonka, Jim Kiick, and Paul Warfield, who all played, of course, on Don Shula's Super Bowl winners. We also had Danny White, who went on to quarterback for the Dallas Cowboys.

Later, I went to the Memphis Blues, the Houston Astros' Triple-A affiliate. I was hired by Denny McLain—yes, *that* Denny McLain, the thirty-game winner who went to jail for extortion. He was their GM at the time. That's a story in itself, but for now let's move on.

A month after Elvis Presley died, I got a connection with the Memphis Chicks. I had met Elvis the year before in the press box at the Liberty Bowl. I became GM of the Chicks in 1977 and was there for two years. We set attendance records. I did all kinds of things to boost their profile—meetings with community folks, giveaways, the kind of things they weren't doing in the major leagues at the time. A man who was a big influence on me was Jim Paul, the owner and GM of the El Paso Diablos, and I later spoke at some of his seminars. He always stressed the value of entertainment—to put on a good show. One game would be hat night, which was not only a good giveaway but great advertising when people saw the hats around town. He always had something good cooked up for Friday and Saturday night when he knew he had to compete with other kinds of entertainment.

Most of the innovations in baseball promotion came from the minor leagues and worked their way up.

I made my Birmingham connection through John Forney, of Lucky and Forney advertising, who was known throughout Alabama as the voice of Alabama football on radio. I had made a very profitable deal with Pepsi while I was with the Memphis Chicks, and Lucky and Forney represented Coca-Cola. He said to me, "Do you think you could come down here and do the same things for Birmingham as you did for Memphis?" I thought about it, and in July drove down to see Rickwood Field. There wasn't any question that it needed a lot of work, but all I could think was "Man, this is a major league ballpark."

Bob Lovell of Coca-Cola really stepped up as one of our sponsors, and things fell into line. The city put in some new seats. I took a lot of heat for replacing the old hand-operated scoreboard and putting in a new electronic one, but the old scoreboard had already fallen apart. Please tell everybody I did *not* tear down the old scoreboard. I don't want to be remembered that way.

A lot of people were skeptical that baseball would work again in Birmingham, because Charlie Finley's teams had never been able to draw crowds like the old Barons had. I thought that had more to do with Finley than with Birmingham fans. I never met him, but I studied his record quite a bit, and I'm convinced he was never much of a promoter. I don't think there's any doubt he had a terrific eye for talent. His 1967 Birmingham A's were probably one of the great minor league teams in history and formed the nucleus of three World Series winners. He knew how to get headlines with that orange baseball thing and with the donkey mascot. But he really didn't know how to sell tickets. I knew that I did.

I'll never forget our opening night. We had staked so much on a big crowd. Bob Lovell called me a few days before opening and said, "Just tell me everything's going to be okay, that we're going to draw some fans." I assured him, "Hell, yes, we're going to have a lot of fans." We opened on a Tuesday night, and the Wednesday before Harry Walker, who was coaching the UAB baseball team, got the St. Louis Cardinals to play an exhibition game in Birmingham, but they only had a few hundred fans. Everyone was nervous that we weren't going to do any better. I admit, I had an anxiety dream the night before that game that no one would show up. What a lot of people didn't know was that I had arranged for the San Diego Chicken to be there. I also had a great opening to bring in black and white fans: three people threw out a ball—Piper Davis, Ben Chapman, and Norm Zauchin.* The gate was almost 10,000.

At that game, I made a friend. I couldn't believe it when I saw Bear Bryant standing in line with his son, Paul Jr., to buy a ticket. I walked over and invited him in. He said, "No, I'll buy a ticket." I said, "Okay, if you want to buy a ticket, buy a ticket." I felt doubly foolish—arguing with a fan who wanted to pay for his ticket and arguing with Bear Bryant. I had my picture taken with him, and we became very good friends. There's only two people I ever met in sports that I was really in awe of. One was Joe DiMaggio, and the other was Coach Bryant.

There's so many memories, it's hard to pick the best. I do remember we had an old-timer's game in 1985—old Barons and old

---

* Zauchin set the Barons all-time home run record in 1950 with 35. He hit 27 home runs and drove in 93 runs for the Red Sox in 1955, but his career was cut short by injuries. He once hit a home run on State of Maine Day and as a prize won a black bear named Homer; not knowing what to do with Homer, Zauchin donated him to the Birmingham Zoo, where Homer lived comfortably until 1987, the Barons' last season in Rickwood.

Black Barons. Piper Davis and Ben Chapman were the managers. You should have seen those old guys play and what fun they had. I like to think it erased some of the bad memories from the segregation years.

I also have some very sad memories. I remember standing on the grandstand roof watching cars pull up the gate and then turning away to go home. We just didn't have enough parking spaces, and we couldn't get the city to help. We couldn't get them to help make basic repairs in the park. I hated to move to Hoover, but I finally felt I had no choice. I guess some people remember me as the Walter O'Malley of Birmingham baseball, and I have to admit that I understand the pressures that caused O'Malley to move the Dodgers to Los Angeles.

I have four championship baseball rings—three from the Barons and one from the 1984 Tigers, when we were their affiliate. It's not the rings or the plaques that matter; it's the wonderful ride I had along the way. To think I was a part of it for ten years is a great honor. I never thought of myself as the owner of the team. The Barons belong to the people of Birmingham. I was just the caretaker.

Art Clarkson was principal owner of the Birmingham Barons from 1980 to 1990. He is currently with an Indoor Football League team in Wisconsin.

• • •

APPENDIX 4

. . .

THIS *IS* A BALLPARK

You can have those new fields with artificial turf and sky boxes. This *is* a *ballpark*. You need the sun and wind in your face....

—DONNIE HARRIS,
former Black Barons center fielder

DURHAM ATHLETIC PARK
Durham, North Carolina

THE ORIGINAL VERSION of "the DAP," as the locals call it, opened in 1926 as El Toro Park—"Bull"–"Toro," get it? Before then, the local minor league ball club, the Durham Bulls, played on the field of a local college, Trinity. (The school's buildings now serve as the east campus of Duke University.) In 1933 it officially became Durham Athletic Park.

According to one legend, six years later, a groundskeeper tossed a lit cigar into a trash can, and the Bulls woke up the next day in need of

DURHAM ATHLETIC PARK *reopened in August 2009, after a $5 million renovation that included a new state-of-the-art playing field and improved seating, restrooms, and concession stands. DAP will be home to North Carolina Central University's baseball team, and minor league baseball will use the park as a training facility for groundskeepers.*

a new home. (A tobacco warehouse supposedly went down with it.) The charming 5,000-seat structure we know today dates from the off-season of 1939. By the spring of 1940, a new mostly steel-and-concrete structure was in place on the same site with the same dimensions and architecture. The major addition is the conical brick tower at the entrance gate. According to a fan on the Endangered Durham website, the bleachers out in center field were cheap seats for black fans, much the way the right field bleachers at Rickwood Field were.

The Bulls were thirteen years younger than El Toro Park, having been first taken to the field in 1913. But over the years the Depression and other economic setbacks caused them to fade away, only to reemerge after a couple of years or so. The DAP, though, was a home for Negro Leagues, Little League, and even company softball games during years when there were no Bulls.

That Durham Athletic Park is the most famous of all minor league ballparks can be attributed to an infielder in the Baltimore system who played several games there. The park isn't remembered for what Ron Shelton did there during his playing career but for what he did afterward, filming there the most famous baseball film of all, *Bull Durham*. In one of the film's most memorable scenes, an opposing batter hits a long home run off Tim Robbins's pitcher Nuke LaLoosh. It strikes a giant red bull perched over the right field wall. The bull bellows and snorts, announcing that the batter has won a free steak at a local restaurant. Shelton admits that the bull was his invention, a tribute to all the different "Win a Free Something" signs he saw during his minor league career.

Shelton, who returned to the DAP in 2008 for a ceremony honoring the ballpark and his film, remembers it fondly. "It's a lovely little place. It was nice because it is located downtown. You could walk to it and not have to spend money on a taxi. There were these old tobacco warehouses around. They gave the neighborhood a nice working-class feel."

In 1995 the city built a new facility for the Bulls but, to its great credit, did not close the DAP, which is now used for concerts and festivals throughout the year, and its sod is still trod each year by thousands of amateur players, both hard and soft ball. Some say the DAP is frequently visited by the ghosts of two fictitious characters, *Bull Durham*'s Crash Davis and Annie Savoy.

For more information see the Endangered Durham website, at http://endangereddurham.blogspot.com/2008/06/durham-athletic-park.html.

• • •

HINCHLIFFE STADIUM

Paterson, New Jersey

"HINCHLIFFE"—also known as City Stadium in Paterson, New Jersey, about twenty minutes across the George Washington Bridge from New York City—"can be said to have hosted some of the most prodigious baseball in America. This significance resonates not just in local and regional or even national sports history, but in national social history, given the enormous significance both of sports and of the racial segregation of sports at the time." So wrote Dr. Flavia Alaya, Paterson resident and cultural historian, in the Hinchliffe Application for Historical Listing. Dr. Alaya did not exaggerate, and in 2004 Hinchliffe was placed on the State and National Registers of Historic Places.

A 9,500-seater when it opened in 1932, the ballpark—named for Mayor John V. Hinchliffe, who backed the project—was a product of the New Deal's public works projects at a cost of around $240,000. Located, like Durham Athletic Park, in a working-class area, Hinchliffe became, from 1933 to 1937 and again from 1939 through the end of World War II, the home of the New York Black Yankees of the Negro National Leagues. In 1936 it was also home park for the NNL's New York Cubans. It is one of the few Negro League stadiums remaining in the United States.

Perhaps Hinchliffe's biggest claim to fame is Larry Doby, Hall of Famer and the first black player in the American League. Doby, who graduated from Paterson's East Side High School, played both baseball and football at Hinchliffe before being scouted there for the Cleveland Indians.

During its heyday, Hinchliffe was the site of professional football

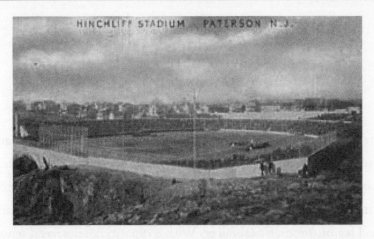

HINCHLIFFE STADIUM, *shown here on opening day in 1932, will be renovated thanks to a $15 million referendum passed by the voters of Paterson, New Jersey, in November 2009.*

games, track and field events, boxing matches, and motorcycles races. It is the only known professional ballpark to have hosted a performance by Abbot and Costello, who did their immortal "Who's on first" skit there.

Hinchliffe was acquired by the Paterson School District in 1963 and used for school events until 1997, when the cost of maintenance became too much for the school system. Although protected by its historic status, it is now in disrepair. Fortunately, local efforts are underway, including the support of Congressman Bill Pascrell Jr. and Councilman Andre Sayegh, to restore the stadium to its former glory and include it in a new sports academy complex. (Councilman Sayegh visited Rickwood Field in October 2009 to see firsthand what has been achieved.)

For more information see the Friends of Hinchliffe website, at http://www.hinchliffestadium.org/history/index.php.

• • •

ENGEL STADIUM

Chattanooga, Tennessee

THE HOME OF the Birmingham Barons' bitter rivals (the Chattanooga Lookouts) and the Black Barons' bitter rivals (the Black Lookouts), Engel Stadium was built in 1930 and named for owner (and ace baseball scout) Joe Engel, called the P. T. Barnum of Baseball for his promotional talent. With a capacity, after several renovations, of more than 12,000, the park has fared better than most surviving minor league parks built before World War II.

The Lookouts departed Engel Stadium in 1999 for the new Bellsouth Park, and the old park is now used for high school baseball games as well as the Tennessee Temple University Crusaders, who won a dazzling 32 of 33 games there during the 2008 season.

Like Rickwood, Engel had a center field fence that seems absurdly distant by today's standards: 471 feet from home. Over the years, adjustable fences were brought in to shorten the outfield dimensions and make it first minor league and then college and high school friendly. Over the decades Engel has seen as much major league talent as any minor league ballpark except Rickwood, including Hall of Famer and old Birmingham Barons spitball ace Burleigh Grimes, Pirates and Cubs great Kiki Cuyler, Babe Ruth, Lou Gehrig, Satchel Paige, Willie Mays, Hank Aaron, Harmon Killebrew, and Ferguson Jenkins.

Perhaps Engle's greatest claim to fame is an exhibition game in 1931 when a seventeen-year-old girl named Jackie Mitchell struck out both Ruth and Gehrig, surely the most astonishing baseball feat never to be made into a movie. (You can find out more about Jackie

Lou Gehrig *takes batting practice in Engel Stadium, April 1937.*

at www.jackiemitchell.net; Engel Stadium historian Andy Broome is completing a book on Mitchell as we go to press.)

Engel Stadium's covered grandstand curves all the way from first base to third, and the roof decking is still the original 1930 slats. Many of the park's old wooden seats remain, although the lower sections were replaced and sold. Behind the left field wall there is a picnic area. The concourse area has a superb concession stand and a nice little souvenir store. Plaques near the front gate commemorate the old Lookouts. In the fall of 2009 an application to register Engel with the National Register of Historic Places was being put together, which would make sure that Engel is safe for future fans.

• • •

DUNCAN PARK

Spartanburg, South Carolina

DUNCAN PARK, named for David Duncan, a former Confederate major and trustee for Wofford and Converse College, was completed in 1926. On July 8 of that year, a capacity crowd of 2,500
watched the hometown Spartans beat the Macon Peaches 5–1.
In 1933 Duncan Park began its seventy-six-year association with
American Legion ball. Temporary bleachers were constructed in
1936—also the year lights were installed—to ensure that 21,000
fans could shoehorn into Duncan to watch the fifth and deciding
game of the American Legion World Series—still the largest crowd
to attend a sporting event in Spartanburg. Later it was home to the
Spartanburg Stingers in the Coastal Plain League and the Spartanburg Crickets in the Southern Collegiate Baseball League.

Duncan has numerous big-league connections. In the 1930s the
Joe DiMaggio–Lou Gehrig Yankees played exhibition games there,
and several National League stars of the 1980s and 1990, such as
the Cubs' Ryne Sandberg and the Braves' Dale Murphy and Tom
Glavine, played there.

In 1967 the park got a makeover on its first base side bleachers, the roof, restrooms, and press box; a new concession stand was
added, but the original was refurbished and is still in use. Some
582 green wooden seats from Philadelphia's Connie Mack Stadium
(originally Shibe Park) were shipped to Duncan after the Phillies
moved to Veterans Stadium in 1971. New lights were installed in
1973. In 1979 the roof was redone and 700 seats added seat in the
grandstand, which was reconditioned. (The park remains one of the

oldest in the country with a wooden grandstand.)

For thirty years, starting in 1963, the Philadelphia Phillies had a Class-A farm team, the Spartanburg Phillies, at Duncan, paced by future Phillies All-Star shortstop and current Los Angeles Dodgers coach Larry Bowa. The Spartanburg Phillies gained national headlines in 1966 by winning 23 consecutive games and were included in minor league baseball's top 100 all-time teams. The Phillies left behind a legacy: by the end of their era in 1994, Duncan was the oldest minor league baseball park hosting full-time minor league baseball (Rickwood had lost the Barons in 1987).

Despite signs of wear and tear over the years, Duncan remains one of the more charming minor league parks. Perhaps the best of Duncan Park's features is its location. Beyond the outfield wall is a man-made lake with pine trees planted around it, as well as Little League diamonds, walking trails, and tennis courts.

Today Duncan is home to the Spartanburg American Legion and Spartanburg High School. The city replaced the outfield wall, and the Spartanburg School District is working on grandstand improvements. There has been talk of applying for National Landmark Status when renovations are complete.

For information on Duncan, see http://www.saveduncanpark .org/.

• • •

CIVIC STADIUM

Eugene, Oregon

IF YOU'VE SEEN OLYMPIC STADIUM in Hoquiam, Washington, you've seen Civic Stadium in Eugene, Oregon, which is on a slightly smaller scale. Civic Stadium has a smaller seating capacity (6,800 to Olympic's 9,000) and slightly shorter dimensions. Civic has also enjoyed a longer and stronger relationship with professional baseball. (Olympic lost its last minor league team in 1999.)

Yet another child of the WPA (in a public-private partnership with the chamber of commerce and Eugene School District), Civic was built in 1938, and the locals will tell you that you can't get there without good directions—it's practically hidden in a charming residential area that is worlds away from downtown city ballparks like Durham Athletic Park and Hinchliffe Stadium in Paterson, New Jersey.

Like Rickwood Field, Civic is known for its hand-operated scoreboard, located down the right field line. In fact, with its distinctive J-shaped covered grandstand, Civic bears a strong resemblance to Rickwood. Moreover, the lovely mountain-view backdrop of Civic is unique in just about all of professional baseball.

Accorded Triple-A status in 1969, the Emeralds—or Ems, as they are affectionately called by their fans—began a fruitful affiliation with the Philadelphia Phillies and future Phillies stars. Larry Bowa, Greg Luzinski, and Hall of Famer Mike Schmidt were all seasoned there. In 2001 they began a hook up with the San Diego Padres, a link that lasted until 2009, when the Ems left Civic for new digs at the University of Oregon's new PK Park. During the

Designed and built in 1938 by the WPA, the covered grandstands in Civic Stadium are strikingly similar to Rickwood's.

Ems' tenure, Civic was one of the ten-oldest minor league ball parks in the country.

Civic Stadium is owned by the Eugene School District, and its primary use is for South Eugene High School. When they decided to move the team, the Emeralds' management cited the need for substantial renovations, including a new electrical system and replacement of broken seats. Fortunately, Civic was named to the National Register of Historic Places in 2008, and a local group, Save Civic Stadium, has launched a campaign to raise support to restore the stadium and find other tenants to help maintain the facility.

• • •

JOE BECKER STADIUM

Joplin, Missouri

To say Joe Becker Stadium is "historic" is one of the biggest understatements in baseball: Satchel Paige, Josh Gibson, and "Cool Papa" Bell played here when on barnstorming tours. It was the home park of Mickey Mantle in 1950 when he was with the Joplin Miners, a Yankees farm team. And he played shortstop!

Legend has it that when Mantle played there, kids at an orphanage beyond the right field fence would hold up signs saying "Mick, Hit It Here" during games. The Mick, of course, often did just that.

Built in 1913 as Miners Park, the park was renamed for Joe Becker, who was well known in Joplin as a professional baseball umpire and scout and business manager of the Miners in the years

Joe Becker Stadium: *Mickey Mantle played here!*

1936–42. Joe Becker Stadium has survived two fires, some terrible storms, and, perhaps worst of all for a ball park, the loss of its professional team when the Miners were disbanded after the 1953 season. After the last fire in 1971, the stadium was rebuilt, in retro style with hand-painted signs in the outfield, with a capacity of about 1,000.

But the city of Joplin, American Legion Post no. 13, and Missouri Southern State College have all stepped up to the plate over the years, and today Joe Becker Stadium is the home of the Missouri Southern Lions, the Joplin High School Eagles, and local American Legion ball. In 2004 it was the host to the USA Baseball Tournament of Stars.

• • •

RAY WINDER FIELD

Little Rock, Arkansas

RAY WINDER FIELD went up during 1931 and the following year became the home of the Arkansas Travelers of the Southern Association. For the next thirty-four seasons, it was called Traveler Field and saw just about every great player from the South, including the Negro Leagues and the Texas League.

The stadium features a covered grandstand, and everyone is seated close to the action; that distinguishes it from Rickwood with its vast area between home plate and the grandstand. From ballparksreview.com: "Ray Winder will take you back in time...."

A game at Ray Winder Field in 2006.

The reviewer also loved the organ music between innings, much preferable to the rock music usually blared out between batters.

In the summer of 1966 the park was renamed Ray Winder Field after the most important man in Little Rock baseball history. Winder began selling minor league baseball tickets in 1915 and sixteen years later became the team's business manager. In 1944 he became part owner.

Traveler Field was unoccupied during the 1959 season after the Travelers moved to Shreveport at a time when the Southern Association was struggling to survive. Funds were raised to purchase the bankrupt New Orleans Pelicans franchise, renamed the Travelers for the 1960 season.

In 1976 the well-known American League umpire Bill Valentine became GM and with limited resources did yeoman work with the old park, stressing Ray Winder Field's rich history.

But the future of Ray Winder Field was the subject of much debate after professional baseball left in 2006. An agreement was finally reached in July 2009 to allow the University of Arkansas for Medical Sciences to buy the stadium and the adjacent Little Rock Zoo to buy the parking lot. However, as we went to press, no plans for the stadium have been announced, and supporters are disappointed that it may not be preserved.

• • •

WARREN BALLPARK

Bisbee, Arizona

LOCATED JUST TWENTY MINUTES south of Tombstone and the legendary O.K. Corral, where Wyatt Earp, his brothers, and Doc Holliday shot it out with the Clantons and McLaurys in 1881, Warren Ballpark in Bisbee might well be the oldest continuously used ball field in the United States. The ballpark which currently surrounds the field, Warren, dates from a 1936 WPA project that replaced the creaking old wooden grandstand with a steel-and-concrete structure still in use today. The original park was built in 1909—the same year as Shibe Park in Philadelphia and the year before Rickwood Field—with lumber from the Warren Company, which was owned by the Calumet, an Arizona mining company and one of the biggest copper producers of the time. Like so many minor league ballparks of the period, Warren was built to provide a home for industrial teams, in Bisbee the industry being almost exclusively copper mining.

During the 1920s Warren became the unofficial home of "Outlaw Baseball," which meant numerous players such as "Prince Hal" Chase, a first baseman who had played for both the New York Giants and the Yankees, Chick Gandil, Happy Felsch, Swede Risberg, Lefty Williams, and Buck Weaver, all of whom had been banned by Commissioner Kennesaw Mountain Landis for fixing baseball games. (The last five were members of the infamous Chicago "Black Sox" team who had conspired to throw the 1919 World Series to the Cincinnati Reds.)

This is only part of the notoriety associated with Warren; in

The Friends of Warren Ballpark call their stadium "The REAL Field of Dreams."

1917 nearly 1,200 striking copper miners and members of the radical union the Industrial Workers of the World ("the Wobblies") were held on the field by the Cochise County sheriff and later deported to New Mexico.

On the plus side of the ledger, the 1952 Copper Kings, an independent minor league team, may have been the first bilingual ball club in America. With no major league affiliation, the Copper Kings reached south of the border to Mexico for talent.

Surrounded by the scenic Arizona desert and mountains, Warren today is a modern concrete structure with seating for 3,000. Warren hosted a number of semipro and minor league teams over the years, including the Ranger Kings and the Bisbee Bees. The Copper Kings returned to Warren in 2007 as a semipro team. The 2009 season kicked off with an exhibition game between two vintage baseball teams from Phoenix. As part of the Pacific Southwest Baseball league, the Copper Kings opened their 2009 season in May, playing the most home games at Warren Ballpark scheduled for a single season since the Bisbee Yankees in 1947.

For more information on Warren Ballpark, visit http://www .friendsofwarrenballpark.com/.

• • •

ACKNOWLEDGMENTS

· IT'S HARD TO SAY EXACTLY when I decided I wanted to write this book. It was more like a process. It might have been the first time I went to Rickwood, in 1966, with my mother, for an exhibition game between the Yankees and Red Sox. It might have been the next year, when I went with my good friend Rob Studin to see the Birmingham A's and Chattanooga Lookouts and Reggie Jackson hit a long home run into the right field seats (Rob remembers the shot as being a foul ball).

Who knows? It might have been back in 1965 when my father, who was from South Philadelphia, took me to a game at Connie Mack Stadium to see Juan Marichal, who was 10–0 at the time. (Bill White, the Phillies first baseman, hit a long home run over the right field stands and into the street to win the game, but Willie Mays hit a home run off the Phillies Chris Short and made a great play to throw Dick Allen out at third, and that's what really counted.) My father explained to me that Connie Mack Stadium in his youth had been named Shibe Park, and I was amazed less than a year later to see how much Rickwood looked like a smaller version of Shibe/ Connie Mack.

Birmingham Barons owner Art Clarkson was a real inspira-

THE AUTHOR'S MOTHER, *Lorraine Arnwine; his sister, Lorrie Rogers; and niece (Jamie Rogers) at Rickwood Field in 1993.*

tion when, in 1987, he took me on a complete tour of the ballpark just before the Barons moved to their new facility in the suburb of Hoover. I wrote a couple of magazine articles about Rickwood at the time, and I suppose the idea of doing a book on Rickwood's history really began to germinate. It definitely kicked into high gear in 1993 when I saw director Ron Shelton filming the baseball scenes for his movie *Cobb* at Rickwood. Watching Tommy Lee Jones, Roger Clemens, and others parading around in those heavy wool uniforms stirred the ghosts of Rockwood's past for me.

The final impetus was definitely ESPN's Classic in 2006, which I attended with the late great Paul Hemphill. Paul and I had both been plugging our books about Alabama greats that day—Paul his biography of Hank Williams, *Lovesick Blues*, and I my biography of Bear Bryant, *The Last Coach*. As we finished up Paul said, "If we hurry, we can catch the end of the game at Rickwood." We did, and I got to see Jim Bouton in a vintage uniform dancing on the roof of the old Barons dugout. It was a great day, and Paul gave me a lifetime of lore about the Barons and Black Barons. A little more than three years later, he died of cancer. Thanks to Paul's wife, Susan Percy, for always responding quickly to our requests for photos and passages from his work.

Also, after twenty-three years of trying, at that game I finally got to do a sit-down interview with Willie Mays.

This book could not have been written without the help, from beginning to end, of David Brewer, executive director of the Friends of Rickwood, who has labored as long and hard as anyone to save Rickwood. If this book does not make a significant contribution to preserving Rickwood and expanding its fame, it will have achieved nothing.

Chris Fullerton, an old friend whose history of the Black Barons, *Every Other Sunday*, was published two years after his death in an auto accident, in 1997, was also an inspiration. His passion for the Black Barons, Rickwood Field, and Birmingham baseball still burn brightly.

Bob Scranton, longtime Barons traveling secretary, was indispensable. I could probably have written this book without him, but it would not have been the same. I also thank his daughter, Caroline Bell, who put me in touch with her father, scanned photos, and served as a liaison when Bob was in the hospital.

The late Alf Van Hoose, through his writing in the *Birmingham News*, and Bill Lumpkin, through both his work in the *Birmingham Post Herald* and his personal recollection, brought me back to a time I've often imagined and now feel as if I have lived through. Thanks to both Ben Cook and Timothy Whitt, who trod these literary base paths years before I got in the game.

Twenty-two years after giving me my first tour of Rickwood, Art Clarkson relived his Birmingham days for me. He also introduced me to Piper Davis.

Ron Shelton and Jim Bouton, two guys who know the game from the perspective of both a player and a writer, shared great stories. By the way, you guys need to get together sometime, and I hope I'm there when you meet.

Thanks to the ballplayers I spoke to, including, in the order I reached them, Jim Piersall, Walt Dropo, the Reverend William Greason (of the Bethel Baptist Church, Berney Points), the late Ben Chapman, Willie Lee, Rollie Fingers, Paul Seitz, Ernie Banks, Donnie Harris, Reggie Jackson, and Bob Veale.

I'm grateful to so many fans of Rickwood, not only for the help they gave me in writing this book but also for their undying devotion to keeping alive the memories of Birmingham baseball and Rickwood Field. They include Lamar Smith, Gerald Watkins, David Wininger, Coke Matthews, Chuck Stewart, John Bird, Rick Bernstein, Buddy Coker, Joe DeLeonard, Courtney Haden, and Rob Studin. Jim McCord provided valuable research material, and Gene and Cindy Worthington shared many firsthand experiences. Carlton Molesworth III, grandson of the first Barons manager, was delightful in relating the stories he had picked up from the dead ball era.

Carry Me Home, by my good friend Diane McWhorter, was an indispensable guide through the civil rights era, and Marshall D. Wright's *The Southern Association in Baseball, 1885–1961* was invaluable for its statistical analysis and recollection of each season in Southern Association history.

In addition to doing extensive research, my wife, Jonelle, typed and edited every line in this book. Those of you astute enough to spot errors may attribute them all to me, but you'll never know how many she stopped before they could get through the infield. For the second book in a row, my daughter, Margaret, contributed some brilliant photography.

My editor, Bob Weil, saw the potential of Rickwood's story from the beginning. This is my third book with him, along with *The Last Coach: A Life of Paul "Bear" Bryant* and *Yogi Berra: Eternal Yankee*, and they just keep getting better. Phil Marino came off the bench in the late innings to do terrific work in getting the manuscript together and into production.

I saved Lorenzo "Piper" Davis for last because, more than anyone else, he was responsible for rekindling he story of the Black Barons and Rickwood for numerous writers before me. Piper's story is the story of all the black ballplayers who had what it took but were born in the wrong time and place and never got their shot at the big time. Without Piper, a world of stories and anecdotes, social history, and folklore would never have been heard. And without Piper we might never have known Willie Mays. I'm not the first person to suggest that Piper Davis deserves to be in the Hall of Fame, and my fervent hope is that this book will spark a move in that direction.

NOTES

PREFACE

1 Ritter, *Lost Ballparks*, p. 178.

CHAPTER ONE: UP FROM THE SLAG PILE

1 Hemphill, *Leaving Birmingham*, p. 15.
2 Fullerton, *Every Other Sunday*, p. 7.
3 Quinlan, *Strange Kin*, p. 17.
4 McMillan, *Yesterday's Birmingham*, p. 16.
5 Hemphill, *Leaving Birmingham*, p. 16.

CHAPTER TWO: BIRMINGHAM MEN DO IT RIGHT

1 Whitt, *Bases Loaded with History*, p. 196.
2 Ibid.

CHAPTER THREE: A TEAM OF THEIR OWN

1 Birmingfind, *The Other Side*, p. 3.
2 Ibid., p. 4.
3 Birmingham Historical Society, *Fourth Avenue History Hunt*.

4 Rosengarten, "Reading the Hops," p. 69.

5 *Birmingham Age-Herald.* September 2, 1919.

6 *Pittsburgh Dispatch,* September 2, 1921.

7 Ribowsky, *A Complete History of the Negro Leagues,* p. xiv.

8 Ibid., p. 116.

9 *Birmingham Age-Herald,* March 31, 1925.

CHAPTER FOUR: THE GOLDEN AGE

1 Paige, *Maybe I'll Pitch Forever,* p. 46.

2 Whitt, *Bases Loaded with History,* p. 40.

3 Paige, *Maybe I'll Pitch Forever,* p. 51.

4 Ibid., p. 49.

5 Holway, *Blackball Tales,* p. 96.

6 Ibid., p. 92.

7 Letter to the author, 2004.

8 Mays and Sahadi, *Say Hey,* pp. 27–28.

9 Fox, *Satchel Paige's America,* p. 29.

10 Ibid., p. 30.

11 Wright, *The Southern Association in Baseball,* p. 261.

CHAPTER FIVE: THE GREATEST GAME EVER PLAYED

1 Gregory, *Diz,* p. 69.

2 *Birmingham News,* September 13, 1931.

3 Gregory, *Diz,* p. 70.

4 *Houston Post,* September 12, 1931.

5 *Birmingham News,* September 15, 1931.

6 Gregory, *Diz,* p. 72.

7 *Birmingham News,* September 17, 1931.

8 Ibid.

9 Ibid., September 24, 1931.

10   Gregory, *Diz*, p. 74.

11   Staten, *Ol' Diz*, p. 72.

12   Gregory, *Diz*, p. 376.

CHAPTER SIX: "THERE WAS JUST SOMETHING ABOUT THE BASEBALL IN THAT PARK"

1   *Birmingham Age-Herald*, September 20, 1907.

2   *Birmingham News*, September 22, 1907.

3   Fullerton, *Every Other Sunday*, p. 61.

4   *Birmingham News*, September 13, 1936.

5   Fullerton, *Every Other Sunday*, p. 67.

6   Whitt, *Bases Loaded with History*, p. 74.

7   Fullerton, *Every Other Sunday*, p. 77.

8   Hemphill, *Leaving Birmingham*, p. 137.

9   Holway, *Voices from the Great Black Baseball Leagues*, p. 182.

10   Ibid.

CHAPTER SEVEN: "WELL, I'M GOING TO THE BALLGAME"

1   Mays and Sahadi, *Say Hey*, p. 20.

2   *The New Bill James Historical Abstract*, p. 168.

CHAPTER EIGHT: "THE BARONS WERE A MEMORY"

1   Hemphill, *Leaving Birmingham*, p. 75.

2   McWhorter, *Carry Me Home*, p. 38.

3   Nunnelley, *Bull Connor*, p. 39.

4   McWhorter, *Carry Me Home*, p. 19.

5   Hemphill, *Leaving Birmingham*, p. 110.

6   Pietrusza et al., eds., p. 829.

7   *Birmingham News*, August 9, 1951.

8   Ibid., August 21, 1951.

9   Hemphill, *Leaving Birmingham*, p. 131.

CHAPTER NINE: EVERYTHING DIES BUT . . .

1   McWhorter, *Carry Me Home*, p. 355.

2   *Birmingham Post Herald*, April 4, 1997.

3   Cook, *Good Wood*, p. 88.

4   Miller, *A Whole Different Ball Game*, p. 369.

5   Ibid.

6   Hemphill, *Leaving Birmingham*, p. 302.

APPENDIX 1: THERE USED TO BE A BALLPARK

1   National Park Service, HABS / HAER Report no. AL-897, "Rickwood Field," 1993, p. 2.

2   Statement by Raymond Doswell, Curator, Negro Leagues Baseball Museum, quoted in article on Hinchliffe Stadium (Paterson, N.J.), by Steve Strunsky, accessible at http://www.nlbm.com/ns/News Detail.cfm?NewsID=69.

3   For a partial list of Rickwood veterans who are Hall of Fame members, see Whitt, *Bases Loaded with History*, p. 103.

4   Recount of this experience first published in the Friends of Rickwood newsletter, *Out of the Park*, Spring 2001.

5   *Rickwood Master Plan*, by Davis Speake & Associates (now Davis Architects), 1993.

6   HABS / HAER Report, p. 2.

7   For example, see Warren Ballpark (Bisbee, Ariz.).

8   Birmingham newspapers during the period covered extensively the play of both the Barons and the Black Barons and contain references to these, and many other, legendary ballplayers.

9   For a discussion of Birmingham as a New South industrial center,

see W. David Lewis, *Sloss Furnaces and the Rise of the Birmingham Industrial District: An Industrial Epic* (Tuscaloosa: University of Alabama Press, 1994).

10 "National Trust's African American Historic Places Initiative: An Update," June 23, 2004.

11 HABS /HAER Report, p. 3; Michael Benson, *Ballparks of North America: A Comprehensive Historical Reference to Baseball Grounds, Yards, and Stadiums, 1845 to Present* (Jefferson, N.C.: McFarland and Co., 1989), p. 33.

12 Whitt, *Bases Loaded with History*, pp. 21–22; caption from 1930s Rickwood Field postcard, Birmingham View Company.

13 *Baseball America*, November 15, 1999, p. 50; ibid., December 22, 2003, p. 39.

14 For example, *Restore America*, HGTV, April 2000; *Three Day Weekend*, Turner South, June 2004; *Blue Ribbon Ballparks*, Turner South, April 2005.

15 Component projects completed to date include the replacement of the original drop-in scoreboard, the installation of a new public address system, the rebuilding of a vintage-style gazebo press box as well as the building of a modern grandstand press box, the restoration of the distinctive front entry building as well as the repainting of the park's entire exterior, improvements to the playing field, the reproduction of vintage-style outfield billboards, the replacement of portions of the grandstand roof and the placement and painting of additional structural support columns, the renovation of the main men's and women's restrooms, and the renovation of the visiting team and home team locker rooms.

Relationships with similar organizations have added credibility to the project and include the National Park Service, National Trust for Historic Preservation, Alabama Historical Commission, Jefferson County Historical Commission, Birmingham Historical Society, Alabama Negro League Players Association, Society of American

Baseball Researchers, International Association of Sports Museums and Halls of Fame, and the Alabama Museums Association.

16 Rickwood web address: www.rickwood.com.

17 For examples of recent travel guide inclusion, see Chris Epting, *Roadside Baseball: Uncovering Hidden Treasures from Our National Pastime* (St. Louis, Mo.: Sporting News, 2003), p. 107; and Jim Carrier, *A Traveler's Guide to the Civil Rights Movement* (New York: Harcourt, 2003), p. 224.

18 *USA Today*, April 8, 2005.

19 Feature-length films shot in part at Rickwood include *Cobb* and *Soul of the Game*; numerous television commercials and print ads have also been shot at Rickwood.

20 Historic parks that have attracted the attention of preservationists include Durham Athletic Park (Durham, N.C.), Bossie Field (Evansville, Ind.), Engel Field (Chattanooga, Tenn.), League Park (Cleveland, Ohio), Luther Williams Field (Macon, Ga.), Hinchliffe Stadium (Paterson, N.J.), Bush Stadium (Indianapolis, Ind.), War Memorial Stadium (Greensboro, N.C.), and Gill Stadium (Manchester, N.H.).

BIBLIOGRAPHY

Bak, Richard. *Turkey Stearnes and the Detroit Stars: The Negro Leagues in Detroit, 1919–1933.* Ventura, Calif.: Gospel Light Publications, 1995.

Birmingfind. *The Other Side: The Story of Birmingham's Black Community.* Birmingham, Ala., 1981.

Birmingham Centennial Corporation. *Portrait of Birmingham.* Birmingham, Ala., 1971.

Birmingham Historical Society. *Fourth Avenue History Hunt: The Historic Black Business District.* http://www.bhistorical.org/education_Hh-4a .pdf.

Cook, Ben. *Good Wood: A Fan's History of Rickwood Field.* Birmingham, Ala.: R. Boozer Press, 2005.

Fox, William Price. *Satchel Paige's America.* Tuscaloosa: University of Alabama Press, 2005.

Fullerton, Christopher D. *Every Other Sunday: The Story of the Birmingham Black Barons.* Birmingham, Ala.: R. Boozer Press, 1999.

Gregory, Robert. *Diz: Dizzy Dean and Baseball during the Great Depression.* New York: Viking, 1992.

Hemphill, Paul. *Leaving Birmingham: Notes of a Native Son.* New York: Viking Penguin, 1993.

Holway, John B. *Blackball Tales.* Springfield, Va.: Scorpio Books, 2008.

———. *Voices from the Great Black Baseball Leagues.* New York: Da Capo Press, 1992.

James, Bill. *The New Bill James Historical Baseball Abstract*. New York: Free Press, 2001.

McMillan, Malcolm C. *Yesterday's Birmingham*. Miami: E. A. Seemann Publishing, 1975.

McWhorter, Diane. *Carry Me Home: Birmingham, Alabama—The Climactic Battle of the Civil Rights Revolution*. New York: Simon and Schuster, 2001.

Mays, Willie, and Lou Sahadi. *Say Hey: The Autobiography of Willie Mays*. New York: Simon and Schuster, 1988.

Miller, Marvin. *A Whole Different Ball Game: The Inside Story of Baseball's New Deal*. New York: Simon and Schuster, 1992.

Nunnelley, William A. *Bull Connor*. Tuscaloosa: University of Alabama Press, 1990.

Paige, LeRoy (Satchel), as told to David Lipman. *Maybe I'll Pitch Forever*. Lincoln: University of Nebraska Press, 1993.

Pietrusza, David, Matthew Silverman, and Michael Gershman, eds. *Baseball: The Biographical Encyclopedia*. Kingston, N.Y.: Total Sports Illustrated, 2000.

Quinlan, Kieran. *Strange Kin: Ireland and the American South*. Baton Rouge: Louisiana State University Press, 2004.

Ribowsky, Mark. *A Complete History of the Negro Leagues, 1884–1955*. New York: Carol Publishing Group, 1995.

Ritter, Lawrence S. *Lost Ballparks: A Celebration of Baseball's Legendary Fields*. New York: Viking Penguin, 1992.

Rosengarten, Theodore. "Reading the Hops: Recollections of Lorenzo 'Piper' Davis and the Negro Baseball League." *Southern Exposure*, Summer/Fall 1977.

Staten, Vince. *Ol' Diz: A Biography of Dizzy Dean*. New York: HarperCollins, 1992.

Tye, Larry. *Satchel: The Life and Times of an American Legend*. New York: Random House, 2009.

Tygiel, Jules. *Baseball's Great Experiment: Jackie Robinson and His Legacy*. New York: Oxford University Press, 2008.

Whitt, Timothy, *Bases Loaded with History: The Story of Rickwood Field, America's Oldest Baseball Park*. Birmingham, Ala.: R. Boozer Press, 1995.

Wright, Marshall D. *The Southern Association in Baseball, 1885–1961*. Jefferson, N.C.: McFarland and Co., 2002.

ILLUSTRATION CREDITS

Page iv–v: Photograph by Chris Epting

Page vii: Susan Percy, photographer

Page 6:   Courtesy of Birmingham Baseball Collection of the Birmingham Public Library

Page 20:   Courtesy of the Birmingham Public Library

Page 23:   Courtesy of William H. Brantley Collection at Samford University, Birmingham Public Library

Page 26:   Courtesy of the National Baseball Hall of Fame Library

Page 28:   Courtesy of Birmingham Chamber of Commerce

Page 29:   From the personal collection of Bruce Kuklick, photographer unknown

Page 34:   From the personal collection of Chuck Stewart

Page 43:   Courtesy of Birmingham Chamber of Commerce

Page 46:   Courtesy of the T. H. Hayes Collection, Memphis Shelby Public Library & Information Center

Page 51:   Courtesy of Alabama State Department of Archives and History

Page 60:   Courtesy of Birmingham Baseball Collection of the Birmingham Public Library

Page 63:   Courtesy of Carlton Molesworth III

Page 65:   From the personal collection of Chuck Stewart

Page 69:   Courtesy of the family of Sam Burr

Page 72:   Courtesy of Bill Chapman

Page 75:   Margaret Barra

Page 77:   Courtesy of Bill Chapman

Page 78:   Margaret Barra

Page 92:   Courtesy of Glynn West

Page 96:   Houston Sports Museum

Page 110:   Courtesy of the National Baseball Hall of Fame Library

Page 112:   Courtesy of Gene Northington

Page 121:   Courtesy of the Birmingham Public Library

Page 128:   Courtesy of Bob Scranton

Page 136:   Courtesy of the *Philadelphia Inquirer*

Page 149:   Courtesy of Birmingham Baseball Collection of the Birmingham Public Library

Page 151:   Courtesy of Birmingham Baseball Collection of the Birmingham Public Library

Page 155:   Courtesy of the T. H. Hayes Collection, Memphis Shelby Public Library & Information Center

Page 157:   Courtesy of the Negro League Baseball Museum

Page 162:   Margaret Barra

Page 164:   Courtesy of the *Tuscaloosa News*

Page 177:   Buddy Coker

Page 184:   Courtesy of the Paul W. Bryant Museum

Page 193:   Buddy Coker

Page 195:   Courtesy of Glynn West

Page 199:   Courtesy of Birmingham Barons

Page 200:   From the personal collection of Gene and Cindy Northington

Page 204:   Courtesy of Ron Shelton

Page 206:   By Birmingham artist Warren Mullins

Page 209:   Bill Chapman

Page 222:   Courtesy of the *Birmingham News*

Page 262:   Courtesy of the *Birmingham News*

Page 267:   Courtesy of Ron Shelton

Page 269:   Courtesy of Birmingham Barons

Page 289:   Photographer Steve Ross, courtesy of the *Birmingham News*

Page 297:   Courtesy of the Paul W. Bryant Museum

Page 318:   Courtesy of Brian Merzbach, ballparkreviews.com

Page 321:   Courtesy of Brian Lopinto

Page 323:   From the personal collection of Andy Broome

Page 327:   Natalie Perrin

Page 328:   Courtesy of Brian Merzbach, ballparkreviews.com

Page 330:   Courtesy of Brian Merzbach, ballparkreviews.com

Page 333:   Courtesy of Mike Anderson and the Friends of Warren Ballpark

Page 336:   Photograph by Jonelle Barra

INDEX

Page numbers in *italics* refer to illustrations.

Aaron, Henry "Hank," 4, 45*n*, 130*n*, 177, 178, 183, 212, 235, 256, 283, 322

Abbott, William "Bud," 321

Abernathy, Woody, 100–101, 107

Adams, Oscar W., 66

Adams, Oscar W., Jr., 66*n*

Alaya, Flavia, 320

Aleno, Chuck, 292

Alexander, Grover Cleveland, 40

Allen, Mel, 130, 168

Allen, Woody, 86

Alston, Tom, 175

Altman, Robert, 263

American Association, 17

American Giants, 133

American League (AL), 3, 4, 24, 38, 69, 83*n*, 88, 94, 130*n*, 131*n*, 134*n*, 146*n*, 147, 153, 164*n*, 167, 175, 180, 254, 271, 290, 298, 310, 320, 331

Andrews, Ivy Paul, 126

Andrews, James, 187*n*

Ankeman, Fred, 105

Anson, Cap, 64*n*

Aparicio, Luis, 180

Arkansas Travelers (Little Rock), 19, 95, 142, 171, 330, 331

Arkeketa, Chief Wood, 273

Armstrong, Louis, 65

Arrington, Richard, 205

Ashburn, Richie, 261

Asheville Tourists, 189

Aspromonte, Ken, 268

Atlanta Black Crackers, 67

Atlanta Braves, 166, 183, 256, 272, 276, 283–84, 324

Atlanta Crackers, 19, 116, 124, 135, 142, 166, 171, 188, 272

Badham, John, 119*n*

Baker, Frank "Home Run," 24, 26

Baltimore Black Sox, 85

Baltimore Elite Giants, 231

Baltimore Orioles, 166, 180, 202, 267, 283, 290

Bancroft, Billy, 98, 102

Bankhead, Tallulah, 290*n*, 296

Banks, Ernie "Mr. Cub," 152, 212, 299–300

Barber, Red, 130

Barnum, P. T., 322

Barra, Alfred, 125*n*

Barry, Jack, 24

Basie, Count, 53, 121

Bassett, Lloyd "Pepper," 123, 135

Battle, Will, 52

Bauer, Hank, 273

Baugh, R. H., 23, 41

Becker, Joe, 328

Beeler, Jodie, 292

Belcher, Albert, 182–83, 188–89

Bell, Herman, 56

Bell, James "Cool Papa," 4, 66, 135, 154, 212, 299, 328

Bellsouth Park (Chattanooga), 322

Bender, Chief, 24

Bennett, Joan, 77

Bernstein, Rick, 256–57

Berra, Lawrence Peter "Yogi," 88, 97n, 147n, 163n, 180, 227, 265, 312

Bigelow, Elliot Allardice, 88–91

Birmingham, 6, 43, 121

Birmingham A's, 184, 191, 193, 195–97, 276, 277, 282, 285, 288, 291, 310, 314

Birmingham Barons, 4, 17–21, 22, 33, 34, 36–41, 44–45, 58, 59, 61n, 62–64, 74–75, 79, 83, 89–90, 92, 94, 95, 97–98, 100–108, 112, 113, 116, 117, 119, 124, 126–28, 142, 144–45, 146n, 148, 161, 162, 164, 165, 168–69, 171–74, 176, 179–80, 181–82, 183, 188–89, 191, 195, 197, 199–202, 200, 205, 208, 212, 216, 221, 228–29, 239, 242–43, 245, 248, 249–51, 258, 268, 269, 271, 272, 278, 280–81, 291, 292–93, 305–6, 307, 311, 315–16, 315n, 322, 325

Birmingham Bees, 126, 128, 306

Birmingham Black Barons, 46, 48, 55, 56, 58, 65, 66–68, 74, 79–86, 110, 118–23, 127, 133–35, 140, 145, 149–51, 153, 155–58, 157, 160, 165, 167, 173, 175, 181–82, 208, 209, 212–13, 218, 222, 225–26, 229, 231, 235, 249–51, 258–59, 261, 262–63, 269, 270, 280–81, 299, 302, 311, 316, 322

Birmingham Giants, 57, 65

Bisbee Bees, 333

Bisbee Copper Kings, 333, 334

Bisbee Ranger Kings, 333

Bisbee Yankees, 334

Black Barons. See Birmingham Black Barons

Black, Joe, 179

Blackwell, Ewell, 83

Blue, Vida, 192, 286

Bostock, Lyman, 150, 159

Bostock, Lyman, Jr., 150n

Boston Braves, 166, 173, 178–79, 181

Boston Red Sox, 2, 90, 94, 126, 130, 131, 140, 144, 147, 153, 158–59, 165n, 171, 172, 174, 175, 179, 203, 222, 231–33, 259, 270, 281n, 283, 290, 315n

Bouton, Jim, 260, 261–63, 262, 264–65

Bowa, Larry, 191n, 325, 326

Boyd, Raymond, 42

Bradley, Gene, 293

Brady, Diamond Jim, 1, 99n

Brashler, William, 119n

Brewer, David, 205, 207, 208, 209

"Bristol Barnstormers," 261, 262, 263, 264–65

Brock, Glenny, 274

Brooklyn Dodgers, 42n, 44n, 61–62, 76, 127, 129, 130, 135, 145, 147, 153, 160, 166, 167, 171, 176, 177, 178–79, 181, 182, 205n, 246, 316

Brooklyn Robins, 44

Broome, Andy, 323

Brown, Charles "Curly," 44

Brown, Johnny Mack, 74

Brown, Tom, 68

Bryant, Paul "Bear," 9, 94n, 100, 137–38,
166, 184, 191, 282, 287–88, 297, 315
Bryant, Paul, Jr., 191, 315
Buchanan, Charles, 122n
Buffett, Jimmy, 266
Burch, Bill, 241
Burgess, Forrest "Smoky," 144
Burns, Jack, 233
Burr, Sam, 68
Burrow, Rube and Jim, 11n
Burt, Jim, 117
Button, Charles, 12

Caldwell, Henry, 14
Caldwell, Ray, 94–95, 96, 98, 101–2, 104,
106, 108–9, 149, 180, 191n, 242,
247
Calloway, Cab, 122n
Cameron, Mike, 198n
Campanella, Roy, 158, 159, 160, 167, 177,
181
Campaneris, Bert "Campy," 189–90, 285,
303
Canseco, Jose, 200
Caple, Jim, 75
Carleton, Tex, 103
Carpenter, Bob, 125
Casey, Hugh "Fireman," 171
Catchings, Ben, 293
Chandler, Albert "Happy," 136
Chapman, Ben "the Alabama Flash," 136,
145–46, 199, 204, 248, 315, 316
Chapman, Ray, 43n
Charleston, Oscar, 65–66, 197
Chase, Harold "Prince Hal," 40, 332
Chattanooga A's, 196
Chattanooga Black Lookouts, 79, 80, 322
Chattanooga Lookouts, 39n, 90, 322
Cherry, Ed, 245
Chicago American Giants, 80
Chicago Cubs, 117, 271, 322, 324

Chicago White Sox, 36, 150n, 175, 198,
201, 203, 271, 290, 332
Cincinnati Buckeyes, 123
Cincinnati Reds, 38, 83, 106n, 117, 118,
124, 129, 290, 332
Civic Stadium (Eugene, Ore.), 326–27,
327
Clancy, Uncle Bud, 273
Clarkson, Jules "Art," 146n, 197–201, 199,
221, 240, 305, 312, 313–16
Clemens, Roger, 203–4
Cleveland Indians, 25, 43n, 86, 94, 117,
126, 134n, 153, 157, 158, 285, 320
Coastal Plain League, 324
Cobb, Ty, 4, 23, 25, 40–41, 60, 66, 177,
197, 202–4, 212, 250, 266, 267, 274,
291
Cochrane, Mickey, 26
Cohen, Octavus Roy, 54–55
Coker, Buddy, 282–84
Colavito, Rocky, 254, 285
Collins, Eddie, 24, 25
Collins, Joe, 128
Combs, Earle, 248
Comiskey Park (Chicago), 23, 30n, 67n,
152
Connie Mack Stadium (Philadelphia),
29, 161, 196, 261, 324; see also Shibe
Park
Connor, Theophilus Eugene "Bull," 74,
132, 148, 168–70, 175, 178, 179, 181,
183, 185–88, 243, 279, 281
Conway, Johnny, 292
Cook, Ben, 35n, 103n, 190
Copper Kings (Bisbee, Ariz.), 333, 334
Corpus Christi Giants, 181–82
Cortazzo, Jess "Shine," 98, 107, 168
Cosby, Tom, 205
Costello, Lou, 321
Coveleski, Harry, 36, 38–39
Coveleski, Stan, 38

Crawford, "Wahoo" Sam, 40
Crenna, Richard, 109*n*
Crockett, Davy, 8, 95
Crosetti, Frank, 248
Crosley Field (Cincinnati), 27
Csonka, Larry, 313
Cuniff, Jack, 68
Cuyler, Kiki, 322

Dahlgren, Babe, 254
Dailey, Dan, 109*n*
Dallas Cowboys, 313
Daniel, Jake, 293
Davis, Lorenzo "Piper," 48, 56, 57, 74, 84,
     99, 118, 119, 121, 133, 134, 145,
     148–54, *149*, 158, 159, 199, 221–37,
     222, 251, 301, 315, 316
Davis, Lorna Perry, 222
Dawson, Andre, 235
Day, Robert, 284
Dean, Clarence, 50–52
Dean, Jay Hanna "Dizzy," 4, 93, 94, 95–98,
     96, 99–100, 101–11, *110*, 149, 180,
     191*n*, 194, 196, 197, 212, 228–29,
     242, 247, 251, 266, 274
Dean, Paul "Daffy," 109*n*
Dejan, Mike, 293
Del Savio, Gar, 273
DeLeonard, Joe, 287–88
DeMoss, Bingo, 66
Dempsey, Jack, 89, 99
Detroit Lions, 87
Detroit Tigers, 39*n*, 40, 130, 165*n*, 177,
     194, 195, 196, 198, 290, 316
Dickey, Bill, 248
Dihigo, Martin, 67*n*
DiMaggio, Joe, 131, 146*n*, 154, 177, 180,
     212, 315, 324
Dobbs, Johnny, 89
Doby, Larry, 134*n*, 153, 158, 320
Doubleday, Abner, 303

Downey, Sunny Jim, 272
Draper, George, 242–43
Dreyfuss, Barney, 32, 62
Dropo, Walt, 131, 176, 202, 242, 244, 251,
     258, 280, 286, 289–90, *289*, 293
Dubois, Roger, 246
Duggleby, Bill, 37
Duncan, Dave, 192, 193, 276, 280, 282,
     296
Duncan, David (Confederate Army offi-
     cer), 324
Duncan Park (Spartanburg, S.C.), 324–25
Durham Athletic Park (DAP; Durham),
     267, 317–19, *318*, 320, 326
Durham Bulls, 317, 318–19
Dykes, Jimmie, 254

Earp, Wyatt, 99*n*, 332
Easter, Luke, 157
Ebbets Field (Brooklyn), 23
Einstein, Charles, 159
El Paso Diablos, 313
El Toro Park (Durham), 317, 318
Ella, Roy, 37
Ellington, Duke, 53, 121
Emory, Lou, 37
Engel, Joe, 322
Engel Stadium (Chattanooga), 97*n*, 196,
     322–23, *323*
Ennis, Del, 261
Ermer, Cal, 303
Erskine, Carl, 179
Eugene Emeralds "Ems," 326–27

Faulkner, William, 118
Feller, Bob, 88, 227
Felsch, Happy, 332
Fenway Park (Boston), 23, 174, 290, 297
Fingers, Roland Glen "Rollie," 191–92,
     193, 196, 260, 276, 280, 285,
     309–10

Finley, Charles "Charlie O," 160, *184*, 190–
     97, 199, 253–55, 291, 303, 314
Fitzpatrick, Jim, 247–48
Fleming, Ian, 122*n*
Flood, Curt, 248
Forbes Field (Pittsburgh), 23, 27, 30, 32,
     214, 261, 289
Forney, John, 197, 214
Fort Worth Cats, 103
Fort Worth Panthers, 142, 144
Foster, Rube, 58, 64, 65, 85–86, 212
Foster, Willie, 150, 228
Fox, Howie, 273
Fox, William Price, 85, 87, 88
Foxx, Jimmie, 26
Frankford Yellow Jackets, 125
Frick, Ford, 182
Fullerton, Chris, 12, 119, 122*n*, 132
Furillo, Carl, 178

Gable, Clark, 13*n*
Gale, Mo, 122*n*
Gandil, Chick, 332
Garcia Marquéz, Gabriel, 10*n*
Gatewood, Bill, 81
Gehrig, Lou, 89, 90, 97*n*, 169, 177, 198*n*,
     212, 248, 254, 322, 323, 324
Gentile, Jim, 254
Gibson, Bob, 224, 227, 283
Gibson, Josh, 4, 68, 135, 154, 197, 328
Gibson, Mel, 21*n*
Gibson, Rufus, 222
Gilbert, Charlie, 144
Gillespie, Dizzy, 122*n*
Gilliam, Junior, 231
Glavine, Tom, 324
Glennon, Eddie "Shorty," 28, 76, 112,
     125–32, *128*, 142, 158, 178, 179–80,
     181, 182, 183, 188, 202, 289, 311,
     312
Glory Days (painting), 206

Gomez, Lefty, 248
Gooch, John, 63, 107
Goodgame, John W., 145
Goodman, Benny, 122*n*
Gould, Elliott, 263
Grady, Henry, 7, 17, 18
Graham, Moonlight, ix
Grange, Red, 89
Gray, Pete, 294
Greason, Bill, 119, 120, 150, 154, 156–57,
     158, 160, 222, 301
Greenberg, Hank, 146*n*
Greenlee, William Augustus "Gus," 146
Gregory, Robert, 98, 103*n*
Griffith, D. W., 77
Grimes, Burleigh Arland, 42–45, 61, 250,
     322
Grote, Jerry, 199
Grzenda, Joe, 303
Guy, Faye, 295

Haden, Courtney, 303–4
Hairston, Jerry, Jr., 150*n*
Hairston, Jerry, Sr., 150*n*
Hairston, Johnny, 150*n*
Hairston, Sam, 150, 223
Hairston, Scott, 150*n*
Hall, Halsey, 102
Hamilton, Milo, 256
Hampton, Lionel, 122*n*, *151*
Handy, W. C., 135*n*
Hardgrove, Omar, 44
Harkins, Caroline, 362
Harlem Globetrotters, 123, 133, 134, 150,
     221, 224, 225–26
Harris, Donnie, 218–19, 317
Hart, William S., 1, 77
Harwell, Ernie, 130
Hasty, Bob, 98, 106, 107
Hatfield, Fred, 163, 164, 165*n*, 278
Hawkins, Erskine Ramsay, 53

Hawkins, Williamson, 49

Hayden, Courtney, 199

Hayes, Tom, 127, 133, 134, 182, 231–32, 280

Heard, Jehosie, 150

Hemphill, Paul, 9–10, 13–14, 111, 114n, 132, 163–65, 169–70, 183, 187n, 201–2, 278–79

Herrmann, Edward, 205

Herskowitz, Mickey, 97n

Heusser, Ed, 292

Higgins, Mike "Pinky," 171

Highbe, Kirby, 273

Hinchliffe, John V., 320

Hinchliffe Stadium (Paterson), 320–21, 321, 326

Hodges, Gil, 221

Holliday, Doc, 332

Holloman, Alva Lee "Bobo," 143n

Holway, John, 83

Homestead Grays, 84, 134–35, 140, 156–58

Hope, Bob (Atlanta Braves PR director), 183

Horne, Lena, 65

Hornsby, Rogers, 4, 25, 60, 90, 177, 212

Houk, Ralph, 283

House of David, 97

Houston Astros, 180, 313

Houston Buffaloes, 93, 96, 100–108

Howard, Elston, 130n, 147, 283

Howard, Frank, 284

Howell, Dixie, 94n

Hubbell, Carl, 110

Huggins, Miller, 36–37

Hunter, Jim "Catfish," 196

Hutson, Don, 94n, 137–38

Indianapolis ABC's, 58, 65–66

Indianapolis Clowns, 123, 177, 178

Indoor Football League, 316

International League, 141, 188

Irvin, Monte, 158, 167

Israel, Melvin Allen. See Allen, Mel

Jackie Robinson All-Stars, 158, 159–60

Jackson, Bo, 150n–51n, 187n, 201

Jackson, Reggie, 4, 138, 176, 192–94, 193, 199, 212, 274, 276, 280, 282, 285, 288, 296–98, 297, 309

Jackson, "Shoeless" Joe, 25, 39, 221, 309

James, Bill, 44n, 64n, 148, 192

James, Frank and Jesse, 11n

Jebeles, Konstantenous John "Gus," 124–25, 126, 129, 182

Jeffers, Thomas, 15

Jemison, Robert, 11

Jenkins, Ferguson, 261, 322

Joe Becker Stadium (Joplin), 328–29, 328

Johnson, Artie, 44

Johnson, Howard, 198

Johnson, Jack, 58n, 99n

Johnson, John J., 147–48

Johnson, Walter "Big Train," 40, 96

Johnston, Jimmy, 41–42

Jones, Bobby, 89

Jones, James Earl, 119n

Jones, John, 8

Jones, Tommy Lee, 203–4, 204, 267

Jones, Willie, 224

Joplin Miners, 328–29

Jordan, Michael, 201

Kansas City A's, 130n, 160, 166, 180n, 181, 191, 253–55, 291

Kansas City Black Monarchs, 299

Kansas City Monarchs, 64, 140, 145, 147, 156, 157, 164, 167, 299

Kansas City Royals, 150n

Keaton, Buster, 77

Keith, Don, 239–40

Kennedy, John F., 186

Kiick, Jim, 313

Killebrew, Harmon, 322

King, Martin Luther, Jr., 169, 185–86

Kinsella, W. P., ix

Kluszewski, Ted, 129*n*

Koufax, Sandy, 228

Kuhn, Bowie, 194, 195, 196–97

LaMacchia, Al, 244

Lamanno, Ray, 273

Landis, Kennesaw Mountain, 332

Lane, Dick "Night Train," 87–88

Lardner, Ring, 2

Lasorda, Tommy, 72, 79, 179, 286

Lauzerique, George, 280, 282

Lazzeri, Tony, 248

League Park (Cleveland), 23

Leavitt, Charles W., 32

Lee, Robert E., 12

Lee, Spike, 205

Lee, Willie, 150, 164, *209*

Leland, Bob, *68*

Leonard, Buck, 135

Levin, Jack, 205

Lieb, Fred, 2*n*

Limmer, Louis "Lou," 303

Lindbergh, Charles, 290*n*

Lindo, Delroy, 205

Lipman, David, 80

Little, Frank and Minnie, 293

Little Rock Travelers, 19, 95, 142, 171, 330, 331

Little Savoy Cafe, *121*

Lockett, Lester, 150

Lombard, Carole, 77

Long, Huey, 170

Longinotti, Frank, 125

Los Angeles Dodgers, 166, 182, 316, 325

Louis, Joe, 58*n*, 122

Lovell, Bob, 313, 315

Lucadello, Tony, 261

Luce, Art, 273

Lucy, Autherine, 278

Lumpkin, Bill, 124*n*, 189, 291–95, 297

Lux, Harvey, 244

Luzinski, Greg, 326

Lyons, Eddie, 292

Mack, Connie, 1–4, 23, 24, 25, 26, 28–30, 31, 32, 41*n*, 125, 126, 127, 130, 143, 160–61, 183, 191, 197, 214

Macon Peaches, 324

MacPhail, Larry, 146, 147, 154

Madjeski, Hank, 273

Madsen, Virginia, 279

Mantle, Mickey, 86, 180, 223, 254, 283, 328

Marion, Marty, 171, 270

Marion, Red, 171, 270

Maris, Roger, 180*n*, 254

Marquard, Rube, 40

Martin, Billy, 174

Martin, J. D., 182

Martin, Steve (journalist), 240

Mason, Charlie, 150

Masterson, Bat, 1, 99*n*

Mathews, Eddie, 171, 176, 178

Mathewson, Christy, 3, 38, 40

Matthews, Coke, 285–86

Maughan, Bill, 173

Mays, Carl, 42*n*–43*n*, 204*n*

Mays, Howard "Cat," 122, 150, 153–54, 225

Mays, Willie, 4, 48, 66, 86–87, 122, 131, 138, 139–40, 147*n*, 148, 150, 153–60, 167, 173, 174*n*, 181, 198*n*, 212, 221, 222, 223, 230–31, 235, 246, 251, 258, 266, 269, 270–71, 274, 276, 280, 286, 289, 297, 301–2, 322

Mazeroski, Bill, 27, 180*n*

McCabe, Dick, 103

McCain, John, 192

McCarver, Tim, 196

McCovey, Willie, 180*n*

McDowell, Jack, 198*n*

McGillicuddy, Cornelius Alexander, Sr.,
    see Mack, Connie

McGilvray, William, 41

McGinnity, Joseph "Ironman Joe," 116*n*

McGraw, John, 2, 3, 38, 198*n*

McInnes, Stuffy, 24

McKechnie, Bill "The Deacon," 63*n*–64*n*

McLain, Denny, 194–96, 195, 284, 313

McQueen, Jay William, 22

McWhorter, Diane, 185

Medwick, Joseph Michael "Ducky," 97,
    100, 106, 107, 108

Mele, Dutch, 273, 292

Memphis Blues, 313

Memphis Chickasaws ("Chicks"), 19, 62,
    90, 125, 129, 174, 182, 197, 294, 312,
    313, 314

Memphis Grizzlies, 313

Memphis Red Sox, 85

Messsenger, Bob, 36

Meusel, Bob, 61

Meusel, Emil "Irish," 61*n*

Milan, Clyde "Deerfoot," 96, 100, 101,
    102, 105

Miller, Marvin, 190, 192–94

Milner, John T., 14

Milwaukee Braves, 166, 176, 188

Minnesota Twins, 150*n*

Minoso, Minnie, 175

Mitchell, Jackie, 97*n*, 322–23

Mitchell, Jesse, 150

Mobile Bears, 19

Molesworth, Carlton, 36–37, 41–42, 44

Monk, Thelonious, 122*n*

Montgomery Black Climbers, 58, 68

Montgomery Climbers, 34, 41

Montreal Expos, 180, 196, 235

Montreal Royals, 141

Moriarty, George, 61, 62

Morney, Leroy, 150

Morris, Willie, 165*n*

Morrison, John "Jughandle Johnny," 59

Mudd, William S., 14

Mullins, Warren, 206

Munson, Thurman, 283

Murcer, Bobby, 283

Murphy, Dale, 324

Murray (catcher), 80

Murrow, Edward R., 168

Musial, Stan "the Man," 175–76, 212, 251

Nashville Volunteers ("Vols"), 19, 142–
    44, 292

National Association, 146, 147

National League (NL), 4, 24*n*, 38, 40, 44,
    57, 60, 83, 94, 97, 116*n*, 144, 146,
    147, 167, 175, 176, 178, 180, 181,
    198, 235, 297, 300, 324

Navin Field (Detroit), 23

Negro American League, 118, 133–34,
    147, 156, 158, 182

Negro Leagues, 55, 56, 58, 64, 68, 82, 85,
    86, 118, 123, 140, 145, 146–48, 152*n*,
    157, 158, 166–67, 177, 182, 183, 205,
    208, 212, 221, 222, 223, 224–25, 226,
    229, 230, 231–32, 235, 236, 237, 299,
    319, 330

Negro National League (NNL), 58,
    64–65, 66, 68, 74, 80, 85, 86, 147,
    157, 302, 320

Negro Southern League, 66, 86

Nelson, Jimmy, 272–73

New Orleans Pelicans, 19, 25*n*, 39, 41, 89,
    126, 182, 311, 312, 331

New York Black Yankees, 320

New York Cubans, 67, 159, 320

New York Giants, 2, 3, 38, 39, 56, 158,
    166, 167, 173, 270, 302, 332

New York Highlanders, 39

New York Metropolitans, 17

New York Mets, 198, 200

New York Yankees, 41, 43n, 44n, 61–62, 69, 76, 94, 96, 103n, 128, 130, 138, 145, 146–47, 150n, 154, 155, 159, 168, 169, 171, 172, 174, 179–80, 192n, 223, 226, 229, 233, 241, 247–48, 263, 265, 268, 273, 282, 283, 298, 324, 328, 332

Newberry, Jimmy "Schoolboy," 150, 159, 160

Newcombe, Don, 158, 167, 181, 226, 286

Newman, Zipp, 93, 98–99, 103, 105, 131n

Newsom, Louis Norman "Bobo," 171–72, 268, 280

Nixon, Richard, 186

Northington, Cindy, 201

Northington, Gene, 112, 201, 305

Northington, Sherry and Pam, 305–6

Norton, Ed, 113, 117

Nunn, William G., 67n

Nunnelley, William A., 168

Nuxhall, Joe, 124

Oakland A's, 160, 184, 190, 191–92, 193, 194, 195, 196–97, 296–97, 298, 310

Odom, Johnny "Blue Moon," 254

Olympic Stadium (Hoquiam, Wash.), 326

Omaha Tigers, 224

O'Malley, Walter, 127, 182, 316

O'Neil, Buck, 156, 299

Ordóñez, Magglio, 198n

Orton, Tim, 241

O'Shea, Katharine, 13n

Pacific Coast League, 56, 158, 166

Pacific Southwest League, 334

Paige, LeRoy "Satchel," 4, 42, 65, 79–88, 99, 109–11, 110, 131, 134, 140, 151, 197, 205, 212, 222, 226, 227–28, 229, 251, 256–57, 266, 274, 309, 322, 328

Palin, Sarah, 192

Parker, Charlie, 122n

Parks, Rosa, 278

Parnell, Charles Stewart, 12–13

Parnell, John, 12–13

Parsons, Charlie, 17

Pascrell, Bill, Jr., 321

Patterson, Floyd, 186

Patterson, James, 170n

Patterson, Willie, 120–21, 122n, 134

Paul, Jim, 313

Peel, Homer, 108

Pennock, Herb, 248

Perdue, Frank M., 66

Perkins, Anthony, 269, 271

Perry, Alonzo, 222

Petersen, William, 279

Petrocelli, Rico, 281

Philadelphia A's, 1, 2, 3, 24–25, 76, 106, 160, 161, 164n, 166, 177, 183, 191

Philadelphia Eagles, 277

Philadelphia Phillies, 37, 40, 125, 146, 196, 261, 325, 326

Pickford, Mary, 77

Piersall, Jim, 172–75, 202, 251, 258, 268–71, 269, 289

Pipgras, George, 248

Pittsburgh Crawfords, 84, 146

Pittsburgh Pirates, 32, 44, 57, 62, 63n, 83, 140, 144, 180, 181, 203n, 259, 322

PK Park (Eugene, Ore.), 326

Plank, Eddie, 24, 25

Polly, Nick, 273, 293

Polo Grounds (New York City), 43n, 198

Pompez, Alex, 159

Ponce de Leon Park (Atlanta), 142
Porter, Dick, 126
Powell, Bill, ix, 56, 132, 150, 222
Powell, James R., 14–16
Pratt, Daniel, 10
Pratt, Derrill, 37
Presley, Elvis, 313
Pryor, Richard, 119n

Quinlan, Kieran, 13

Radcliffe, Ted "Double Duty," 133–34
Rampersad, Arnold, 186n
Ranger Kings (Bisbee, Ariz.), 333
Ray Winder Field (Little Rock), 142,
    330–31, 330
Reese, Harold "Pee Wee," 109n, 152, 177
Regan, Phil, 303
Reynolds, Allie, 226–27
Ribowsky, Mark, 64–65, 68, 86
Rice, Grantland, 67n
Rickard, Tex, 98–99
Rickey, Branch, 145–46, 152, 203n, 205
Rickwood Field illustrations, 28, 34, 46,
    72, 75, 77, 78, 92, 162, 177, 206, 262
Risberg, Swede, 332
Ritter, Lawrence S., 1, 30n
Rizzuto, Phil, 152, 163n–64n
Robbins, Tim, 319
Robertson, Debra S., 249–52
Robertson, Dick, 44
Robinson, Bill "Bojangles," 65
Robinson, Jack Roosevelt "Jackie," 122,
    127, 136, 145–46, 147, 152, 153,
    158, 159–60, 167, 177, 178, 181,
    186–87, 188, 203n, 205, 212, 226,
    235, 299
Robinson, Jeff, 200
Robinson, Wilbert "Uncle Robbie," 44, 61
Rock Hill Owls, 273

Rogers, Cowboy, 102, 280
Roosevelt, Franklin "FDR," 115
Roosevelt, Theodore "Teddy," 51, 114
Rose, Pete, 221
Rosengarten, Theodore, 56
Rudi, Joe, 192, 193, 196, 276, 282, 296
Ruffing, Red, 248
Runyon, Damon, 54, 55, 134
Rush, Joe, 120
Rust, Art, Jr., 30n
Ruth, George Herman "Babe," Jr., 4, 25,
    31, 36n, 45n, 61, 66, 68–71, 89, 90,
    97n, 131, 159, 177, 180, 197, 212,
    246, 248, 250, 256, 274, 322

Sahadi, Lou, 139
Salmon, Harry, 82–84
Sampson, Tommy, 135, 222
San Diego Padres, 326
San Francisco Giants, 166, 196
Sandberg, Ryne, 324
Saperstein, Abe, 133–35, 226
Sauer, Hank, 293
Savoy, Bob, 156
Sayegh, Andre, 321
Schmidt, Mike, 198n, 261, 326
Schultz, Joe, 107
Scott, George, 264
Scranton, Bob, 123, 126, 127, 128, 129,
    131n, 144, 152, 161, 174, 176, 182,
    198, 205, 258, 311–12
Seattle Mariners, 198n
Seitz, Paul, 260
Sewell, Joe, 248
Shantz, Bobby, 164n
Shaughnessy, Frank, 141
Shaut, Art, 103n
Shea Stadium, 198
Shelton, Ron, 202, 204, 266–67, 267, 319
Sherman, William Tecumseh, 7

Shibe, Benjamin F., 1

Shibe Park (Philadelphia), 1, 4, 23, 25, 27, 28, 29, 30–32, 125, 126, 136, 196, 214, 261, 289, 324, 332; see also Connie Mack Stadium

Shor, Bernard "Toots," 125n

Shoun, Clyde, 273

Shuba, George "Shotgun," 129n

Siebern, Norm, 180

Sinatra, Frank, 207

Sipek, Dick, 294

Skowron, Bill, 130n

Slag Pile, 19, 24, 32

Slaughter, Terry, 205

Sloss, Jacob, 21

Smith, Bill, 307

Smith, Fred, 104

Smith, Lamar, 264–65

Smith, Pistol, 102

Smith, Sam, 181

Smith, Wayne C., 307

Snider, Edwin Donald "Duke," 177, 178

South Atlantic League, 188

Southern Association, 18–19, 24n, 25n, 35, 37, 39, 41, 59, 63, 74, 89, 91, 96, 100, 106, 116, 126, 129, 141–42, 144, 165, 166, 168, 180–83, 188, 260, 278, 294, 312, 330, 331

Southern California Suns, 313

Southern League, 4, 17, 18, 110, 188, 189, 192, 193, 199, 296

Spahn, Warren, 176–77, 179

Spartanburg Phillies, 325

Spartanburg Spartans, 324

Spartanburg Stingers, 324

Speaker, Tris, 25, 66, 95

Sportsman's Park (St. Louis), 100

Springsteen, Bruce, 199

St. Louis Browns, 143n, 153, 166, 167, 171, 294

St. Louis Cardinals, 95, 96, 167, 175–76, 177, 180, 203n, 260, 270, 315

St. Louis Stars, 80

Staten, Vince, 94n, 109

Stearnes, Norman "Turkey," 67–68, 85

steel mill (Ensley), 51

Steele, Ed "Stainless," 56, 123, 159

Steers, Dallas, 92

Steinbrenner, George, 41, 138, 193, 196, 297

Stengel, Casey, 44n, 271

Stephenson, Riggs, 117

Sterling, Bob, 239

Stern, Bill, 70–71

Stewart, Charles, 103n, 253–55

Stone, Rocky, 292

Stottlemyre, Mel, 283

Strawberry, Darryl, 198

Studin, Rob, 275–77

Sturdivant, Tom, 180

Sugar, Bert Randolph, 94n, 109n

Sullivan, Ed, 194

Sulphur Dell (Nashville), 142–44

Susko, Piccolo Pete, 168

Suttles, George "Mule," 67–68, 85, 175, 251

Sutton, James, 294–95

Taft, William Howard, 33

Tauby, Fred, 273

Taylor, Charles Isham "C. I.," 55–59, 64

Taylor, Zach, 101–2

Tenace, Gene, 192

Terry, Ralph, 180

Texas League, 92, 96, 100, 103n, 141, 181, 234, 311, 330

Texas Rangers, 271

Thaxton, Bill, 293

Thomas, Frank, 4, 138, 240

Thompson, Hank, 157–58, 167

Thoreau, Henry David, 185

Tiger Stadium (Detroit), 23

Tilden, Bill, 89

Till, Emmett, 278

Topping, Dan, 109*n*, 179–80

Traveler Field (Little Rock), 330, 331

Travis, William Barret, 8*n*

Traynor, Harold Joseph "Pie," 62–64, 63, 83, 251, 266

Triandos, Gus, 180

Tropical Park (Miami), 67

Twenty–fourth Street Red Sox, 258

Tye, Larry, 109*n*, 111

Tygiel, Jules, 146

Underwood, Blair, 205

Valentine, Bill, 331

Van Hoose, Alf, 131, 152, 172, 173, 176, 280–81, 297

Vance, Hy, 102

Veale, Bob, 3*n*, 130, 152, 153, 203*n*, 204, 258–59, 261

Veeck, Bill, 134

Ventura, Robin, 240

Veterans Stadium (Philadelphia), 324

Virdon, Bill, 180

Virginia League, 44

Vulcanites, 20

Wagner, Honus, 40, 57, 212

Wahconah Park (Pittsfield, Mass.), 263

Walker, Bill, 294

Walker, Fred "Dixie," 203*n*

Walker, Harry "the Hat," 203*n*, 204, 315

Walkup, Jim, 98

Wallace, George, 9, 170

Walsh, Ed, 203

Walters, Fred, 142

Warfield, Paul, 313

Warren Ballpark (Bisbee, Ariz.), 332–34, 333

Washington, Dinah, 87*n*

Washington Generals, 221

Washington Senators, 69, 83, 167, 171, 194, 283–84

Weaver, Buck, 332

Webb, Chick, 122*n*

Weis, Art, 97, 105, 107

Weiss, George, 109*n*, 179–80

Welch, Gus, 151, 226, 232

Wells, Oscar, 115

Wertz, Vic, 198*n*

West Baden Sprudels, 57

West, Glenn, 188, 190

West, Sam, 83

Western League, 106*n*

Wheat, Zack "Buck," 61–62

White, Danny, 313

Whitt, Timothy, 32, 35–36, 45*n*, 80, 85*n*, 89*n*

Wilkinson, John Leslie "J. L.," 64

Williams, Billy Dee, 119*n*

Williams, "Bulldog" (umpire), 42*n*

Williams, Lefty, 332

Williams, "Noble" Bob, 121–22

Williams, Ted, 131, 194, 212, 270, 283

Wills, Gary, 186*n*

Wilson, Artie, 56, 121, 150, 158, 159, 301

Wilson, Bobby, 223

Wilson, George, 280

Winder, Ray, 331

Wininger, D. B., 307

Wininger, David, 307–8

Wood, Obadiah Washington, 49

Woodward, A. H. "Rick" III, 205

Woodward, Allen Harvey. *See* Woodward, Rick

Woodward, Joe (son of Rick), 161
Woodward, Joseph Hersey, 3, 21–22, 38, 45
Woodward, Rick, 2–4, 21–25, 23, 26, 32, 33, 34, 36, 41, 42, 44, 58–59, 66, 75–76, 78–79, 99n, 104, 113–14, 117, 160, 161, 162, 212, 214
Woodward, Stimson Harvey, 21
Woodward, William, 21
Wooster, Lou, 16n
Workman, Charlie, 143–44, 292
World Football League, 313

Wright, Marshall D., 90
Wrigley Field (Chicago), 23, 299

Yakima (Washington) Browns, 224
Yankee Stadium (New York City), 134, 262
Yawkey, Tom, 130, 233
Yielding, F. B., 16n
Young, Leandy, 135
Young, Loretta, 77–78

Zapp, Jimmy, 150, 157, 158, 222, 301
Zauchin, Norman, 199, 295, 315

ABOUT THE AUTHOR

Birmingham native ALLEN BARRA writes about sports regularly for the *Wall Street Journal* and Bloomberg News. He is a regular contributor to the *Daily Beast*, the *Washington Post*, the *Village Voice*, and *Salon*.

His books include *Inventing Wyatt Earp: His Life and Many Legends* (recently reissued by the University of Nebraska Press); *Clearing the Bases: The Greatest Baseball Debates of the Century*, a 2003 *Sports Illustrated* book of the year; *The Last Coach: A Life of Paul "Bear" Bryant*; and *Yogi Berra: Eternal Yankee*, named one of the top ten biographies of the year by *Booklist*. He lives in South Orange, N.J., with his wife, daughter, and a menagerie of adopted cats.